OEDIPUS UNBOUND

OEDIPUS UNBOUND

Selected Writings on Rivalry and Desire

René Girard

Edited and with an Introduction by
Mark R. Anspach

STANFORD UNIVERSITY PRESS

STANFORD, CALIFORNIA

2004

Stanford University Press
Stanford, California

"From the Novelistic Experience to the Oedipal Myth" was first published under the title "De l'expérience romanesque au mythe œdipien" in *Critique* 222 (Nov. 1965): 899–924. "*Oedipus* Analyzed," the text of a lecture delivered at a symposium in 1965, was first published under the title "Une analyse d'Œdipe roi" in *Critique sociologique et critique psychanalytique* (Institut de Sociologie, Université Libre de Bruxelles, 1970), pp. 127–55. "Symmetry and Dissymmetry in the Myth of Oedipus" was first published under the title "Symétrie et dissymétrie dans le mythe d'Œdipe" in *Critique* 249 (Feb. 1968): 99–135. "Doubles and the *Pharmakos*: Lévi-Strauss, Frye, Derrida, and Shakespeare" was first published under the title "Lévi-Strauss, Frye, Derrida and Shakespearean Criticism" in *diacritics* 3 (Fall 1973): 34–38. "The Myth of Oedipus, the Truth of Joseph" is adapted from "The Bible Is Not a Myth," in *Literature and Belief* 4 (1985): 7–15.

Printed in the United States of America on acid-free, archival-quality paper.

Library of Congress Cataloging-in-Publication Data

Girard, René, 1923–
    Oedipus unbound : selected writings on rivalry and desire / René Girard ; edited and with an introduction by Mark R. Anspach.
        p.   cm.
    Includes bibliographical references and index.
    ISBN 0-8047-4779-2 (alk. paper)—
    ISBN 0-8047-4780-6 (pbk. : alk. paper)
    1. Sophocles. Oedipus rex.   2. Sophocles—Characters—Oedipus.
3. Oedipus (Greek mythology) in literature.   4. Oedipus complex in literature.
5. Psychology in literature.   6. Competition (Psychology)   7. Sophocles—
Influence.   8. Incest in literature.   9. Desire in literature.
I. Anspach, Mark Rogin, 1959–   II. Title.
PA4413.O7 G57 2004
882'.01—DC22

                                                        2003022278

Original Printing 2004

Last figure below indicates year of this printing:
13   12   11   10   09   08   07   06   05   04

Typeset by Tim Roberts in 11/13.5 Adobe Garamond

Contents

Editor's Note

Presented in chronological order, these previously uncollected essays offer the full spectrum of René Girard's reflections on Oedipus, while illuminating the evolution of his ideas over time. I have updated and completed the source references (editorial additions are indicated by square brackets).

I would like to express my indebtedness to Professor Jørgen Jørgensen, editor and translator of René Girard's work in Denmark, who was the first to recognize the importance of René Girard's early essays.

I would also like to thank Professor Girard for his generous and patient assistance in every stage of the preparation of this book.

Finally, I would like to thank my brother, William Anspach, who made a number of helpful comments on the introduction.

Mark R. Anspach
Centre de Recherche en Epistémologie Appliquée
Ecole Polytechnique
Paris, France

Editor's Introduction: Imitating Oedipus

> "'There is none but Chu-bu.'
> . . . 'There is also Sheemish.'"
> —Lord Dunsany, "Chu-bu and Sheemish"

What happens when a new god is installed in the temple of Chu-bu? In Dunsany's fable,[1] Chu-bu is a small god, but a proud one. He could not but resent the worship given to that callow upstart, Sheemish. One night, to Chu-bu's deep satisfaction, a bird soiled the newcomer's head. "There is dirt upon thy head, O Sheemish," exulted Chu-bu. "Dirt, dirt, dirt, upon the head of Sheemish."

Alas, the time came when a bird soiled Chu-bu's own head. This turn of events could scarcely go unremarked by Sheemish. "Dirty Chu-bu," he cried triumphantly, setting off an endless exchange of accusations between the two gods. "All night long they spake," writes Dunsany, "and all night said these words only: 'Dirty Chu-bu,' 'Dirty Sheemish.' 'Dirty Chu-bu,' 'Dirty Sheemish.' . . . And gradually Chu-bu came to realize that he was nothing more than the equal of Sheemish."

To Chu-bu, there may be something tragic in this hard-won realization. Yet nobody would mistake him for a tragic hero. Dunsany's protagonist lacks gravitas. His squabbling is hopelessly childish.

Children, of course, like nothing better than to trade insults. The object is to come up with a sally so devastating it cannot possibly be topped. However, the target of the sharpest barb always has a sure-fire retort available. All she has to do is say: *I know you are, but what am I?*

Pronounced in the mocking tones of a smug big sister, the annoyance value of this all-purpose formula is hard to beat. Like some improbable Star Wars antimissile system, it swoops down from above and intercepts oncoming insults before they land, automatically lobbing them back at the assailant without even stopping to scan their contents.

Such a mechanical response is effective because, however varied the content of insults may be, the structure of the exchange is always the same.

"Who are you calling a dummy? You're the dummy!" *I know you are, but what am I?* tops all comers by operating at the meta-level of pure structure. It reduces schoolyard repartee to a mathematical equation through the principle of the "dummy" variable. Just plug in your rival's favorite jibe and apply it to him. "Who are you calling an (x)? You're the (x)!"

Although the structure in question may be simple, there is a paradox to it. When I hurl your own insult back at you, I mirror your behavior as precisely as possible, taking you as my model at the very moment I make you my target. I know you are worthy of insult, since you just insulted me, but, since I just insulted you . . . what am I? If I imitate you, can I be anything more than your equal?

A Plague of Doubles

The paradoxical tendency of rivalry to beget imitation—and of imitation to beget rivalry—is the point of departure for the theory of human culture that René Girard has patiently elaborated and refined over the past four decades. Of course, Girard takes on subjects more serious than schoolyard quarrels. He has tackled literary criticism and psychoanalysis, structural anthropology, comparative religion, and Continental philosophy; he has given us fresh readings of Shakespeare, Dostoyevsky, Proust, Freud, and the Bible, not to mention of primitive mythology and Greek tragedy. His range is staggering. And yet, wherever he looks, he cannot help turning up the selfsame structure of imitation and rivalry.

Take *Oedipus the King*, for example. It would be hard to think of a more serious work than this. After having solved the riddle of the sphinx, Oedipus must confront the deepest, darkest secret of all, the secret of patricide and incest. So fearsome is this secret that even the famed seer Tiresias hesitates to reveal it. Indeed, when Oedipus asks him who killed Laius, Tiresias will only say, in effect: "That's for me to know and you to find out."

Increasingly exasperated by the other's refusal to answer, Oedipus finally accuses Tiresias of having plotted the murder himself. But as soon as Oedipus launches this accusation, his target lobs it right back at him, accusing Oedipus of having carried out the murder *himself*. And when Oedipus dares Tiresias to repeat his harsh words, Tiresias not only repeats them, he tops them off with an inflammatory insinuation involving the other's mama.

Oedipus then reacts the same way anyone might upon being called a murderous mother-lover. "Oh yeah," he says in so many words, "well, you're a blind fool!" This is a low blow because Tiresias, as it happens, *is* blind, so now he really loses his cool. "Who are you calling blind?" he demands. "You're the one who's blind, since you don't even see the truth about yourself." At this point, Girard steps in and asks whether Tiresias sees the truth about *himself.* Does Tiresias realize that he is *imitating Oedipus?* Does he understand that the more he lashes back at his adversary, the more he becomes his equal?

I know what you are—but what am I? "Every man is Oedipus, the guilty party, *to the Other*," remarks Girard, "and Tiresias, the misjudged prophet, *to himself.*"[2] "Dirty Tiresias," "Dirty Oedipus." "Dirty Tiresias," "Dirty Oedipus": as the debate between the prophet and the king degenerates, the members of the chorus look on with growing dismay. Barely able to get a word in edgewise, they do manage to admonish Oedipus that anger "inspires Tiresias's words, and yours too" (lines 404–5).

Animosity is contagious. Tiresias "'catches' Oedipus's hate the way one catches a contagious disease," writes Girard.[3] The chorus fears that, as Oedipus and Tiresias bicker, they are losing sight of what should be paramount: the need to rid Thebes of the plague. In a bold stroke, Girard ties these two threads together. Violent conflict is itself a form of plague, he observes. By virtue of its imitative nature, it can spread like a devastating contagion, and like a contagion it obliterates distinctions, turning individuals into symmetrical doubles.

Every plague is a plague of doubles. Girard has commented elsewhere on the striking similarities that mark literary and mythical treatments of plagues: "The curious thing about these similarities is that they ultimately involve the very notion of the similar. The plague is universally presented as a process of undifferentiation, a destruction of specificities."[4] Girard could have illustrated this observation by quoting the following lines from Thucydides' description of the plague that struck Athens in 430 B.C.: "Some of the sufferers died from want of care, others equally who were receiving the greatest attention. No single remedy could be deemed a specific; for that which did good to one did harm to another. No constitution was of itself strong enough to resist or weak enough to escape the attacks; the disease carried off all alike."[5] Thucydides' words are all the more relevant in that the *Oedipus the King* is believed to have originally been produced some time between 429 and 425 B.C.—during or immediately following the outbreak of the Athenian plague. Since a Theban plague was not part of the earlier Oedipus tradition, Sophocles must have been inspired by the epidemic in his own city.[6]

If Girard does not dwell on the specific historical context in which the play was written, that is doubtless because he prefers to stress its universal import. In *Violence and the Sacred*, he remarks: "Even if Sophocles had in mind the famous Athenian plague of 430 B.C., he clearly did not mean to limit his reference to one specific microbiotic visitation. The epidemic that interrupts all the vital functions of the city is surely not unrelated to violence and the loss of distinctions."[7] However, given Girard's avowed tendency to find similarities among all great works of literature, some readers may wonder whether he is not himself heedless of distinctions. An intruder in the temple of classical studies, he is automatically suspect. It seems only fair to ask whether his interpretation of *Oedipus* respects the specificity of the ancient Greek text.

The most frequently used word for "plague" in both Sophocles' play and in Thucydides is *nosos*. According to American classics scholar Frederick Ahl:

The meaning of *nosos* may also be extended into a political metaphor. Plato describes in book 5 of the *Republic* (470C) the conflicts among the Greek states not just as civil wars but as themselves a kind of *nosos*, "sickness": "in such a situation Greece is sick." Many in Sophocles' audience may have shared Plato's view that the internecine wars among Greeks are "the ultimate sickness (*nosêma*) of the *polis*" (*Republic* 8.544C).[8]

Historically speaking, the two kinds of "sickness" coincided. The microbial plague descended on Athens while it was caught up in the Peloponnesian War, which was still raging when Sophocles wrote *Oedipus*. Moreover, Sophocles links his Theban epidemic to war in mythical terms by having the chorus blame the city's affliction on the god of war, Ares. Ahl comments: "In the chorus' thoughts, then, the plague is accompanied by a war, and it is above all the war that they want ended. The verb they use to ask Zeus to destroy Ares, *phthison* (201), is the same verb the priest uses twice to describe the destructive effects of the plague upon Thebes in lines 25–26 (*phthinousa*)."[9] The use of the same verb points to a loss of distinctions of the kind Girard associates with the contagious spread of violence. Zeus must combat the destructive power of Ares by wielding the same destructive power himself.

This pattern recurs again and again, not only in *Oedipus*, but in Sophocles' other plays as well. French classics scholar Suzanne Saïd finds a typical example in his *Electra*, where the title character plots the murder of her mother as revenge for the mother's murder of the father: "In Sophocles' tragedy as in the recent analyses of R. Girard, the avenger necessarily becomes her adversary's double. Electra, who wishes to be her father's daughter and his alone, must acknowledge that she is also the worthy daughter of her mother, since she has become, like the latter, 'ill-tempered, shrill, shameless' and has learned to commit infamy from her example."[10]

But if the adversaries are doubles, *each* learns from the other's example. Hence the heartfelt cry common to tragic antagonists and squabbling schoolchildren alike: "She started it!" Saïd draws attention to a debate between Electra and her mother in which "each of the two women denies having been the one to start": when the mother proclaims that she has never done more than "answer with harsh words the harsh words she has heard," Electra observes pointedly that the same cannot be said "this time."[11] In other words, "Who are you to accuse me of being the first to use harsh words? *You* are the first to launch a harsh accusation against me right now!" This exchange of harsh words between Electra and her mother not only follows the pattern identified by Girard in the similar exchange between Oedipus and Tiresias, it also refers to the pattern explicitly, thus confirming Sophocles' conscious interest in the symmetrical structure of such exchanges.

By zeroing in on what one critic has called the "festooning of quasi-mathematical symmetries" in *Oedipus*,[12] Girard seeks to show that the structural equivalences between characters outweigh any distinguishing features they may seem to possess. Now, this is clearly a challenge in the case of the title character, who may be said, without exaggeration, to possess the mother of all distinguishing features. Oedipus is, after all, the only character who can claim to have possessed his mother. For Freud, of course, he has acted out a universal impulse, but one which normally lies hidden. When Oedipus concludes at the end of the play that his wife Jocasta was the woman who bore him, the incomparable horror of the situation prompts him to gouge his eyes out. Where is the loss of distinctions there?

Before coming to Girard's interpretation of the incest theme, let us see how far the posited equivalence between Oedipus and Tiresias will take us. The events at the end of the play are framed by the earlier dispute between the two in which Tiresias voices the first hint that Oedipus is guilty of incest and predicts that he will soon be as blind as the aged Tiresias is himself. When Oedipus ultimately accepts his guilt and puts out his own eyes, Tiresias is vindicated on both counts. Oedipus has become Tiresias's physical double, but the parallel ends there. The unique circumstances of Oedipus's blindness set him apart, or so it seems.

In reality, we cannot be sure where the parallel ends without knowing the circumstances of Tiresias's blindness. Although the play does not tell us, the story would have been familiar to Sophocles' Athenian spectators. Indeed, it was their city's namesake, the goddess Athena herself, who struck Tiresias blind when he was still a small child. Athena was bathing; Tiresias's offense—as inadvertent as Oedipus's—was to have accidentally seen her unclothed. Having misused his eyes, Tiresias was condemned to lose them. If we return now to the play, we will notice that Oedipus blinds himself with brooches torn from Jocasta's dress (1268–70)—the very brooches that failed to keep him from seeing her unclothed. Thus, Oedipus's punishment fits the crime in the same way that Tiresias's punishment fit the crime. He too loses his eyes after misusing them. Oedipus is therefore Tiresias's equal not only in his blindness but in the reason for it.

A Freudian might object that this demonstration of the loss of distinctions conveniently leaves the element of incest out of account. But it is easy enough to restore this element to the equation by assuming, in Freudian fashion, that when little Tiresias glimpsed the adult Athena bathing, he must have been filled with unconscious lust for her as a mother-figure. In fact, Roheim, who does not hesitate to equate Oedipus and Tiresias, he even cites a version of the myth, in Callimachus's *Lavacrum Palladis*, in which Tiresias encounters the goddess bathing *with his mother*.[13] It follows that Tiresias's offense was "oedipal" before the fact—in which case it might be just as apt to call Oedipus's offense "tiresian." Either way, the distinction between the two is lost.

Filthy Oedipus

For Girard, the theme of incest is itself significant primarily as an extreme indicator of the loss of distinctions. By erasing the line dividing the roles of son and husband or mother and wife, an incestuous union undermines the most fundamental differences on which the social order rests. Moreover, any offspring such a union produces will necessarily suffer from the same loss of distinctions,[14] so that Oedipus laments having sired "children brothers of their father." As Greek classics scholar Maria Daraki observes, "what the king of Thebes accuses himself of in horror, is of having mixed generations. In Sophocles' tragedy, incest is not strictly speaking a *sexual* transgression; it offends the laws of a certain type of *descent*."[15] Following Sophocles' own lead, Girard emphasizes this "scandalous scrambling of kinship,"[16] which is cited repeatedly throughout the play as the monstrous consequence of incest.

In its power to confound distinctions, incest is akin to violence. Just as incest turns family members into doubles, violent conflict turns enemies into doubles. The accusation of incest gives symbolic expression to the same process of undifferentiation that unfolds before our eyes as we witness the conflict between Oedipus and Tiresias. But that is only half the story. The accusation of incest is not just a symbol, it is also a weapon used by one antagonist against the other. When Tiresias calls Oedipus a father-killing mother-lover, he is hitting him with the biggest insult he can muster. It would be hard to charge anyone with a viler crime, except perhaps raping a nun (and, as we shall see, this omission is easily repaired).

While incest destroys specificities, the *accusation* of incest has the power to destroy a specific individual: the accused. If the accusation is made to stick, the latter will be destroyed in the eyes of the community, singled out as the sole source of what may actually be a more general process of undifferentiation. In the first part of Sophocles' play, for instance, the city is already in the grip of a plague, which the Delphic oracle attributes to an act of regicide. Oedipus and Tiresias each blame the other for this initial violation of a fundamental distinction. As they defend with equal vehemence and an equal lack of evidence their equal and opposite accusations, they only deepen the pre-existing crisis of differences. But once Tiresias succeeds in definitively pinning on his adversary the blame for the regicide, along with shocking new charges of patricide and incest, Oedipus stands alone as a unique embodiment of the breakdown of distinctions. "In Oedipus," observes Girard, "difference is so radically destroyed that all men shrink back in horror. And this shrinking back, this putting at a distance, is the restoration of the lost difference."[17]

Here we have reached the turning point in the dynamic of the crisis described by Girard and in Girard's own argument. At the very moment when all differences are imperiled and each antagonist seems to be nothing more than the equal of the other, a paradoxical reversal occurs: by virtue of being concentrated in a single individual, undifferentiation itself is transmuted into the basis for a new difference. Incest represents an excess of undifferentiation sufficient to make Oedipus "more equal" than—

and therefore different from—everyone else: this is not merely Girard's interpretation, it is what Tiresias himself affirms through a play on words analyzed by Jean-Pierre Vernant, France's leading authority on classical Greece. In "Ambiguity and Reversal," an article on *Oedipus* published not long after Girard's "Symmetry and Dissymmetry," Vernant writes:

> The equalization of Oedipus and his sons is expressed in a series of brutal images. . . . But it is Tiresias who gives all its tragic weight to this vocabulary of equality when he addresses himself to Oedipus in these terms: there will come evils that "will make you equal to yourself by making you equal to your children" (425). The identification of Oedipus with his own father and his own children, the assimilation in Jocasta of mother and wife, make Oedipus equal to himself, that is, they make him an *agos* ["thing of faith"], a being *apolis*, without common dimensions, without equality with other men.[18]

Tiresias stigmatizes Oedipus for his distinctive lack of distinctions. Being equal to his children makes him unequalled in his iniquity. No one is as filthy as he. "There is dirt upon thy head, O Oedipus," Tiresias proclaims. "Dirt, dirt, dirt, upon the head of Oedipus."

But isn't Tiresias right? By the end of the play, everyone agrees that Oedipus killed his father and married his mother, including the accused himself. Isn't Oedipus guilty as charged?

Looking for Clues

Sophocles' *Oedipus* is often deemed the world's first mystery story, and a very sophisticated one at that. After questioning witnesses and assembling evidence, the hero deduces that he himself is the villain. This twist is so dramatic that we may lose track of what the mystery was about in the first place. The question the hero originally set out to answer was not, after all, "Who killed his father and married his mother?" It was not even, strictly speaking, "Who killed Laius?" As the story opens, no one is even thinking about Laius. His death has been forgotten amidst the generalized death and destruction caused by the plague. It is this crisis, not one man's murder, that the people of Thebes call upon their ruler to solve. And from the standpoint of the crisis, the relevant question is not so much "Who done it?" as "Who started it?" When Oedipus sends to Delphi for advice, the oracle's reply addresses the latter question.

Every good mystery story includes a red herring to throw alert readers off the track. In *Oedipus,* the oracle supplies what modern readers would ordinarily regard as an obvious red herring. According to the oracle, Thebes is harboring an unpunished killer whose festering presence is responsible for the plague. Now, this cannot be right. We know that plagues are not caused by the mere presence of miscreants, no matter how foul the deeds they may have committed. Yet Oedipus and the Thebans immediately swallow this colossal red herring hook, line, and sinker. To Girard, there is something fishy about the way they drop everything to go chasing after Laius's killer.

There is, of course, an easy explanation for their behavior: being ancient Greeks, they would presumably have shared a cultural belief in the magical potency of blood pollution. To demonstrate how "strongly this superstition worked, even in the days of the 'enlightenment,'" J. T. Sheppard quotes from a speech composed for Athenian prosecutors by the orator Antiphon as a model of "the kind of argument to which a jury will respond": "It is against your own advantage that this person, so bloodstained and so foul, should have access to the sacred precincts of your gods and should pollute their purity; should sit at the same table with yourselves, and should infect the guiltless by his presence. It is this that causes barrenness in the land. It is this that brings misfortune upon men's undertakings."[19] If one believes that contact with a person bloodstained and foul can cause pestilence, sterility, or all-around misfortune, then it is only logical, when a plague or similar calamity strikes, to go hunting for the foul individual responsible.

The extent to which enlightened Greeks of Sophocles' era still gave credence to such archaic beliefs is open to debate. In the end, however, the precise nature of their beliefs is of secondary importance here. Culturally specific beliefs cannot account for behavior which is not culturally specific, and there is little that is culturally specific about the behavior of the characters in *Oedipus*. All over the world, people of widely varying beliefs have responded to calamity by going hunting for the foul individuals responsible.

The reference to culturally specific Greek beliefs is therefore itself something of a red herring. It allows us to feel guiltless by making sure the holders of such bloodthirsty beliefs do not sit at our table and infect us by their presence. Yet, though we ourselves do not believe that a Theban plague could be cured by tracking down the individual responsible, we too are caught up in the thrill of the hunt.

This thrill doubtless explains in large measure the popularity of both *Oedipus* and modern crime fiction.[20] Girard quotes Northrop Frye's observation that the "growing brutality" of the mystery story comes "as close as it is normally possible for art to come to the pure self-righteousness of the lynching mob."[21] If *Oedipus* is a detective story, Girard is a meta-detective who sniffs out the evidence of mob violence hidden behind the surface details of the narrative. These details fit together like the pieces of a puzzle. On the one hand, we have a disaster threatening the community. On the other, we have a single individual who is blamed for the disaster, while at the same time being accused of unspeakable moral transgressions. Between these alleged transgressions and the general disaster, no rational causal link is possible. For that very reason, the conjunction of the two disparate types of charges is all the more striking.

This conjunction provides Girard with a vital clue, for hapless individuals have been the victims of such two-pronged accusations throughout much of Western history. "During the great medieval plague epidemics, for instance, the Jews were often the victims of these accusations, and so were the foreigners and strangers who happened to find themselves in some panic-stricken town. A century or two later, the same pattern of accusation reappears in the great epidemic of witch-hunting in the Western world."[22]

Girard identifies a further clue in the lameness of Oedipus, whose very name is an epithet meaning "swollen foot": "In a panicked community, an individual's chances of being selected as a victim are greatly increased if, in addition to being a highly visible and powerful stranger who became successful too fast, he is afflicted with some physical infirmity that the multitude regards as uncanny."[23] The inelegant manner in which Oedipus's name alludes to his infirmity is lost on non-Greek ears. Shelley remedied this problem in a parody whose inspired title, "Swellfoot the Tyrant," conveys the meaning of the original better than more reverent versions.

When things fall apart, it doesn't take the clairvoyance of a Tiresias to figure out where to lay the blame. Any child could point a finger at the newcomer who walks funny. "Swellfoot started it! It's Swellfoot's fault." The pure self-righteousness of the accuser is contagious. Soon everyone will take up the refrain. "There is dirt upon Swellfoot's head. Dirt, dirt, dirt, upon the head of Swellfoot."

By joining together to heap abuse on a common target, the members of the community can surmount the quarrels that are bound to divide them in a time of crisis. This is especially true when, as in the case of disease or drought, little can be done to attack the real causes. "Through its recourse to arbitrary violence," writes Girard, "the helpless populace manages to forget its helplessness in the face of uncontrollable events."[24]

Naturally, the populace does not regard its violence as arbitrary. It feels fully justified in going after an individual so bloodstained and so foul. "A lynching mob must believe in the malevolence of its victim," Girard observes. "Which means that a lynching process described by the lynchers themselves must necessarily come out as something other than itself, as the Oedipus myth for instance."[25]

The myth does not present Oedipus as an arbitrary victim; it tells us that he really did commit patricide and incest and that he really did cause the plague. Now, when it comes to the plague, we know he cannot possibly be guilty as charged, but we may still hesitate to reject the accusation of patricide and incest. After all, a son of the king and queen of Thebes could conceivably be abandoned as an infant, saved by herdsmen and raised as the son of the king and queen of Corinth before chancing to kill the king of Thebes and chancing to wed his widow. It is not likely, but it *could* happen. We might therefore conclude that although the myth has arbitrarily accused this club-footed stranger of being a provoker of plagues, it has nonetheless credibly identified him as a father-killing mother-lover.

What if it further alleged that the same individual had begun by defiling hundreds of nuns? In a Russian folk variant on the Oedipus myth,[26] there is no microbial plague, but a veritable epidemic of sin sweeps through a convent when the devil inspires a stranger who had been abandoned as an infant to "defile the nuns one by one, sometimes by force, other times with love in secret." We may apply to this onslaught Thucydides' comment on the Athenian plague quoted earlier: "No constitution was of itself strong enough to resist or weak enough to escape the attacks." Indeed, only after the diabolical stranger has violated all three hundred inmates of the convent, including the Mother Superior, is he expelled by the assembled nuns. He then goes on to kill his father, marry his mother, and murder three priests for good measure—or so we are told. By this time, however, we may doubt the narrative's credibility. Although the enormities it alleges could conceivably happen, they are so unlikely we are liable to acquit the accused of all charges.

This Russian folk narrative demonstrates the vanity of treating the accusation of patricide and incest differently from the other accusations made against Oedipus and similar mythic figures. Whether we are told that they defiled their mothers and hordes of nuns or, as in further variants on the Oedipus myth, that they devoured their own baby sons,[27] these allegations do not deserve to be taken seriously any more than the allegation that Oedipus caused a plague by committing regicide.

But why should we take seriously anything that mythic narratives tell us? Aren't they just stories in the first place—pure fiction from beginning to end?

René Girard was originally trained as a medieval historian.[28] When he later turned his attention to primitive and classical myths, he was struck by their similarity to medieval accounts of persecutions written from the persecutors' viewpoint.[29] The authors of these accounts believe self-righteously in the malevolence of the victims despite the manifestly fanciful nature of the charges made against them. We may be told, for example, that in a time of plague Jews were put to death as diabolical traitors by an angry populace after being accused of devouring Christian babies and poisoning the water supply. Although we reject both of these fanciful charges, we do not dismiss the entire account as pure fiction from beginning to end. Instead, we take it seriously as evidence that, in a time of plague, Jews may well have been put to death as diabolical traitors by an angry populace after being accused of devouring Christian babies and poisoning the water supply.

Girard takes myths seriously in the same way. He sees them as evidence of real persecutions. Even when the link to particular historical events is irretrievably lost, the types of accusations we find in myths betray their origin. The more outlandish these accusations are, however, the easier it is for us to view them as harmless poetic conceits. This outlandishness gradually fades as we near the modern period. Our Russian folktale is already less fantastic than the Greek myth, since the diabolical stranger is not blamed for provoking an actual plague, but the notion that he defiled three hundred nuns is still extravagant enough to pass for an innocuous flight of fancy. But what if a century-old narrative from the American South stated that a diabolical black mother-lover had defiled, one by one, sometimes by force, other times by love in secret, a series of virginal white maidens? Surely we would then conclude, as Girard concludes of mythology, that the "conjunction of themes" displayed could not be the product of a "purely poetic imagination."[30]

A change in the identities of the characters and locations may suffice to make us treat a narrative differently. When we read an overwrought account of a Southern lynching or medieval witch-hunt written from the persecutors' viewpoint, we do not praise it as a colorful contribution to world mythology. But when a narrative comes to us cloaked in the glorious mantle of ancient Greece, we approach it with different assumptions.

In his book *The Scapegoat*, Girard proposed a "simple experiment": "I'm going to give the story of Oedipus a homely disguise; I shall remove his Greek clothing. . . . In so doing, the myth will descend several steps on the social ladder":

Harvests are bad, the cows give birth to dead calves, no one is on good terms with anyone else. It is as if a spell had been cast on the village. Clearly, the cripple is to blame. He arrived one fine morning, no one knows from where, and made himself at home. He even took the liberty of marrying the most prominent heiress in the village and had two children by her. They say the wildest things go on in their house! The stranger is suspected of having done away with his wife's first husband, a sort of local potentate, who disappeared under mysterious circumstances and was rather too quickly replaced in both roles by the newcomer. One day the fellows in the village had had enough; they took their pitch forks and forced the disturbing character to clear out.[31]

By stripping the myth of its familiar trappings, Girard's experiment allows us to see it in a new light.

Frederick Ahl conducted a similar experiment on a more elaborate scale in the classroom, using the students in his Greek literature courses as guinea pigs. This time, the focus of the experiment was not the myth of Oedipus, but Sophocles' tragedy. Over a period of two years, Ahl gave some classes an undisguised translation of *Oedipus* and others a second version in which the names and locations were changed. Even though he presented the play identically to both groups as "the story of a man who discovered that he had killed his father and contracted an incestuous marriage," Ahl observed a "marked difference" in the students' responses:

Those given the disguised version read the play much more carefully than those who knew from the outset that they were reading Sophocles' tragedy. And they asked far more questions and expressed a great deal more skepticism about the conventional interpretation I offered them. It became clear that those familiar with the Oedipus myth were beginning with assumptions about what the play *must* mean, and that they tended to privilege that assumption even when the language of the play did not itself tend to support it. Thus I began to realize that there was a very special tension in *Oedipus* between the "received" myth and the structure of the drama itself.[32]

Prodded by his students' questions, Ahl undertook his own word-by-word study of the play in the original Greek, the results of which he presents in his landmark 1991 book *Sophocles' Oedipus: Evidence and Self-Conviction.*

Ahl's examination of the evidence suggests that Girard may have been too cautious, if anything, in formulating his interpretation of Sophocles.

In *Violence and the Sacred*, Girard ventures a "strange and well-nigh fantastic thought": "If we eliminate the testimony brought against Oedipus in the second half of the tragedy, then the conclusion of the myth, far from seeming a sudden lightning flash of the truth, striking down the guilty party and illuminating all the mortal participants, seems nothing more than the camouflaged victory of one version of the story over the other."[33] But if Ahl is right, it should be possible to sustain Girard's interpretation without eliminating the testimony found in the play's second half, for, in reality, "no conclusive evidence is presented that Oedipus killed his father and married his mother." If we decide that he did, Ahl contends, "we are doing so on the basis of assumptions external to the arguments presented."[34]

Such assumptions may stem not only from our knowledge of the myth, but also from our understanding of the way mystery stories operate. Once the Delphic oracle launches the hunt for Laius's killer, we have a right to expect that the culprit will ultimately be identified. What kind of detective story ends with the hero fingering the wrong man? Unless we can be sure that the accused is the guilty party, we will be cheated of the *katharsis* so reliably delivered by modern mysteries and ancient tragedies alike. But perhaps Sophocles has concocted a mystery even more sophisticated than we thought. At the risk of lessening the satisfaction produced by a tidy ending, let us go back and ask whether Oedipus is really the man the oracle was talking about.

Phrased in this way, the question is misleading because it implies that the oracle blamed a single individual for Laius's death. In fact, as Sandor Goodhart emphasizes in a seminal essay cited by Ahl, the oracle in Creon's report "speaks distinctly of a multiplicity of murderers. 'Apollo now clearly commands us to punish with [heavy] hand his murderers, whoever they may be'" (line 107).[35] Creon goes on to add that the only member of Laius's party to escape "insisted [*ephaske*] that many brigands [*lêistas*] waylaid him: many hands, not one man's force" (122–23).[36] Indeed, the fact that the assailants were numerous was the "one thing" of which the witness was "certain." The chorus and Jocasta later confirm having heard the same thing. Some critics have opined that a witness who flees in fear might lie about the number of attackers. Perhaps, but there is no suggestion to this effect in the text. Oedipus himself affirms that, when he is able to question the witness, the apparent discrepancy as to the number of murderers will be the key point: "if he still says the same number, I was not the killer; for one cannot be equal to many" (843–45). Moreover, a similar discrepancy exists, not mentioned by Oedipus, concerning an equally crucial point: the number of victims. Since Oedipus recalls having killed an unidentified old man and "all" the members of his party, the very fact that one member of Laius's party lived to tell the tale is good evidence that Laius and his party were not the victims of Oedipus.[37] All save one cannot be equal to all.

Now, surely the ancient Greeks were capable of doing the math. It doesn't take a rocket scientist to see that, unless the interrogation of the murder witness produces dramatic new evidence regarding these points, Oedipus cannot be convicted of killing Laius. But when the witness arrives, Oedipus fails to ask him a single question about Laius's death. He is distracted by questions about his own birth raised by a visitor from Corinth who claims first to have found Oedipus as a baby, then to have received him from none other than the murder witness.[38] The latter then states he gave Jocasta's baby to the Corinthian, telling Oedipus: "If you're who he says you are, then you were born to a grim fate" (1180–81).[39]

But *is* Oedipus who the other says? Ahl maintains there is no evidence he is: "We have only the anonymous Corinthian's word for it."[40] One might object that we also have the evidence of Oedipus's feet. Since the feet of Jocasta's baby were pinned together, the Corinthian fastens on Swellfoot's infirmity to clinch his case. The argument is hardly decisive, however. If Jocasta's husband has bad feet and Jocasta's son has bad feet, it does not follow that her husband is her son. To conclude that he is, we are still obliged to rely on the anonymous Corinthian's word.

Most translators confer an aura of authority on this nameless stranger by labeling him a "messenger." In reality, as R. D. Dawe notes, he is "not an official representative, but one hoping to earn a reward on his own account by enterprisingly informing Oedipus of local gossip."[41] Having heard a rumor in Corinth that Oedipus will succeed to the throne following the death of his father, the stranger hurried to Thebes with the news, aiming to ingratiate himself with the incoming king. But Oedipus will not think of regaining his homeland as long as his mother still lives. When he explains that he has long feared fulfilling a prophecy of incest and patricide, the Corinthian asks: "why have I not yet freed you from this fear?" (1003). The following dialogue then takes place (1004–7):

OEDIPUS: And I'd reward you well if you still could.

CORINTHIAN: And I came here primarily for this: the hope that I'd do well
when you came home.

OEDIPUS: I'll never go where my begetters live.[42]

The Corinthian then proceeds to tell Oedipus the one thing he can tell
him if he still wants to collect a royal recompense, namely, that Oedipus
was not begotten in Corinth.

The anonymous Corinthian might be telling the truth, but Sophocles has supplied him with a good reason for lying, and Oedipus is Jocasta's
son only if the Corinthian is not lying. Had Sophocles wished to place the
belief in Oedipus's incest on a firm basis, he could have made its source an
official envoy rather than a self-seeking gossipmonger. And yet, swept
along by the momentum of a drama in which all suspicion comes to center on a single individual—Oedipus—we are not apt to stop and question
the motives of other characters. "Sophocles' great achievement here," Ahl
comments, "is to make us do what Oedipus does: to disregard or rational-
ize away everything that might demonstrate the hero's innocence."[43]

In ruling out the hero's innocence, we are following the lead of the
hero himself: in a word, we are *imitating Oedipus.* When the murder witness, after telling how he disposed of Jocasta's baby, says Oedipus was born
to a grim fate *if* he is who the Corinthian says (1180–81), Oedipus ignores
this prudent caveat and leaps to the conclusion that he has committed
both incest and patricide: "how it all could come so clear! . . . forbidden
marriage and killings I should not have carried out!" (1182, 1185). Not only
does Oedipus accept without question that he has married his mother, he
instantly assumes that he has murdered his father as well. But the murder
witness's testimony about Jocasta's baby has brought us no closer to knowing who killed Laius. As one critic observed long ago, the fulfillment of the
prophecy of patricide is not "directly established," it is "inferred" from the
fulfillment of the prophecy of incest.[44]

This "inference" is not a logical deduction but a mythological one.
Logically, the incest charge should have no bearing on the murder investigation. Even if Oedipus is Jocasta's son, it does not follow that he killed
Laius. But an incestuous son is a transgressor of mythic proportions; as one
capable of anything, he can be accused of anything. No proof is needed to
blame him for further crimes, and the hunt for Laius's killer may cease on
the spot, the niceties of detective work forgotten now that the taint of incest has turned Oedipus into an all-purpose culprit: a scapegoat.

Thus, what began as a mystery story stands revealed as something else, something more like the tale of a lynching. If the object were to find Laius's killer, the alleged incest would be no more than a red herring. But, as we noted at the outset, the question of who killed Laius was already a red herring with regard to the crisis brought on by the plague. Since no single individual is responsible for this general disaster, the investigation was bound to end by imputing guilt to a scapegoat. Oedipus's suitability as a scapegoat was made evident by his infirmity. Once this was used to identify him with Jocasta's baby, his conviction on all charges was a foregone conclusion. "Swellfoot is a dirty mother-lover; therefore he must be the foul individual who killed the king and caused the plague": this spurious chain of reasoning is all the more persuasive for being adopted by the interested party. "There is dirt upon my head," proclaims Swellfoot. "Dirt, dirt, dirt, upon the head of Swellfoot."

Oedipus "joins in the unanimous chorus that proclaims him to be the most abominable filth; he is repulsed by himself and beseeches the city of Thebes to repulse him literally from its midst." The cooperation of victims with their persecutors has often been observed, notes Girard: "We are told in the sixteenth century that witches themselves choose the stake; they were made to understand the horror of their misdeeds. Heretics, too, often call for the punishment merited by their abominable beliefs," a phenomenon visible in our time with the Stalinist show trials.[45] A persecution best succeeds in replacing dissension with consensus when no member of the community questions the myth of the victim's guilt: "The victim must participate if there is to be perfect unanimity. . . . The perspective of the persecutors is transformed into indisputable truth by Oedipus' final submission to the imbecilic judgment of the crowd."[46]

The pivotal role played by the crowd in Oedipus's downfall is demonstrated by the chorus's speech that immediately follows the words of Oedipus quoted above: "forbidden marriage and killings I should not have carried out!" When Oedipus speaks, he is still king; once the chorus has spoken, he is king no longer. The chorus's speech includes a line whose significance was pointed out by Michel Foucault: "He was our bastion against disaster, our honoured King" (1200–1202).[47] Foucault drew attention to the chorus's use of the past tense here, "meaning that the people of Thebes, at the same time that they recognize in Oedipus the one who had been their king . . . declare him now stripped of his kingship."[48] Oedipus is summarily deposed by collective fiat.

"The ritual expulsion demanded by Oedipus at the end of the play echoes the collective violence which constitutes the true mainspring of mythological creation," Girard affirms.[49] If we imitate Oedipus in assuming that he actually committed incest and patricide, then we join in the chorus of those who contribute to keeping the myth alive. That is why, for Goodhart, "Sophocles' play is a critique via Oedipus of us," a "critique of mythogenesis."[50] Of course, Sophocles does not tell us that Oedipus is innocent any more than the myth does. Rather, what both Goodhart and Ahl argue, in effect, is that Sophocles' play operates at two levels, just as Girard has argued that the plays of Shakespeare operate at two levels.[51] Sophocles has constructed his drama so artfully that, in Ahl's words, we "are lured into overlooking the same sort of detail that Oedipus overlooks until, at the end, we share his conviction of guilt."[52] At the same time, however, Sophocles has strewn the trail with clues indicating that there is more to the story than meets the eye.

When One is Equal to Many

The biggest clue is the statement "one cannot be equal to many," which Goodhart's article brought to the attention of Girard. We saw that Oedipus makes this statement after hearing that the murder witness had said Laius's killers were many: "if he still says the same number, I was not the killer; for one cannot be equal to many" (843–45). In *Job: The Victim of His People*, Girard observes that this sentence echoes an earlier sentence spoken by Oedipus that implies, on the contrary, one *can* be substituted for many: "In the first scene the king said to the Thebans, who had come to beg him to cure them: 'I suffer more than any one of you for I, your king, must suffer for everyone at once.'" It is the king's job to take upon his own head all the ills that afflict his people, even at the price of becoming the victim of his people. As king, he must be willing to sacrifice himself for the good of the kingdom. Thus, Oedipus's suitability as a scapegoat is determined not only by his infirmity but also by the lofty position he occupies. "By accepting the kingship," Girard comments, "every man runs the risk of becoming a scapegoat, and that is what Oedipus implicitly recognized in his first sentence."[53]

The two contradictory sentences spoken by Oedipus embody the dilemma he faces. In purely rational terms, he cannot be guilty, for "one" and "many" are not interchangeable. But if no culprit is found, the crisis will continue indefinitely. In the last resort, Oedipus must assume the role of culprit himself. This entails arbitrarily ignoring the witness's testimony and forsaking the rational logic in which "one" and "many" are not inter-changeable for the scapegoating logic in which a single man may be made to suffer in the place of many.

"If it is I, the Singular Man, who is guilty, let (the punishment) spare the many! If it is the many who are guilty, let the (punishment) be for me, the Singular Man!" These words, which so well express the heads-you-win /tails-I-lose logic of the scapegoat, are said to have been uttered by an ancient Chinese emperor who offered himself as "victim" to end a drought.[54] Oedipus and the Chinese ruler both exemplify what is in fact an intrinsic aspect of kingship. Since any crisis affecting a kingdom is the king's responsibility, he functions by the very nature of things as an all-purpose culprit. The chorus told us that when Oedipus was their "honored King," they counted on him to be their "bastion against disaster." It is only natural that when disaster struck, they would deem it to be the bastion's fault. Like the African monarchs described by Simon Simonse, Oedipus is a "king of disaster," destined to be sacrificed when all else fails.[55]

"In Homer and Hesiod," notes Jean-Pierre Vernant, "the fecundity of the earth, of the flocks, of women depends on the person of the king, off-spring of Zeus. . . . Thus the normal solution, when the divine scourge strikes a people, is to sacrifice the king." But less drastic remedies were also available, which involved delegating the part of the unfit king to a substitute victim:

Such is the *pharmakos*: double of the king, but in reverse, like those carnival rulers crowned for the duration of a festival, when order is set upside down, social hierarchies reversed: sexual prohibitions are lifted, theft becomes legal, the slaves take their masters' place. . . . But when the festival is over, the counter-king is expelled or put to death, taking with him all the disorder which he incarnates and of which the community is purged at one blow.[56]

Once he is charged with subverting social hierarchy and sexual prohibitions through patricide and incest, Oedipus embodies all the disorder of which the community must be purged.[57] In the opening scene, he had promised the crowd of Thebans complaining of the plague that, as their king, he would take their ills upon himself; in the closing scene, the plague has been forgotten and Oedipus, king no longer, tells the Thebans to expel him, saying: "My ills are mine, no other mortal was made to bear them" (1414–15). As one critic observes, "the sense in which his downfall means his city's salvation is immediate and intimate."[58] May we conclude, then, that Oedipus is a *pharmakos*?

It would be more accurate to say that Oedipus becomes a scape-goat—a "*pharmakos* figure" in Northrop Frye's sense[59]—for want of a rit-ual *pharmakos* in the strict sense. It is precisely because he does not delegate the scapegoat's role to a substitute victim that Oedipus ends up becoming the victim himself. His victimhood is the outcome of a spontaneous process, not a ritual procedure. "Oedipus is a scapegoat in the fullest sense *because he is never designated as such*," Girard stresses.[60] Oedipus is not des-ignated as a *pharmakos*; he is designated as the father-killing mother-lover who caused the plague. Sophocles' play is not the dramatization of a ritual. But it is not the dramatization of a myth, either. Sophocles never shows Oedipus killing his father or marrying his mother. Instead, he stages the process through which, in a time of crisis, everyone comes to *believe* that Oedipus killed his father and married his mother. In this sense, Sophocles' *Oedipus* is indeed "a play about the genesis of a myth."[61]

Perhaps the best way to make clear this understanding of *Oedipus* is through a comparison with the story of another Oedipal figure, Anwar:

A faraway land across the sea enjoyed many years of prosperity under the firm hand of a proud ruler until one day, out of the blue, disaster struck. The land fell prey to a dangerous contagion, and prosperity gave way to blight and misery. The ruler's suffering subjects looked to him for a solution. After conducting an inves-tigation, he announced that a guilty party had been found: the culprit was none other than Anwar, his heir-apparent. Anwar was seized by the ruler's men and charged with subverting the land's social hierarchy and sexual prohibitions through abuse of power and sodomy.

Thus far, the tale of Anwar is not unlike that of Oedipus. The main differ-ence lies in the fact that the ruler in this story does not take the people's ills upon his own head, preferring instead to delegate the scapegoat's role to a substitute victim. But Anwar is not explicitly designated as a substitute vic-tim any more than Oedipus is; he is designated as a seditious sodomite. At this point, however, the tale of Anwar takes a rather unexpected turn:

Throngs of Anwar's supporters gathered throughout the land to proclaim his in-nocence. They accused the ruler of ordering him seized on trumped-up charges having nothing to do with the crisis at hand.

Has there ever been a myth that ends with such a surprising reversal?

The answer is no. There never has been a myth that ends with mem-bers of the community questioning the fantastic accusations made against the protagonist. In reality, the tale of Anwar is not a myth at all, it is a true story. The faraway land is Malaysia, whose economic success caused many observers in the mid-1990s to class it with the so-called "Asian tigers." The contagion that struck out of the blue was the financial panic of 1997 in which foreign investors fled en masse.[62] In 1998, faced with an unprecedented crisis, Malaysia's ruler ordered the arrest of his political heir-apparent, Anwar Ibrahim, on charges of "abuse of power" and "sodomy."[63] Most Malaysians found these accusations unconvincing. They know very well that sodomy cannot be responsible for a financial contagion. For this reason, the story of Anwar will never become a myth. Anwar is a failed scapegoat because he was rightly believed *to be* a scapegoat. By contrast, "Oedipus is a successful scapegoat, because he is never recognized as such."[64]

Oedipus is a successful scapegoat because he is wrongly believed to have committed the crimes of which he is accused. Does this mean he is innocent?

The answer seems obvious. Readers who have followed our argument thus far may understandably suppose Girard to be an unstinting defender of Oedipus's innocence, and most of his more recent writings on the subject could certainly lead one to this conclusion. In reality, his position is a little more complicated, as we shall soon see.

First, let us leave aside momentarily the question of the accused's guilt or innocence and consider what is involved in the very act of accusation. François Tricaud has suggested that every accusation involves an element of scapegoating inasmuch as it creates a feeling that all guilt must necessarily be concentrated in a single direction:

it magically removes guilt from the accuser by establishing between the accused and him a sort of highly polarized vector in which all moral purity has gone to one extremity and all impurity to the other. Whereas a sick man is not disqualified, by his state, from recognizing the sickness in another, in the world of accusation everything takes place as if the only possible revealer of the accusation were scandalized innocence. This is the scapegoater's sleight of hand.[65]

We may take Tricaud's reasoning one step further by asking what will happen should the accusation of guilt be refuted. The "highly polarized vector" magically established by the initial accusation is not liable to disappear in a puff of smoke; more likely, it will simply reverse polarities. The accused will now embody scandalized innocence, while all impurity will shift to the other extremity, the accuser standing accused in turn of having made a false accusation.

In ancient Greece, such a reversal of the vector of guilt was clearly observed in the case of trials by ordeal, which left the sentence to the judgment of the gods. If the accused survived a life-threatening physical test, then his innocence was proven. But one must not imagine that matters ended there. According to Marie Delcourt, "those who have studied the ordeal have neglected one of its aspects. They have interested themselves only in the fate of the accused, never in the fate of the accuser." But, as many Greek legends testify, "one cannot appeal to the justice of the gods without putting oneself in danger": "The trial always ends with an acquittal and with a condemnation. If the accused is proclaimed innocent, his adversary, even if he had been in good faith, pays for his mistake."[66]

Delcourt discerns a reversal of this type in the myth of the Flood. Although in the biblical story of Noah the ark is rationalized as a boat, an "ark" was originally a chest. The Hebrew word for Noah's vessel, *têbâ*, appears in only one other passage, where it designates the chest in which Moses's mother cast her baby upon the waters. To be cast adrift in a chest is to undergo an ordeal. The myth of the Flood concludes, Delcourt remarks, "with the salvation of the protagonist of the ordeal and with the death of all other men."[67]

Delcourt finds the same type of reversal at work in the myth of Oedipus, whose father commands that the baby be exposed on the mountainside or, in a variant, cast adrift. If Oedipus had been born clubfooted, this would have been reason enough to condemn him in the eyes of the ancient Greeks, who viewed such congenital deformities as "proof of divine wrath." But exposing a baby on land or sea, rather than killing it outright, was a means of leaving its ultimate fate to the "judgment of God." Now, as we have just seen, a "judgment of God always ends with a condemnation." If the accused survives, "it is the accuser who will perish." And in legends, the instrument of divine justice in such cases is none other than the accused himself. So it is that "Oedipus, exposed by his father, will take his revenge on him."[68]

"The tragedy presents itself as an investigation into the 'murder of Laius.' But the real theme," Girard writes, "is the universal impurity which, thanks to the expulsion of the scapegoat, passes for a consequence of this one murder."[69] Accusing Oedipus magically removes guilt from all the other members of the plague-stricken community. If Oedipus is guilty as charged, then they are the victims of an act of violence which he alone committed. But if Girard is right and Oedipus is a scapegoat, then he is the victim of an act of violence committed by all the other members of the community. It is they who are guilty of wrongfully accusing him. As soon as we rehabilitate Oedipus, the vector of guilt appears to reverse direction, just as it does in the myth of the Flood. All the impurity which his expulsion would have drained away comes billowing back to submerge the rest of the community, leaving the victim as the lone embodiment of scandalized innocence, the sole survivor of the judgment of God.

The Scapegoat's Guilt

If Oedipus were burdened with no sins of his own, his moral status would be as felicitous as that of the scapegoat in Sylvia Townsend Warner's poem:

> See the scapegoat, happy beast,
> From every personal sin released,
> And in the desert hidden apart,
> Dancing with a careless heart.
>
> "Lightly weigh the sins of others."
> See him skip! "Am I my brother's
> Keeper? O never, no, no, no!
> Lightly come and lightly go!"[70]

Can Oedipus really be the only member of the community with no dirt on his head? Girard does not let him off so easily. Although Oedipus is not guilty *as charged*, that does not mean he is innocent. For Girard, "Oedipus is guilty, even if he did not kill his father and marry his mother. The violence to which he falls victim in the end is no different from that which he contemplated against his brother. His responsibility for everybody's misfortunes is real: it is exactly the same as the responsibility of anybody else."[71]

Our starting point was the conflict of doubles, the struggle of enemy brothers symbolized by the dispute between Oedipus and Tiresias. We have now come full circle. Tiresias accused Oedipus of responsibility for the death of Laius after Oedipus accused Tiresias of responsibility for the death of Laius. Each sought to make a victim of the other. *I know you are a scapegoater—but what am I?* If Tiresias is no more than Oedipus's equal, Oedipus is no more than Tiresias's equal. In fact, Oedipus himself initiated the hunt for the foul individual who killed the king and caused the plague. "If the scapegoat is first of all a hunter," comments Girard, "that is precisely because he is identical to everyone. The investigation that ends badly for Oedipus is not his alone, it is that of all the Thebans."[72]

All the Thebans want to discover who started the plague. Each believes it must be somebody else, and Oedipus is no exception. Girard compares him to the hero of Albert Camus's novel *The Plague*: "He presents himself as a man of good will, moved by a disaster which, at bottom, hardly touches him. . . . He is certainly not sick with the plague," or so he thinks.[73] But a sick man is not disqualified from recognizing the sickness in others; the fact that he sees it in those around him does not mean he is immune to the disease himself. For Girard, the disease is of a piece with the mounting violence and undifferentiation that accompany the hunt for the culprit who started it. Once Oedipus is convicted of patricide and incest, he stands as the unique embodiment of violence and undifferentiation; a mythological difference is established.

If we view Oedipus as a scapegoat, we consider that he has been arbitrarily singled out as the only one guilty. But if we view the scapegoat as *innocent*, we arbitrarily single him out as the only one *not* guilty, thereby establishing a new mythological difference. Like the *pharmakos* in Northrop Frye's definition, the scapegoat "is neither innocent nor guilty. He is innocent in the sense that what happens to him is far greater than anything he has done provokes, like the mountaineer whose shout brings down an avalanche. He is guilty in the sense that he is a member of a guilty society . . . or living in a world where such injustices are an inescapable part of existence."[74]

When Oedipus first pronounced his curse on Laius's killer, he did not know he was triggering an avalanche that would end up falling on his own head. Before it came to that, however, he had shown himself ready to direct the curse at his rivals for the roles of sage and king, his "enemy brothers" Tiresias and Creon, arbitrarily accusing them of having plotted Laius's death. Yet at the critical moment, as Girard emphasizes, he pulls back and refrains from violence: "Oedipus replies to the chorus, which has pleaded with him to spare Creon: 'What you are asking, if the truth be told, is neither more nor less than my death or exile.' . . . To spare an enemy brother from death or exile is to condemn oneself to death or exile: 'Well, then, let him depart—though his departure means my certain death, or else my ignominious expulsion from Thebes.'"[75] If there is a prophetic moment in the tragedy, it is this one. Here Oedipus breaks out of the circle of violence that circumscribes the myth. In the myth, the prophecy that Oedipus will kill Laius prompts Laius to condemn Oedipus; when Oedipus unknowingly takes his revenge on Laius, the circle of violence is closed. In the play, Oedipus knowingly renounces revenge on those who condemn him, despite his own prophecy that this renunciation will spell his downfall.

Having first contributed to the rivalries that plague Thebes, Oedipus abstains from further violence, even at the price of sacrificing himself. His curse on Laius's killer had been intended to target the culprit responsible for the plague; in the end, Oedipus identifies himself as the one responsible. Girard's approach leaves room for two different interpretations of this conclusion. If the plague is seen strictly as a microbial epidemic, then, whether or not he committed patricide and incest, Oedipus did not cause the Thebans' sufferings and must therefore be regarded as no more than a compliant scapegoat. But if the plague is understood in broader terms as a symbol of the violence and undifferentiation that become increasingly apparent as the hunt for a culprit progresses and the microbial epidemic itself fades from view, then, although he is still a scapegoat, Oedipus is not wrong to accept his own share of guilt for his city's ills.

The view of Oedipus as no more than an innocent victim is doubtless the one most familiar to Girard's readers. The two brief texts that conclude the present volume are representative of this view, which came to dominate Girard's writings after he refined his hypothesis that myth and ritual originate in the scapegoating process. Since this hypothesis undeniably marks a decisive advance in the anthropology of religion, Girard can hardly be blamed for seeking to formulate it in the most clearcut fashion possible by emphasizing the scapegoat's innocence. This seems to entail toppling Oedipus from the pedestal where he stands as a hero of the Western quest for knowledge and reducing him to the less-exalted status of a mere hapless victim. As Girard remarked in a 1978 interview, he does not "grant the Oedipus myth as myth the same privilege as Freud": "To me it is only one myth like any other." At the same time, however, he acknowledged the role played by Sophocles' tragedy in his own discovery of the structural power of scapegoating: "In *Violence and the Sacred*, this mechanism is first reached at the end and through the means of an analysis of *Oedipus Rex*."[76]

Written before *Violence and the Sacred*, the first three essays in this volume open a window onto the early evolution of Girard's thought. They demonstrate that his anthropological theory did not spring forth already full-blown, but emerged gradually out of his persistent reading and rereading of Sophocles' tragedy. In some ways, these early essays paint a richer and more nuanced portrait of Oedipus than Girard's later writings, one not yet bound by the tenets his theory was to lay down in its final form. The Oedipus who appears here betrays a greater family resemblance to Freud's Oedipus, but he is not bound by the assumptions of psychoanalytic theory either.

Freud's Oedipus is a hero of the quest for knowledge because, as the tragedy unfolds, he unearths the truth about himself in the same manner that patients in psychoanalysis must unearth the truth about themselves:

The action of the play consists in nothing other than the process of revealing, with cunning delays and ever-mounting excitement—a process that can be likened to the work of a psychoanalysis—that Oedipus himself is the murderer of Laïus, but further that he is the son of the murdered man and of Jocasta. . . . While the poet, as he unravels the past, brings to light the guilt of Oedipus, he is at the same time compelling us to recognize our own inner minds, in which those same impulses, though suppressed, are still to be found.[77]

The work of psychoanalysis comes down to imitating Oedipus by confronting these omnipresent impulses as unflinchingly as he did. Yet the extent of this imitation is limited by the assumption that, unlike the rest of us, Oedipus is guilty of actually carrying out those impulses: "Here is one in whom these primaeval wishes of our childhood have been fulfilled, and we shrink back from him with the whole force of the repression by which those wishes have since that time been held down within us."[78] We shrink back from him just as the Thebans shrink back from him, convinced that he and he alone has killed his father and married his mother. Like the culture heroes of countless foundation myths, who show what to do by showing what not to do, Freud's Oedipus is at once a universal model and a uniquely guilty transgressor.

Girard's Oedipus also becomes a hero of the quest for knowledge by unflinchingly confronting the truth about himself, but the truth this time involves the scapegoating impulse rather than a drive to incest or patricide. In the first part of Sophocles' play, Oedipus pursues the culprit responsible for a plague that he believes to be unrelated to his own behavior; he tries to scapegoat his rivals while accusing them of trying to scapegoat him. When Oedipus ultimately accepts his own responsibility for his city's ills, he turns against himself the accusation that he had previously directed at his rivals. We need not shrink back from him, for where scapegoating is concerned, Oedipus is not a uniquely guilty transgressor. *Imitating Oedipus* no longer means discovering within ourselves an impulse toward certain specific crimes which he alone committed, it means recognizing within ourselves the general impulse to single out others for behaving as we ourselves behave.

Contagious Desires

"The edge of wisdom is turned against the wise man": such is the moral that Nietzsche drew from *Oedipus*.[79] Girard's position is best captured by giving Nietzsche's maxim a twist: the wise man is the one who turns the edge of wisdom against himself. This is in effect the moral that Girard drew from the study of great Western writers in his first book, *Deceit, Desire, and the Novel: Self and Other in Literary Structure*. The "deceit" of the title is above all a form of self-deceit, the reassuring belief in one's own uniqueness, the Romantic faith in the Self's innate superiority to the contemptible mass of uncomprehending Others. The greatest novelists are distinguished by their shared ability to transcend the Manichean opposition between Self and Other and to see through "the illusion of spontaneous desire and of a subjectivity almost divine in its autonomy." This egoistic illusion is the "Romantic lie" that the book's original French title, *Mensonge romantique et vérité romanesque*, contrasts with "novelistic (*romanesque*) truth," the truth that the great novelist attains through a painfully acquired identification with the once-disdained Others: "There is novelistic genius when what is true about Others becomes true about the hero, in fact true about the novelist himself. After cursing Others the Oedipus-novelist realizes he himself is guilty."[80]

I know you are, but what am I? "The subject's indignant knowledge of the Other returns in a circle to strike him when he is least expecting it," writes Girard. "The sickest persons are always the ones obsessed with the sickness of Others."[81] Here we already have, in a nutshell, the argument Girard would later develop with regard to Oedipus and the plague. But the disease that he diagnoses in his first book is an "ontological sickness"; it is the chronic suffering caused by the deep-seated sensation, endemic to novelistic heroes, that they lack *being*. Proust supplies a clinical case history in *Remembrance of Things Past*, whose narrator recalls having felt that everyone else around him seemed "more precious and more important, endowed with a more real existence."[82]

I know you *are*—but what am I? If you *exist* more surely than I, if you possess the precious *being* that I so sorely lack, the best I can do is to imitate you. Imitation is the sincerest form of flattery, and the most widespread. From infancy on, humans learn how to comport themselves in the world by imitating others. The necessity of "role models" is readily acknowledged. What is not usually perceived is the influence of models in determining an individual's *desires*. Romantic thinking assumes desire is elicited directly by the presence of an intrinsically attractive object. In Girard's analysis, the presence of a model is essential to orient desire by designating the object as worthy of possession. This is especially clear in *Remembrance of Things Past*: "Proustian desire is *always* a borrowed desire." If the underlying desire is a metaphysical one, a desire for *being*, no object can truly satisfy it; the object is coveted only as an emblem of that "more real existence" seemingly displayed by the model who acts as the mediator of desire: "The impulse toward the object is at bottom an impulse toward the mediator."[83]

When an insuperable distance separates the mediator from the imitator, the relationship between the two remains relatively uncomplicated. Don Quixote tilts at windmills in his zeal to obtain the kind of knightly fame won by the legendary *chevalier* Amadis of Gaul. Quixote can safely avow his desire to imitate Amadis, for there is no chance of running into him in real life: the two knights will never tilt at each other. As to Sancho Panza, he is content to share in the pursuit of Quixote's aims by serving as a faithful vassal; he would never dream of jousting with his master. The one-sided relationships between Amadis and Quixote or Quixote and Sancho exemplify what Girard calls *external mediation*, where the mediator and imitator move in separate spheres, insuring that their paths will never collide.[84]

But when the mediation is *internal*, when the mediator moves within the same "sphere of possibilities" as the imitator, the relationship becomes much more symmetrical, and the very distinction between mediator and imitator threatens to collapse. The impulse toward the object "is checked by the mediator himself since he desires, or perhaps possesses, the object." The imitator, ever fascinated by the mediator, "inevitably sees, in the mechanical obstacle which he puts in his way, proof of the ill will borne him. Far from declaring himself a faithful vassal, he thinks only of repudiating the bonds of mediation." He therefore "reverses the logical and chronological order of desires in order to hide his imitation," persuading himself that his own desire is spontaneous and denouncing the mediator as a pesky intruder.[85]

According to Girard, "it is in internal mediation that the profoundest meaning of the *modern* is found." The erosion of traditional social barriers favors the rise of internal mediation, and this in turn leads to a loss of distinctions between mediator and imitator, who are destined to end up as symmetrical rivals. Thus, before Girard came to interpret the Theban plague as a crisis of differences, he had begun by linking the metaphysical affliction of novelistic heroes to the long, steady process of undifferentiation through which modernity emerges from the decline of the traditional order. In *Deceit, Desire, and the Novel*, Girard traces the progress of the "ontological sickness" from Cervantes through Stendhal and Flaubert to Dostoyevsky and Proust: "Proust's work describes new forms of alienation that succeed the old forms when 'needs' have been satisfied and when concrete differences no longer dominate relationships among men."[86]

As the distance between the novelistic hero and his mediator diminishes, the ontological sickness worsens, and metaphysical desire becomes ever more contagious. Indeed, the communicability of desire is the defining trait of internal mediation: "Internal mediation is present when one 'catches' a nearby desire just as one would catch the plague or cholera, simply by contact with an infected person." Since the contact allows for transmission of the infection in both directions, the mediator "will be tempted to copy the copy of his own desire," thus intensifying it beyond all measure. In this way, mediator and imitator become interchangeable doubles: "Each imitates the other while claiming that his own desire is prior and previous. Each looks on the other as an atrociously cruel persecutor."[87]

Rather than revealing this mechanism, the Romantic writer reflects it, depicting an exceptional hero at odds with a horde of persecuting Others. The solitary protagonist is the lone embodiment of scandalized innocence, the sole survivor of a universal judgment, as in Camus's novel *The Stranger*: "Meursault alone is innocent in a sea of guilt; he dies the victim of the Others. . . . He is the judge of his judges, like all the romantics before him. The hero always escapes the curse which his creator hurls at the rest of mankind."[88]

The wise man turns the edge of wisdom against himself. The novelistic hero transcends the Romantic lie when he "sees himself in the loathed rival" and "renounces the 'differences' suggested by hatred." In fact, it is the novelist himself who avows "his similarity to the fascinating Other through the voice of his hero." "The novelist recognizes that he is guilty of the sin of which he accuses his mediator," concludes Girard. "The curse which Oedipus hurled at Others falls on his own head."[89]

Like Oedipus, the novelist brings to light the hidden truth of his own guilt, but this does not mean that all guilt is concentrated in a single direction. The truth he discovers deep within himself is identical to everyone else's truth; indeed, it is the truth of the identity between himself and everyone else:

At a certain depth there is no difference between our own secret and the secret of Others. Everything is revealed to the novelist when he penetrates this Self, a truer Self than that which each of us displays. This Self imitates constantly, on its knees before the mediator.

This profound Self is also a universal Self, for everyone imitates constantly, everyone is on his knees before the mediator.[90]

Everyone imitates, everyone is just the same: compared to the deep, dark secret unearthed by Freud's Oedipus, the fearsome secret of patricide and incest, this secret seems disappointingly tame.

There is something seductive in Freud's notion that the king's "destiny moves us only because it might have been ours—because the oracle laid the same curse upon us."[91] Freud allows each of us to play the hero's part in our own private drama. Girard, by contrast, casts us in a decidedly unheroic posture, kneeling before the model whose desire we copy. It would be hard to imagine anything more humiliating than that. While incestuous and patricidal impulses are no doubt shameful, they also appear gratifyingly spontaneous, powerful, and extreme. In a world that places a premium on originality and authenticity, the most shameful thing for the Self may be to admit that it "imitates constantly, on its knees before the mediator."

Unbinding Oedipus

If Freud's Oedipus is a *desiring Oedipus*, Girard's Oedipus is an *imitating Oedipus*. For Girard, the mediator comes first; the model of desire precedes the object. Of course, for a small boy, the first and most important model is likely to be his father; for a small girl, her mother. Out of eagerness to imitate his father, a small boy will naturally desire to marry the very woman his father married, just as a small girl will want to marry the man her mother married. But even though such a desire is conceived out of the purest fidelity to the model, the model can only be an obstacle to possession of the object. In short, Girard's imitating Oedipus is liable to find himself caught in the same triangle as Freud's desiring Oedipus.

Girard does not deny the existence of the Oedipal triangle discovered by Freud, but he understands it differently: "The main difference between the mediation principle and psychoanalysis is that, in Freud, the desire for the mother is intrinsic,"[92] when, in reality, the son's "oedipal" urges "actually derive from the father himself in his role as model." But the "Oedipus complex waxes as the father wanes"; the father can be perceived as an obstacle and rival only "when the diminution of his paternal authority has brought him into a direct confrontation with his son, obliging him to occupy the same sphere"—in other words, only when the father-son relationship has succumbed to the spread of internal mediation. Girard implicitly places Freud in the same historical context as the novelists he analyzed earlier, associating the Oedipus complex with the social transformations characteristic of modernity: "The Oedipus complex appears most plausible in a society in which the father's authority has been greatly weakened but not completely destroyed; that is, in Western society during the course of recent centuries."[93]

While recognizing the existence of the Oedipal triangle, Girard does not confer on it the privileged status that Freud does. Instead, he derives it from the operation of a universal mechanism equally capable of producing other triangles. The trouble with the Oedipal triangle from Girard's viewpoint is that it "is not functional. One does not really know why it should go on generating substitute triangles."[94] Freud's Oedipus is forever bound to a primordial object, the mother, and a primordial rival, the father; later relationships perpetually re-enact, for better or worse, this original triangle. Girard unbinds Oedipus, cutting him loose from any particular object and endowing him with a primordial desire that, being abstract or metaphysical, is utterly open-ended, capable of remolding itself in protean fashion to fit the mediator of the moment: "There is only one metaphysical desire but the particular desires which instantiate this primordial desire are of infinite variety."[95]

The variety of possible desires is as great as the variety of possible mediators. But even if the son's mediator is the father, the resulting triangle will not necessarily be "oedipal" in Freud's sense. Take the triangle in Dostoyevsky's *A Raw Youth*, for example: "Son and father love the same woman. Dolgorouki's passion for Akhmakova, the general's wife, is copied from that of his father."[96] The son does not desire the general's wife because she is a substitute for his mother, but because she is the woman his father desires: the independent operation of the imitation mechanism makes it possible to account directly for the father-son rivalry without a need to interpret it as the repetition of a childhood triangle.

Just as Girard's imitating Oedipus may enter into rivalry with the father for an object other than the mother, so, too, may he take the mother as object in imitation of a mediator other than the father. This mediator may even be the mother herself. The identity between object and mediator is a configuration that Girard envisages when analyzing *coquetterie*: "The coquette's indifference toward her lover's sufferings" spurs him on because he views it as proof of her possessive desire for *herself*, a rival desire which stands as model and obstacle to his own desire for her.[97] Proust depicts something similar at work in the case of little Marcel's desperate longing for a goodnight kiss after being sent to bed early so that his parents can dine with Swann undisturbed: "When the mother refuses her son a kiss she is already playing the double role characteristic of internal mediation: she is both the instigator of desire and a relentless guardian forbidding its fulfillment."[98]

Here the son's desire for the mother, rather than manifesting itself spontaneously, is kindled by his chagrin at being excluded from an enchanting soirée reserved for grown-ups. By withholding herself from him, Marcel's mother has unwittingly inflamed his passion, just as a coquette inflames a suitor's passion by rebuffing his advances. Mother and son form an unorthodox triangle in which she singlehandedly occupies the positions of both object and rival. One might add that the father, by contrast, shows little sign of rivalry with the son; when he sees that Marcel has waited to intercept the mother on her way upstairs at the end of the evening, the father urges her to do more than kiss the boy goodnight: "Go along with him, then. . . . There are two beds in his room; tell Françoise to make up the big one for you, and stay with him for the rest of the night."[99]

The agonies suffered by Proust's narrator when his mother withholds her kiss "foreshadow the agonies of the snob and of the lover," Girard remarks.[100] Does this mean that the triangle involving the mother is somehow the original matrix responsible for generating the subject's later erotic entanglements? Proust's own comments on the incident, which Girard does not quote, suggest a different interpretation. Marcel compares his anguish at being excluded while his mother dined with Swann to the anguish Swann himself felt in different circumstances:

to him, the anguish that comes from knowing that the creature one adores is in some place of enjoyment where oneself is not and cannot follow—to him that anguish came through love, to which it is in a sense predestined, by which it will be seized upon and exploited; but when, as had befallen me, it possesses one's soul before love has yet entered into one's life, then it must drift, awaiting love's coming, vague and free, without precise attachment, at the disposal of one sentiment today, of another tomorrow, of filial piety or affection for a friend.[101]

The anguish Marcel suffers so precociously, whether with his mother or with a childhood friend, is but a vague warning of suffering to come, the floating signifier of an inchoate metaphysical affliction waiting to be instantiated through future love relationships. Rather than seeing these relationships as repeated attempts to recover an identical *object*, the mother, we may see them as resulting from the repeated operation of an identical *mechanism*, which renders desirable the object one cannot have, the object that resides "in some place of enjoyment where oneself is not and cannot follow."

"Psychoanalytic man is forever an Adam driven from paradise because he devoured or coveted the forbidden fruit," writes Girard.[102] But mimetic man covets the fruit *because* it is forbidden; he covets whatever is withheld from him by the mediator, who acts as both model and rival: "The obsession with forbidden fruit is not primary, it is not the cause but the consequence of the rivalry."[103] The paradise of mimetic man is not a place of enjoyment he had to leave, it is the place he cannot go: "the model shows his disciple the gate of paradise and forbids him to enter with one and the same gesture."[104] Thus, it "is with the model and not the obstacle that the dialectic begins. But this hierarchy will soon reverse itself, dissimulating the true genesis of desire."[105]

When the model blocks the disciple's access to the object, his "apparent hostility does not diminish his prestige but instead augments it." It does not cross the disciple's mind that someone as formidable as the model could possibly be threatened by him. On the contrary, he "is convinced that the model considers himself too superior to accept him as a disciple."[106] Once he interprets the model's injunction to stay away as a sentence condemning him from on high, an individual may come to perceive any condemnation, any obstacle thrown in his way, as itself a sign of the Other's superiority. As a result of this reversal, apparent hostility or even indifference will be enough to arouse his fascination, and countless potential mediators will crowd his path.

"Beginning with Proust," Girard remarks, "the mediator may be literally *anyone at all* and he may pop up *anywhere*." So it is that a "chance encounter along the promenade at Balbec decides Marcel's fate."[107] He is entranced by a close-knit band of adolescent girls who display "insolent indifference" to everyone they pass. "For the narrator, they form an obstacle that is fascinating precisely because it is impenetrable. For the girls, on the other hand, there are no obstacles at all":

they . . . forced those who had stopped to talk to step aside, as though from the path of a machine which has been set going by itself and which could not be expected to avoid pedestrians. . . . But they could not set eyes on an obstacle without amusing themselves by clearing it, either in a running jump or with both feet together.[108]

One girl in particular, Albertine, captivates Proust's narrator: "he watches Albertine jump over the head of a terrified old man and he identifies with the victim."[109]

In *Notes from Underground*, Dostoyevsky's narrator is the helpless victim of a similar public humiliation when he is brusquely pushed out of the way by an unknown officer in a billiard room, an incident that turns the officer into the permanent object of the underground man's fascination. "In this case as in others," Girard observes, "Dostoyevsky presents us with the truth of the Proustian experience in an exaggerated form," pushing to farcical extremes the idea that the mediator may be *anyone at all*.[110]

Girard does not mention how the underground man comes to enter the billiard room in the first place. Passing by chance before a tavern in which men are fighting with billiard cues, Dostoyevsky's narrator sees one man go flying out the window and instantly takes him as his model, demonstrating that the mediator may quite literally "pop up" anywhere: "I envied the gentleman who'd been tossed out; I envied him so much that I even walked into the tavern and entered the billiard room. 'Perhaps,' I thought, 'I'll get into a fight, and they'll throw me out the window, too.'" It is hard to imagine a desire more purely imitative, a desire whose object is more futile, than the desire to follow the Other out the window. Alas, the underground man fails in the attempt to satisfy even this seemingly modest desire: "It turned out that I wasn't capable of getting tossed out the window."[111] But perhaps a desire for expulsion is not so modest after all; perhaps it is the Romantic desire to be the lone victim at the center of everyone's attention. Instead, everyone ignores the underground man, even the officer who blithely removes him from his path.

With the inexorability of a mechanical reaction caused by the collision of two billiard balls, the narrator is seized by an impulse to do to the officer what the officer did to him. For years to come, he is obsessed by the thought that, one day, in an equal and opposite movement, he must force the officer to step out of *his* path. Discovering that his nemesis goes for walks along Nevsky Prospect, he stalks him on the crowded promenade, where he finds himself obliged to make way for a ceaseless flow of passersby: "I darted in and out like a fish among the strollers, constantly stepping aside before generals, cavalry officers, hussars, and young ladies."[112] Even the officer makes way for his social superiors, the underground man notices, but when faced with those of lesser rank he charges ahead as if they were not there.

The underground man dresses up to place himself on a more equal footing, even asking for an advance on his salary so that he may buy a new fur cap. But when he stands in the other's path, the officer looks right through him, heedless of the fur cap, and forces him to yield yet again, plunging him into the depths of despair. Finally, on the spur of the moment, Dostoyevsky's narrator resolves that if the other will not step aside, neither will he: "I closed my eyes and—we bumped into each other forcefully, shoulder to shoulder!" Although the officer marches on as if nothing had happened, the underground man returns home "feeling completely avenged."[113]

In both Proust and Dostoyevsky, Girard writes, "the mediator's arrogant bearing as he forces his way through the crowd, his disdainful indifference," appear as the outward signs of "a calm and serene superiority of *essence* which the miserable victim, crushed and trembling with hatred and adoration, tries in vain to steal": "Marcel imitates Albertine's language and manners; he even adopts her tastes. The underground man strives in a grotesque fashion to copy the impudent swagger of the man who insulted him." Such imitation demonstrates the reversal by which the obstacle is transformed into model. Girard quotes Denis de Rougemont's observation, in *Love in the Western World*, that the "most serious obstacle" is "the one preferred above all. It is the one most suited to intensifying passion." The "most impassable obstacle has this value only because it indicates the presence of the most divine mediator," Girard adds. He notes: "In the episode of the officer there is in the most literal sense of the word an obstacle: the underground man is actually forced off the sidewalk by the officer's insolence."[114]

The Difficulty in Giving Way

When, following *Deceit, Desire, and the Novel*, Girard turns his attention to the story of Oedipus, we should not be surprised to see him focus on a comparable episode, the hero's violent encounter with an arrogant old man on the road to Thebes:

As soon as Oedipus detects an obstacle—for example, this stranger absurdly blocking his way—he thinks he hears the mysterious sentence condemning him, he thinks he perceives, behind the obstacle, the secret path of paternal being. The possessions of the man who chances to stand in the way—his throne and his wife—acquire sacramental status. They become the one and only throne, the one and only wife, Thebes and Jocasta.[115]

Whether or not the stranger was really Oedipus's father is of secondary importance in the present context. When he was face to face with the rival who sought to push him out of the way, Oedipus did not know the other's identity any more than the underground man knew the identity of the officer. If the obstacle is automatically transmuted into the model, the mediator may be *anyone at all* and he may pop up *anywhere*: why not this stranger on the road to Thebes?

Once the stranger becomes the model to be imitated, his possessions become the objects to be desired. Jocasta becomes the "one and only wife" for Girard's imitating Oedipus, not because she is his mother, but because she is his model's wife. Even if we grant that Oedipus kills his father and marries his mother, he does not commit the murder in order to satisfy an incestuous desire since he is unaware what woman lies behind the obstacle. The rivalry comes before the forbidden fruit. Unless, of course, what Girard terms a "quarrel over *priority*"[116] actually has hidden sexual significance. In a 1922 paper, one of Freud's early followers, Karl Abraham, ventured that the "road over which father and son quarrel hardly needs further commentary": it could only be a thinly veiled symbol of maternal genitalia.[117]

However promising Abraham's gambit may appear from a psychoanalytic standpoint, it quickly encountered an objection from an unexpected source: Freud himself. In a letter to Abraham, Freud pointed to

an awkward feature of the Oedipus passage which has already caused me a great deal of trouble. You write of the "hollow way" as the place of meeting [between Laius and Oedipus], and that is just as suitable to us as a symbol of the genitals as it is suitable as a spot for giving way. . . . But the Greek text known to me talks of a . . . not "hollow way," but cross-roads, at which one would suppose giving way would not be difficult.[118]

In a follow-up note, "'The Trifurcation of the Road' in the Oedipus Myth," Abraham proposed an ingenious means of reconciling his previous interpretation of the hollow way with the reference in the Greek text to a "triple-branching," or Y-shaped, crossroads: "The two roads which merge to form a wide highway are the two thighs which join at the trunk. The junction is the site of the genitalia." Therefore "the trifurcation has the same meaning."[119] But one suspects Abraham could have found the "same meaning" in any other configuration just as well. One can't help thinking here of the patient who was told he had a sexual obsession after he saw genitalia in every Rorschach blot he was shown. "But doc," he protested, "you're the one who drew all the dirty pictures!"

In the end, of course, anybody is free to see the same thing in the crossroads as Abraham. The real question is whether his solution truly addresses Freud's objection, which does not concern the hidden sexual meaning of the place where Oedipus and Laius quarrel, but its overt significance. The "awkward feature" that has already given Freud "a great deal of trouble" is not the unsuitability of the crossroads as a symbol of the genitals, but its unsuitability as a site for a quarrel. Why fight at a place where two roads merge into a "wide highway" when, in Freud's words, "one would suppose giving way would not be difficult"?

It is the idea that Oedipus and Laius could come to blows for no good reason that troubles Freud. He is unable to account for the intensity of a rivalry that is not rooted in the desire for a concrete object. What would he make of the underground man on Nevsky Prospect in his new fur cap, determined to jostle the officer in his thirst for vengeance even though "giving way would not be difficult"?

In *The Interpretation of Dreams*, Freud recalls how, when he was ten or twelve years old, his father began taking him on walks and talking to him about the world. One story his father told him particularly marked Freud:

"When I was a young man," he said, "I went for a walk in the streets of your birthplace; I was well dressed, and had a new fur cap on my head. A Christian came up to me and with a single blow knocked off my cap into the mud and shouted: 'Jew! get off the pavement!'" "And what did you do?" I asked. "I went into the roadway and picked up my cap," was his quiet reply. This struck me as unheroic conduct on the part of the big, strong man who was holding the little boy by the hand. I contrasted this situation with another which fitted my feelings better: the scene in which Hannibal's father, Hamilcar Barca, made his boy swear before the household altar to take vengeance on the Romans. Ever since that time Hannibal had had a place in my phantasies.

Freud explains that when he studied the Punic Wars as a boy, he had always identified with the Semitic Hannibal: "To my youthful mind Hannibal and Rome symbolized the conflict between the tenacity of Jewry and the organization of the Catholic church."[120]

According to Ernest Jones, Freud's father "never regained the place he had held in his esteem after the painful occasion when he told his twelve-year-old boy how a Gentile knocked off his new fur cap into the mud and shouted at him: 'Jew, get off the pavement.'"[121] Freud himself refers to this painful occasion as "the event in my youth whose power was still being shown in all these emotions and dreams."[122] In his brilliant work *The Ordeal of Civility*, John Murray Cuddihy argues that this traumatic event constitutes the "primal scene" holding the secret to Freud's fascination with Sophocles' *Oedipus*: "the *idée fixe* that Oedipus was to become for Freud, I maintain, hinges on a small detail (small, but structurally indispensable for the action of the story) that Freud never mentions . . . the whole plot starts from a social insult, a discourtesy on the road, stemming from someone in a position of social superiority." To drive his point home, Cuddihy quotes the speech in which Oedipus relates what took place when he met a man in a carriage "near the triple-branching roads":

> The herald in front and the old man himself
> Threatened to thrust me rudely from the path,
> Then jostled by the driver in wrath
> I struck him, and the old man, seeing this,
> Watched till I passed and from his carriage brought down
> Full on my head his two-pointed goad.
> Yet was I quits with him and more; one stroke
> Of my good staff sufficed to fling him clean
> Out of his seat and laid him prone. (804–13)

When "jostled" by the driver, Sophocles' hero "strikes back in anger," Cuddihy comments. "Then, just as with Freud's father years back, Oedipus is struck 'full on the head' . . . but this time, instead of the 'unheroic conduct' of his father meekly fetching his cap out of the muddy gutter, Oedipus in his fury strikes back again and kills ... his father."[123]

Cuddihy contends that Freud had metaphorically killed his own father when he heard him relate his passive humiliation at the hands of the Christian: "To be ashamed of a father is a kind of 'moral parricide.'" Freud then experienced guilt toward his father: "not the guilt of having entertained the forbidden wish to kill him in order to possess the mother," but the even more unspeakable guilt of having been ashamed of him.[124] What Cuddihy dubs the "guilt of shame" is, he suggests, the distinctive form of guilt felt by members of ethnic minorities who assimilate successfully into the larger culture, leaving their embarrassingly alien parents behind.

Here Cuddihy cites Peter L. Berger's account of "massive social mobility" as entailing "a kind of symbolic murder of the parent in 'a sacrificial ritual of the mind'": "It is no wonder, incidentally," Berger remarks, "that the Freudian mythology of parricide has found ready credence in American society and especially in those recently middle-class segments of it."[125] This observation recalls Girard's assertion that the "Oedipus complex waxes when the father wanes." As social mobility breaks down traditional hierarchical differences, internal mediation replaces external mediation and children come to rival their parents.

In Freud's case, however, the rivalry with the father plays out in a more complex manner than a purely sociological interpretation could lead one to believe. Cuddihy's thesis is that Freud's Oedipal theory allows him to disguise from himself the real "moral parricide" of shame by substituting for it an imaginary parricide: "It is more permissible and tolerable to own up, to blame yourself for being a parricide (in fantasy), than to be ashamed of your father (in reality) for his, and consequently your, misfortune in having been born a Jew." But Cuddihy also notes that, in striking back at the man who tried to push him out of the way, "Oedipus *does* what the young Freud *wished* his father had done."[126] In fact, Freud was ashamed of his father not so much for being born a Jew as for passively accepting the Christian's assault.

Cuddihy relates a similar incident in which Freud himself reacted much more aggressively. Travelling by train in 1883, Freud opened a window to get some fresh air and other passengers demanded that he shut it. When one shouted "He's a dirty Jew!" the dispute took on an anti-Semitic tone. Rather than back down, Freud held his ground and quieted his adversaries by offering to fight the ringleader. "All the essential elements of the paternal encounter repeated themselves," Cuddihy observes, but "with one important difference: Freud's calling their bluff by an open challenge to stand up and fight."[127]

It follows that not only did Oedipus do what the young Freud wished his father had done, but so did Freud himself. When he successfully faced down the Christian, Freud bested his own paternal model. But by positing the existence of a rivalry for the mother, Freud conjured up an alternative scenario in which the paternal model had bested him. If marriage with the mother were to be the measure of success, Freud's father was destined to remain an unsurpassed external mediator. Freud could never marry the woman his father had married; he could not outdo his father in an imaginary contest for the maternal object, but he had already outdone him in the real-world rivalry with Christians—a rivalry in which Freud had demonstrated he could hold his ground even when "giving way would not be difficult."

"I Hit Him 'Cos He Hit Me"

Freud's enduring disappointment with his father over the cap incident was confirmed by a slip he made when he recounted the incident in the first edition of *The Interpretation of Dreams*. Recalling how his thoughts had turned to the scene in which Hannibal swore to avenge his father against the Romans, Freud mistakenly identified Hannibal's father as "Hasdrubal," which was actually the name of Hannibal's brother. He later analyzed this slip in *The Psychopathology of Everyday Life*:

The error of putting *Hasdrubal* instead of *Hamilcar*, the brother's name instead of the father's, occurred precisely in a context that concerned the Hannibal-phantasies of my school-years and my dissatisfaction with my father's behaviour towards the "enemies of our people." I could have gone on to tell how my relationship with my father was changed by a visit to England, which resulted in my getting to know my half-brother, the eldest son of my father's first marriage, who lived there. My brother's eldest son is the same age as I am. Thus the relations between our ages were no hindrance to my phantasies of how different things would have been if I had been born the son not of my father but of my brother.[128]

This admission lends new meaning to a maxim formulated by Girard in "Symmetry and Dissymmetry in the Oedipus Myth": "Brotherhood is the truth of fatherhood."

Ernest Jones held that the discovery of the Oedipus complex was "potently facilitated" by Freud's "own unusual family constellation." In the opening chapter of his useful and stimulating book *Freud and Oedipus*, Peter L. Rudnytsky expands upon Jones's remark, noting that the "coincidence between Freud's biographical accidents of birth and the Oedipus drama is staggering." When Freud's parents wed, his father was twice his mother's age and already had two grown sons from a prior marriage. His father's eldest son had a daughter who was Freud's age and a son, John, who was but one year older. Thus, Freud's "niece and nephew were, for practical purposes, his siblings, and his half-brothers were old enough to be his father." This confusion of generations creates a striking parallel between Freud's family and that of Oedipus, Rudnytsky observes, for "it is the consequence of Oedipus's commission of incest with his mother that his kin-ship ties display an analogous involution." Rudnytsky quotes Tiresias's warning:

> He shall be shown to be to his own children
> at once brother and father, and of the woman
> from whom he was born son and husband, and of his father
> sharer of the same seed and murderer. (457–60)

"There could scarcely be a more vivid illustration of Oscar Wilde's para-doxical dictum that 'Life imitates Art,'" Rudnytsky concludes.[129]

What are we to make of this? Was Freud, with his unusual family constellation, *imitating Oedipus*? In reality, only Tiresias's reference to confusion in the roles of brother and father applies to Freud's case, at least in part: Freud's half-brother is old enough to be his father, and his half-brother's son—his nephew—is old enough to be his brother. On the other hand, the age of Freud's real father is that of a grandfather, not a brother. Freud is not "sharer of the same seed and murderer" of his father, nor is he "son and husband" of the woman from whom he was born. In-deed, since she is the right age to be his mother, she is the only family member whose generational relationship to Freud is straightforward. Thus, while the parallel between Oedipus's family and Freud's is undeni-ably striking, it is limited to an undifferentiation of kinship roles on the paternal side and—curiously enough from a psychoanalytic standpoint—does not involve the mother.

The absence of the mother from this picture makes it difficult to in-terpret the parallel between Oedipus's family and Freud's in the light of Freud's own reading of *Oedipus*. What about Girard's reading? We saw earlier that he interprets the incest and patricide in Sophocles' play as sig-nifiers of a general crisis of undifferentiation, the same crisis symbolized by the plague. Like Sophocles, Girard puts the emphasis less on incest as such than on the collapse of differences it entails—what he calls the "scandalous scrambling of kinship" in Oedipus's family. And it is precisely this feature of Oedipus's "unusual family constellation" that must have impressed Freud the most, since it could not fail to remind him of the "scandalous scrambling of kinship" in Freud's own family. If we want to understand why Freud was drawn to *Oedipus*, then, incest as such turns out to be a red herring.

Indeed, rivalry for possession of the mother plays no more part in the confusion of kinship roles in Freud's family than it did in his father's road-way confrontation with a stranger. These two elements came together in

Freud's fantasy of substituting his more imposing half-brother for his aged father, who had demonstrated his inadequacy by letting the stranger push him out of the way. As we saw, Freud contrasts his father's behavior unfavorably with that of Hannibal's father, who made his son swear a warrior's oath of vengeance. Freud then remarks that his own "martial ideal" may be "traceable still further back" to the "close relation, sometimes friendly but sometimes warlike," in which he found himself, at the age of three, "with a boy a year older," presumably his half-brother's son, John.[130]

In the course of his dream interpretations, Freud provides a revealing glimpse of his "sometimes warlike" relation with John by describing a dimly remembered incident in which he got the better of the older boy:

The two children had a dispute about some object. . . . Each of them claimed to have *got there before the other* and therefore to have a better right to it. They came to blows. . . . The vanquished party hurried to his grandfather—my father—and complained about me, and I defended myself in the words which I know from my father's account: "I hit him 'cos he hit me." . . . From this point the dream thoughts proceeded along some such lines as these: "It serves you right if you had to make way for me. Why did you try to push me out of the way? I don't need you, I can easily find someone else to play with," and so on.[131]

Freud was determined not to be pushed out of the way by his older playmate even though—to quote his comment on Oedipus at the crossroads—"one would suppose giving way would not be difficult."

Rudnytsky observes that "Freud's justification for his retaliation against John—'I hit him 'cos he hit me'—has an exact counterpart in *Oedipus the King* in the fact that Oedipus kills Laius in self-defense," since "Oedipus declares that he struck back only after the old man" hit him first. Although Rudnytsky is a staunch defender of psychoanalysis who devotes the better part of an appendix to a spirited attack on Girard's ideas, he acknowledges that "Girard's concept of 'reciprocal violence' certainly applies to the confrontation between Freud and John." At the same time, Rudnytsky maintains that "the scene is wholly explicable in oedipal terms":

The dispute between Freud and John is specifically over the question of priority, the claim by both boys "to have *got there before the other*." Exactly this issue is at stake in the battle between Oedipus and Laius at the crossroads, which represent symbolically the genitals of the mother. The oedipal dimensions of this scene with John extend beyond the purely sexual sphere to evoke the controversies over intellectual priority and originality in which Freud became embroiled throughout his life.[132]

Rudnytsky is surely right to identify the issue of priority as the fundamental link between Oedipus's dispute with the stranger at the crossroads and Freud's disputes with both his childhood playmate and his adult colleagues. But this important insight is fully able to stand on its own; since it extends "beyond the purely sexual sphere," it is not strengthened by reference to the genitals of the mother or by the suggestion that the unspecified "object" over which the boys fought was John's little sister, "who, as a female coming between two males, is a substitute for the mother."[133]

The question here is not whether an incestuous desire for the parent of the opposite sex exists. Even if we accept the existence of such a desire, we need not invoke it every time we are faced with a dispute between members of the same sex. The real question is whether all conflicts are rooted in the desire for a single primordial object or whether, as Girard holds, they are diverse manifestations of an open-ended tendency to rivalry unbound to any specific object.

If Freud does not specify the identity of the object over which he and John clashed, that is probably because it had no special significance. The imitative nature of the conflict is made evident by the words "I hit him 'cos he hit me." Two small boys are quite capable of fighting over any object that one of them gets his hands on before the other. They may even come to blows with *no* concrete object at stake—and so, for that matter, may two grown men,[134] as in Oedipus's battle over priority at the crossroads.

Many scholars have remarked on the "controversies over intellectual priority and originality" which dogged Freud throughout his adult life. Refuting Ernest Jones's claim that Freud was above such matters, Robert K. Merton states: "In point of fact, Elinor Barber and I have identified more than one hundred and fifty occasions on which Freud exhibited an interest in priority."[135] Needless to say, dispute over priority is the defining feature of internal mediation: Who is the original and who the copy? Who the model and who the disciple? When each person imitates the other and both reach for the same object—whether it be the same plaything or the same claim to have made a scientific discovery—each will become an obstacle in the way of the other's desire to get there first. If left unchecked, the operation of this simple mechanism is enough to turn the most intimate friend into the most hated enemy. It is a mechanism that would swing into operation again and again in the course of Freud's life.

In *The Interpretation of Dreams*, Freud notes that "all my friends have in a certain sense been re-incarnations" of John, adding: "My emotional life has always insisted that I should have an intimate friend and a hated enemy . . . and it has not infrequently happened that the ideal situation of childhood has been so completely reproduced that friend and enemy have come together in a single individual—though not, of course, both at once."[136] Examining Freud's dreams that provide the bulk of the material in the first edition of the work, Lucien Scubla remarks that "what is played out on the dream stage is not incest but the confusion of doubles, not the murder of the father but the rivalry of brothers."[137]

In a similar comment on Freud's dreams, Marthe Robert observes that the important thing in his "inner life does not at all appear to be sexuality, but rather the desire to succeed, to make a name for himself . . . with all the violence and absence of scruples that always characterize such exigencies."[138] Although Robert later suggests that intellectual ambition may function as a dream substitute for censored sexual desire, Scubla proposes that the reverse is true: "sexual desire, which is much too voluble if it so badly wants to pass unnoticed, itself serves in reality to mask the power of envy, vanity and conceit, to the point of covering them over more and more completely with each new edition of *The Interpretation of Dreams*."[139]

The Underground Freud

Why did Freud insist so tenaciously on the primacy of concealed sexual impulses? Cuddihy quotes Vincent Brome's question in *Freud and His Early Circle*: "Could it be that, when Viennese medical circles ordered him off the medical pavement because of his sexual theories, he refused to move with such indomitable will because the humiliating picture of his father remained an unconscious driving force within him?" The shout that Freud's father had heard from the Christian who forced him off the pavement "was probably the ancient command that a Jew frequently heard when he encountered one of the *goyim* in a narrow street or defile—'*Machmores Jud!*' ('Mind your manners, Jew!')—whereupon the Jew would obediently step into the gutter, allowing the Gentile to pass," Cuddihy notes.[140] By defending his sexual theories in blunt, uncensored language, Freud refused to "mind his manners." But Cuddihy takes this intuition much further, arguing that the entire psychoanalytic discourse on the repression of hidden impulses can be read as a kind of allegory for the experience of the Jew forced to disguise his identity if he wants to "pass" in the world of Gentile "manners."

In *The Interpretation of Dreams*, the agent of repression that disguises the expression of the dream wish is the "censor," which, Cuddihy comments,

stands at the borders of consciousness and says: "Thou shalt not pass." All through the nineteenth century, the Eastern European Jew had sought admission to bourgeois Western civil society. At first he experienced economic and political exclusion; by Freud's time he was seeking social acceptance and experiencing social rejection. This importunate "Yid," released from ghetto and *shtetl*, is the model, I contend, for Freud's coarse, importunate "id." Both are saddled with the problem of "passing" from a latent existence "beyond the pale" of Western respectability into an open and manifest relation to Gentile society *within* Gentile society, from a state of unconsciousness to a state of consciousness.[141]

Although Cuddihy does not spell out the connection himself, this gloss on the Freudian mechanism of repression takes us back once more to the episode of Sophocles' play which seems to have played the decisive role in Freud's thinking. For what is the old man who blocks Oedipus's path, if not a sentinel standing at the borders of Thebes and saying: "Thou shalt not pass"? And what is the Gentile who monitors the Jews' entry into respectable Western society if not a new avatar of the Girardian obstacle, the model who "shows his disciple the gate of paradise and forbids him to enter with one and the same gesture"?

Freud's ambivalence toward Gentile society—his eagerness to attract Christian followers who could shield psychoanalysis from the accusation of being "a Jewish science,"[142] his proud rejection of compromises that might have facilitated the acceptance he craved from the *goyim*—is the typical ambivalence of the disciple toward the mediator. It is not unlike the ambivalence that Girard attributes to the underground man: "He wants to become the Other and still be himself."[143] After being jostled by the officer in the billiard room, Dostoyevsky's narrator writes his nemesis a letter that he never sends, a letter motivated by a secret hope not so different, perhaps, from the unspoken dream wish of a defiant Jewish thinker with regard to the "enemy of his people":

I composed a splendid, charming letter to him, imploring him to apologize to me, and hinting rather plainly at a duel in case of refusal. The letter was so composed that if the officer had had the least understanding of the good and the beautiful he would certainly have flung himself on my neck and have offered me his friendship. And how fine that would have been! How we should have got on together! "He

lii   *Introduction*

could have shielded me with his higher rank, while I could have improved his mind with my culture, and, well . . . my ideas, and all sorts of things might have happened."[144]

If Cuddihy is right, Freud resolved the problem of becoming the other while remaining himself by exposing the other's hidden kinship to the self. His theory of repressed urges offered a way to "unmask the gentility of the Gentile" by showing that the same uncouth "id" lurked beneath the surface of *goy* and "Yid" alike. To "the sexual naturalism of Freud, 'love in the Western world' (de Rougemont) is 'id' tricked out as 'Eros,'" Cuddihy writes, quoting Freud's insistence that the "fundamental processes which promote erotic excitation remain always the same. Excremental things are all too intimately and inseparably bound up with sexual things; the position of the genital organs—*inter urinas et faeces*—remains the decisive and unchangeable factor."[145]

In short, to the cry "Dirty Jew!" Freud replied: "Dirty Christian!" A Christian had knocked the cap from the head of Freud's father and sent it tumbling into the mud; Freud picked up the mud and hurled it back onto the head of the Christian: "There is dirt upon thy head, O Christian. Dirt, dirt, dirt, upon the head of the Christian."

Like Jew, Like Christian

Jews and Christians, enemy brothers locked in an age-old struggle. By charging the Gentile with harboring unspeakable urges, Freud was, in a sense, merely settling an old account. In medieval Christendom, legends had arisen about an individual guilty of committing unspeakable crimes. Abandoned as an infant, this man unwittingly returned as a youth to his parents' home, where he killed his father and married his mother before going on to join the disciples of Jesus, whom he betrayed to be crucified. Thus it was that the story of Oedipus, unbound from its ancient Greek origins, fused with the story of Judas—that dirty, father-killing, Jewish mother-lover.[146] By positing a universal Oedipus complex, Freud universalized the scapegoat's part, making father-killing mother-lovers of Jews and Christians alike.

Jews and Christians, enemy brothers. A two-thousand-year-old drama that, in the final years of Freud's life, erupted in catastrophe. Once again, in a time of crisis, Jews were put to death as diabolical traitors: Judases. What can explain a conflict so long-lasting and so intense?

From Girard's point of view, Jews and Christians should be united by the condemnation of scapegoating that distinguishes the religions of the Bible from mythological cults. In the essay that closes this volume, Girard compares the myth of Oedipus with the Old Testament story of Joseph. While both are marked by scapegoat-type accusations, in the biblical account, far from being taken at face value, as happens in the myth, these accusations are refuted in the course of the story itself.[147] In his later works, Girard argues that this distinctive impulse to defend the victims appears for the first time in the Old Testament and reaches fulfillment in the New. Many questions could be raised here, questions that go well beyond the scope of the present essay.[148] We will conclude by asking a single question: If Girard is right, if the defense of victims in Judaism served as a model for Christianity, why have Jews historically been hated victims of Christians? If the Bible looks forward to a world where men will treat each other as real brothers, not enemy brothers, how did Jews and Christians end up being enemy brothers themselves? What can explain a conflict so long-lasting and so intense?

To the Jew in Gentile society, we said, the Christian is the model and obstacle. But to the Christian, what is the Jew?

—Good News, says the Christian, knocking at the door of the Jew. He is here, the Messiah you desire so ardently. You taught me to desire Him too, and it is I who have found Him. Join me in rejoicing.

—No, says the Jew. Not yet. This Messiah of yours leaves me indifferent. He is not the one I wanted. Try again later.

To the Christian, what is the Jew, if not the original model and ultimate obstacle? The model who "considers himself too superior to accept him as a disciple," provoking the very type of passionate reaction described by Girard in his analysis of internal mediation:

The subject is torn between two opposite feelings toward his model—the most submissive reverence and the most intense malice. This is the passion we call *hatred*.

Only someone who prevents us from satisfying a desire which he himself has inspired in us is truly an object of hatred. The person who hates first hates himself for the secret admiration concealed by his hatred. In an effort to hide this desperate admiration from others, and from himself, he no longer wants to see in his mediator anything but an obstacle. . . . Now the mediator is a shrewd and diabolical enemy; he tries to rob the subject of his most prized possessions; he obstinately thwarts his most legitimate ambitions.[149]

To the Christian, what is the Jew, if not the original model and ultimate obstacle?

Christianity is, after all, the offspring of Judaism.

Brotherhood is the truth of fatherhood. Laius and Oedipus, father and son, enemy brothers . . .

Imitating Oedipus. Perhaps that is explanation enough?

~

When Chu-bu and Sheemish had wearied of exchanging identical accusations, each resolved to assert himself over the other by performing a miracle. By chance, they both chose the same miracle, each willing a small earthquake. And the earthquake came, with unintended consequences:

It was a very local earthquake, for there are other gods than Chu-bu or even Sheemish, and it was only a little one as the gods had willed, but it loosened some monoliths in a colonnade that supported one side of the temple and the whole of one wall fell in . . . and the temple of Chu-bu quivered and then stood still, swayed once and was overthrown, on the heads of Chu-bu and Sheemish.

No one rebuilt it, for nobody dared go near such terrible gods. Some said that Chu-bu wrought the miracle, but some said Sheemish, and thereof schism was born. The weakly amiable . . . sought compromise and said that both had wrought it, but no one guessed the truth that the thing was done in rivalry.[150]

OEDIPUS UNBOUND

CHAPTER I

From the Novelistic Experience
to the Oedipal Myth

Desire is not of this world. That is what Proust shows us at his best: it is in order to penetrate into *another world* that one desires, it is in order to be initiated into a radically foreign existence. The desired object frequently presents itself in the guise of an impenetrable sphere: the roundness of Albertine's cheeks, beyond the reach of any kiss; the breast-plate molded to the warrior's chest, bruising love-struck maids. Behind every closed door, every insurmountable barrier, the hero senses the presence of the absolute mastery that eludes him, the divine serenity of which he feels deprived.

To desire is to believe in the transcendence of the world suggested by the Other. As soon as it yields to the desire that lays siege to it, the enchanting totality reveals itself to be illusory. It bursts like a soap bubble at the slightest contact, but the mirage springs up anew a bit farther on. To imagine Albertine faithful, to penetrate among the Guermantes, means hurdling the chasm and abolishing transcendence. This desire is masochistic at heart. The most colossal obstacle, the most humiliating prohibition, signify the most authentic royalty, the most stable idol. Here Proust is heir to the writers he admires. With her piercing blue eyes and her beak like a bird of prey's, Madame de Guermantes represents the outer limit of impassive Baudelairean beauty, the ultimate metamorphosis of the *breast of stone,* that cold, hard globe on which the poet bloodies his fingernails.

Lost in the anonymous crowd of the orchestra pit, the narrator of *Within a Budding Grove* contemplates the inaccessible *loge* where the Guermantes are enthroned, just as, in the tympanum of a Roman church, the chosen are gloriously arrayed in the bosom of Abraham. The chapter of *Jean Santeuil* on the premiere of "Frédégonde" offers us a quite different earlier version of this great scene. The poetry of desire, the specifically Proustian emotion, is absent. The intersubjective conditions of its presence are not fulfilled. Words like "imagination" and "sensibility" are of no help here. Nor is it in the writer's technique that the key to the mystery must be sought. The difference lies in the relative positions of the characters. This time the hero is not languishing in the orchestra. He is happily ensconced in the balcony, basking in attention, the envy of everyone. Two or three duchesses are at his feet. A king straightens his necktie. We are in the very heart of what in the masterpiece will never be more than the inaccessible goal of desire.

Jean Santeuil experiences neither desire nor true disillusionment. He possesses everything which the narrator of the later work lacks. Elegant, gifted, sure of himself, he exercises an irresistible charm over Others. But we recognize him to be a projection of the desire that *Remembrance of Things Past* will reveal. This desire still has such a hold over the author of *Jean Santeuil* that its failure remains *unthinkable*. To turn away from this failure and to persevere in this desire are one and the same. What is desired is mastery and its absence is conjured at each moment through a furtive recourse to the Other's mastery, through a panicked but secret flight toward the Other. Failure, so as to remain unacknowledged, perpetuates failure, ever conferring upon the Other the magical power of which the Self feels inexplicably and, it hopes, temporarily deprived.

The Proust of *Jean Santeuil* takes himself for an Other, at once imaginary and real, and it is this Other that he depicts. The originality with which he believes he has endowed his hero is illusory. Jean's ideas are the fashionable ideas of his day. This first novel bears the imprint of its age to a greater extent than *Remembrance*. Not that the author is unaware that such a desire as possesses him exists. He refers to it incessantly and he defines it, already, in quite precise fashion. But he always attributes it to the Other; he regards the Other alone as contaminated by it. It is not Jean, at the premiere of "Frédégonde," who contemplates the desirable from the outside, it is the future Verdurins of *Remembrance*. We find here an intersubjective system that is foreign to the great Proust but very frequent in his early novelistic efforts. After "Frédégonde" comes the exit from the theater: Jean gets into the car of the highest-ranking duchess. Once more he disappears into the mystic enclosure while the future Verdurins, green with rage, behold the fascinating spectacle from the sidewalk. Only *Others* desire, in the unfinished work.

Only *Others* are snobs. The author embodies himself in a hero uncontaminated by snobbery. That is the proof he has not stopped being a snob. Failure manifests itself but in a veiled form. Everything would be for the best in the best of all possible high societies if only those jealous meanies, the snobs, didn't occasionally come between the hero and his delightful friends. The snobs go about spreading vicious slanders. It looks as if all is lost for Jean until the Réveillons—the Guermantes of *Remembrance*—intervene *in extremis* and restore their favorite to his rightful position with a wave of the hand. The good fairy is there to watch over Cinderella's happiness. Virtue is rewarded; the snobs are banished into the outer darkness.

The snob has no other model than the snob. He therefore has no other rival. That is why introspection reveals nothing to the snob but his hate of snobbery. The other snob becomes the evil double. In this *alter ego*, in this enemy brother, the snob thinks he detects absolute alterity, maximal difference. He gives himself over to moral indignation. He resembles those snobbish foes of snobbery of whom Legrandin provides us, from the opening pages of *Remembrance*, with a magnificent example.

The Proust of *Jean Santeuil* talks about snobs the way Legrandin would. But he is no more capable of describing them than he is of describing himself. To depict snobs properly, when one really wants to, one must first recognize oneself in them. The novelist's "know thyself" is always achieved via the Other. The Self must grasp itself as Self in the mirror of the Double. This recognition looks easy from the outside, it looks easy to the Other, that is. But it is beyond every psychology. The Proust of *Jean Santeuil* is a discerning psychologist. He knows very well how to recognize in the moral indignation of *Others* the sign of an ambivalent desire. His own indignation, by contrast, appears to him as justified, if only by the blindness of the Others. The writer is not able to turn his perspicacity against itself. He does not avert his gaze from the *signs* that are addressed to him, far from it. He even deciphers them with passion, but only to identify in them the signs of the Other, only to remain blind to his own destiny.

Jean Santeuil is located at the paroxysm of a debate that is sterile in itself but pregnant with truth. The novelistic genius lies beyond this conflict between an equally false Self and Other. It therefore lies beyond desire, in a certain sense at least. *Jean Santeuil* and the early manuscripts published since the war do not contradict but confirm the genetic significance of *Time Regained.* These drafts date back to long before the revelation from which the definitive novel is supposed to derive. This led to the conclusion that the definitive novel was the product of a long gestation rather than of the dramatic upheavals to which it was formerly attributed, on the testimony of *Time Regained.* These two truths are not mutually exclusive, they are complementary. It is because the "revelation" of *Time Regained* was lacking that *Jean Santeuil* remains unfinished.

To inquire into the genesis of Proust's art is to ask the masterpiece to provide a "psychoanalysis" of its antecedents. (The limits of this operation would be quickly reached, and sexual desire would not yield the results that "snobbery" does.) But the fact that this psychoanalysis internal to the Proustian *œuvre* is possible, even if only in a privileged sector, is enough for us to assert that the relations between literature and psychoanalysis are not simple. To maintain dogmatically the subordinate or independent status of the one relative to the other means just about nothing. One must ask oneself, in every instance, with what kind of literature one is dealing, and with what kind of psychoanalysis.

A writer only becomes great, Proust asserts in *Time Regained,* the day that he stops carrying on, in his work if not in his life, the interminable monologue that confirms for him at every moment the justice of "his" cause in the quarrel of snobs and lovers. This tells us that the writer once did carry on such a monologue, by means of sometimes quite complex identifications well-calculated to conceal their underlying intention. Nothing could be more illusory at this stage than the much-celebrated rupture between the active life and the esthetic life.

The project of blissful autonomy is one with the passion that pulls the Self towards the Other, transforming the latter into a fascinating double. The Self does its best to reinforce the certainties that are tearing it apart. At this stage the work is an attempt to perpetuate and exalt the differential gap that we all posit between ourselves and the Other. The writer strives, but in vain, to give this gap a concrete content.

Jean Santeuil represents only an initial variation on this literary project. The bland perfection of the hero shows him to be the "angelic double" of the creative subjectivity. The writer can equally well center his work on the Other. The wholly positive hero is then replaced by a wholly negative one, a caricature, the evil double. Both types of work are rooted in the same dualism. The Other is never absent from the lyrical, idealist works organized around the Self. The Self is never absent from the bitter, satirical, realist works organized around the Other. The masterpiece defies this system of oppositions. That is why it defies any critical approach whose categories are founded on dualism and any critical approach determined to evade this essential problem. The masterpiece demands a questioning of dualism. It is no longer "realist" or "idealist" or "subjective" or "objective." This means it always departs from an original intention inevitably informed by the dualist outlook. Mere craftsmanlike revision, in the spirit of Boileau's dictum "Twenty times set your work back onto the anvil," cannot account for the gulf separating the intention from the completed work.

Stendhal's late masterpieces suggest such a radical break. According to Henri Martineau, the creation of *The Red and the Black* falls into two periods separated by an interval of nearly two years. In what way did the first *Red and the Black* differ from the one we read today? Doubtless we will never know, but we can easily imagine the impression that the bleak story of Louis Jenrel first made on Stendhal. How could one not see in this criminal a hypocrite bent on using women and the Church to climb the social ladder? In 1828, Stendhal is forty-five years old. He has gotten himself run out of Italy: doubly exiled, he has been making a living, since his return, from rather miserable expedients. To paint a damning portrait of Louis Jenrel and of a whole society with him is a way of convincing oneself, when one's name is Henri Beyle, that one is deliberately resisting temptations to which Others succumb; it is a way of affirming that one has chosen one's fate, a way of defending a certain image of oneself, "true" no doubt, but superficial.

It is not hard for us to conceive of a negative and "realist" point of departure for *The Red and the Black*. But we could just as easily imagine an "idealist" point of departure. Julien the pure victim of those Others whom he in no way resembles. Julien the angelic double of Stendhal. The first point of view, it may be noted, is the one which the nineteenth century seldom transcends in its reading of Stendhal. The second fairly well sums up the attitude of contemporary criticism. It is difficult not to read Stendhal in terms of these dualist schemes that he himself has a hard time overcoming. Yet the definitive *Red and the Black* is irreducible to either of the antithetical and secretly analogous projects that we have just outlined. The only point of departure not conceivable is the point of arrival.

This is what is confirmed for us by the relative failure of *Armance*. Here the point of departure is realist to the point of caricature. The Octave with which Stendhal ultimately leaves us, however, can no longer be defined by sexual impotence. And that is why the novel is obscure. *Armance* is already a work that contradicts the original intention of its creator, but this contradiction does not bear fruit. Seeking to give the work the life it lacks, the novelist is led to reverse the initial perspective. True enough, this initial perspective is incompatible with life; dead itself, it is secretly a source of death, but the reverse perspective is no less so. The writer overturns his cage without succeeding in breaking out of it. Meanings reserved for the Other are replaced by or mixed with meanings reserved for the Self. The novelistic approach is present as an unfulfilled promise. The work is a hybrid, lacking cohesiveness. It does not avoid the stereotypes defined above, it combines them. The hero partakes of an Other and a Self both equally abstract. He is at once the angelic double and the evil Other, a noble romantic hero and an impotent figure of fun.

Reality is still structured by oppositions. Novelistic genius is approached through inverse errors and stumbles in opposite directions that exhaust the forms of truth conceivable in the world of alienation. The juxtapositions of incompatible elements, the sudden reversals and flagrant contradictions are a prelude to authentic novelistic creation. *Armance* does not get past this preparatory stage. *The Red and the Black* does go beyond it, but only belatedly. The detailed analyses of Georges Blin reveal contradictions that we believe to be as interesting to a critic concerned with the problem of genesis as certain geological faults are to the historian of our planet. These contradictions would not have escaped a writer in full control. One must imagine extremely confused creative about-faces accomplished not, as a rule, by complete rewrites but by returns to previous versions or by the addition of little touches inspired now by one, now by the other of the two dualist perspectives. One must imagine a succession of always-partial restructurings conceived in a very different spirit each time.

Julien is the happy lover of Madame de Rênal: Stendhal describes his hero's feelings in these terms:

Within a few days, Julien, restored to all the ardor of his age, was head-over-heels in love. One must admit, he said to himself, that she has an angelic goodness of the soul, and no one is prettier.

Some fifteen lines further down, the novelist speaks of this passion again, but in quite different terms:

His love was still a form of ambition: it was the joy of possessing, poor despised and unhappy creature that he was, a woman so noble and so beautiful.

Georges Blin comments on these two passages as follows:

It is clear that we find ourselves here in the presence of two feelings that cannot be reconciled, but of which the author could have made us accept the simultaneity by specifying that the hero's heart was torn between them, that it was in fact a case of emotional conflict, a contradiction experienced as such. In the absence of like clarification, the discrepancy, instead of being imputed to the ambiguity of the passion under examination, can only be counted as proof of the narrator's inconsistency (*Problèmes du roman*, p. 194).

The contradiction cannot in our view be reduced to a conflict between love and ambition. One need only reread the pages from which the two passages are excerpted. Julien made it his duty to conquer Madame de Rênal. He has just succeeded. The hero's fundamental passion momentarily coincides with a surrender to pleasure. There is no heart-rending conflict. It will not pay to drown the contradiction in the novelistic context. We must reject solutions that are located at the same level as the problem and that re-establish the momentarily-compromised unity of the work. It is this unity that we must consent to put in doubt here.

The first quotation illustrates the idealist and introspective point of departure. It makes Julien into a "positive" lover, his internal discourse a bit too much in tune with the Beylist mythology of passion. The second quotation illustrates the objective and "realist" point of departure. Its presence confirms the existence, in the first stages of the creation, of an *Ur-*Julien, radically *Other*.

Stendhal switches for no apparent reason from a *Self*-Julien to an *Other*-Julien because he is obscurely seeking to transcend the dualist schemas. But language itself disposes of no term to designate the dual nature of desire, a force oriented toward the Self, an energy which is strictly narcissistic and yet which tears the individual away from himself to make him into the satellite of an Other. Language is alienated from desire. The oppositions of traditional morality and psychology skate over desire without ever gaining a foothold on it. Observer of my own desire, I dub it *love* after suppressing reference to the Self; observer of a foreign desire, I dub it *ambition* after suppressing reference to the Other. The "egotistic" morality sometimes recommended by Stendhal and later taken up by his disciples does little more than invert the original system. It suppresses reference to the Other in the desire that I recognize as mine and it reproaches the Other with being powerless to desire on his own. It unveils desire's double reference to Self and Other, *but only in the Other's desire*. It denies its own duality. It expresses in a psychological, polemical, and ideological language the paroxysm of the debate between Self and Other, the dual progress—in lucidity and in blindness—that marks the approaches of novelistic genius. Stendhal, too, turns ardently towards the signs of the Others; he does not want to recognize his own signs. It is under the banner of "egotism" that he fights rearguard battles against the invading truth.

Neither "altruism" nor "egotism" is able to recognize that love is always present in ambition and ambition in love. Stendhal juxtaposes these two incomplete *sentiments*, the mutilated signs of an ineffable desire, because he is headed obscurely towards the revelation of the latter. The writer strives to transcend the abstract divisions, but he strives equally hard to maintain them; in the last resort, his Self is at stake. It is always at the least possible cost to the Self that one would like to write masterpieces.

The Red and the Black at its best is beyond "ambition" and "love." The decisive experience occurs at last, with Stendhal as with Proust. The fragments of Proustian archives published under the title *Contre Sainte-Beuve* allow us to get some notion of its contours. These texts were written shortly before work on the definitive version of *Remembrance* began. The most important ones already lead up to *Time Regained*. We need to understand what distinguishes them from the definitive version. The event is not yet in the past. Proust senses its proximity and foretells its coming more than he analyzes its nature. He displays the infinite patience of a writer awaiting the creative moment. And he speaks to us of works that are:

interrupted, resumed, begun again and again, sometimes finished after sixty years like Goethe's *Faust*, sometimes left unfinished, genius having passed them by, so that at the last moment, seeing clearly in the hour of death like Don Quixote, a Mallarmé who has been laboring fiercely for ten years on an immense *œuvre* will tell his daughter to burn his manuscripts.[1]

Will Proust die as sterile as Don Quixote and Mallarmé? He is suffering the agonies of such a lucid death. (The intrinsic value of the judgment on Mallarmé is not important here.)

Proust identifies with those who discover only in dying their delusion and wretchedness; no longer does he fancy himself a Jean Santeuil, a Prince Charming. This is a crucial change. In another revelatory text, *The Filial Feelings of a Parricide*, he tells the story of a man with whom he was vaguely acquainted who killed himself after killing his mother. Proust endows this suicide with the same clairvoyant significance as the deaths of Don Quixote and Mallarmé; he even compares the parricide's final illumination "to that belated moment of lucidity that the most chimera-be-witched lives may have, since even Don Quixote's had its."

It is no longer the existence of the Other, this time, it is his own that Proust sees as "chimera-bewitched" to the point of being criminal. The writer recognizes himself in this snob, this bad son, this wrongdoer whom he had sought outside himself in his previous works. The signs of the Other have become the signs of the Self. The double is revealed *to be* a double. Here is where the operation occurs that we characterized above as being indispensable to the emergence of novelistic genius.

This Copernican revolution of the aggressive literary "psychology" puts an end to the oppositions that structure the psyche; it destroys the initial subjectivity and the dualist world which that subjectivity reflected. Proust's early art reflects this dualism. It too must therefore come apart. Certain pages of *Contre Sainte-Beuve* describe this process. Proust mourns his lost talent. His former virtuosity eludes him. In the depths of his ordeal, however, a ray of hope gleams. The discovery of a "link" between two "ideas," two "sensations" confers on the artist a new Self, intermittent and delectable.

It is often when I am sickest, when I have no more ideas in my head nor any strength, that this Self . . . perceives these links between two ideas, just as it is often in the fall when there are no more flowers nor leaves, that one senses the most profound harmonies in the landscapes. And this boy inside me who thus plays among the ruins has no need for any food, he subsists simply on the pleasure that the sight of the idea that he is discovering gives him, he creates it, it creates him, he dies, but an idea revives him, like those seeds that stop germinating in too dry a climate and die, but a little moisture and warmth are enough for them to be born anew.[2]

One should notice above all the unifying, synthetic character of the intuitions that spring up on the ruins of the dualist universe. These are the properly novelistic intuitions. To turn back against oneself the curse first hurled at the Other, to discover that this wicked Other and the Self are one, means discovering the Same in what once passed for absolute Difference, it means unifying reality. But first of all it means *dying*.

Here we have the experience in the process of being lived through, and not the experience already lived through as in *Time Regained*. The dualist values are merely shaken. The joys of the "boy who plays on the ruins" remain insubstantial; they are not yet capable of restructuring the world. Proust wonders, further on, if the work that could be produced with them would be "beautiful." He has left *Jean Santeuil*'s way; he has not yet found the way to *Remembrance*. This is the novelistic moment *par excellence*; the initial subjectivity, in the process of being transcended, experiences a descent into hell that will end with the reversal of all signs.

"Except a grain of wheat fall into the ground and die . . . " The symbolism of death and resurrection is already in place. We are able to verify its "operational" quality here. In *Time Regained* it takes on a rhetorical flavor for it has become too sure of itself.

The novelistic message is already concealed in the reference to Don Quixote. Proust *recognizes* the death of this hero. But it is not he, it is Cervantes who was the first to charge this death with his novelistic experience. The repeated allusions to this hero point us beyond death to the vacant niche of the novelist, the one Proust is now going to fill.

The hero embodies the novelist's "chimera," his desire. But he initially embodies it as if it were truth. In the novelistic masterpiece, he embodies it as the chimera that it is. The transition from the reflected illusion to the represented illusion demands identification with the wicked Other, which implies death. The novelist succeeds in experiencing this death *in the work*, through the intermediary of a hero who is sick, wounded, mutilated, dying.

Perhaps this novelist had contemplated giving his work a tragic conclusion all along, and had done so for reasons that were superficial but later took on depth. Between the mechanically planned tragic conclusion and the novelistic experience no external, biographical link is necessary. Tragedy always offers a possibility of symbolic expression for the anguished transcendence of dualisms. *The ordeal, death, becomes the invasion of the Other, the invasion of a truth that the previous existence refused.*

In *The Filial Feelings of a Parricide*, Proust strives, like the Stendhal of *The Red and the Black*, like the Flaubert of *Madame Bovary*, but too consciously this time, to encompass his experience in a mundane tragedy. He ends up renouncing this "classic" conclusion. He understands its mechanism too well. In *Time Regained*, therefore, he sets forth clearly, not without diluting them on occasion, the essential elements of the experience.

~

The novelistic conclusions of Stendhal, Cervantes or Dostoyevsky can be understood in the light of *Time Regained*—in the light, that is, of the creative experience. Why is the conclusion the privileged locus of the novelistic experience? Can the structural analogies between such different works be made intelligible?

The masterpiece contradicts the artist's original intention. That means the first draft is a failure, and sometimes the second and third as well. But the trajectory which unfolds within a single novel in Proust can also be accomplished over the course of several works of which the first appear "finished" only because they were published. The early novelist does not really grasp his failure. But, once more, he can only grasp it in the face of a work which in principle is finished; he must always arrive at the conclusion of the projected work. Having reached what he believes to be the end of his toils, he gazes back at last upon the work that he had dreamed of as perfect and discovers its weakness. On the seventh day of creation, the God of Genesis looks at his work and finds it to be good. The novelist looks at his and finds it to be bad. In short, he recognizes that he is not God. That is the first step of true art, the most essential perhaps and the least recognized. A merely skillful writer would never see this weakness; perhaps he would know better how to conceal it.

The real labor begins, the labor to which, in the manner of Proust's unpublished manuscripts, the contradictions in *The Red and the Black* bear witness. The novelistic miracle is always the pursuit of the work amidst an esthetic despair that seems liable to divert the artist from it. A site of failure, the place where the writer's first attempts collapse and dissolve, the conclusion is also the springboard for each new effort. It is the end and a new beginning. The authentically novelistic energy that transcends little by little the initial subjectivity, denying every time the artist's prior intention, springs up in this testamentary place where an equally false Self and Other die, where the death of the hero becomes the birth of the novelist. The death to the Self, necessary for the transcendence of dualisms, is cloaked and concealed by the "classic" novelists in the tragic death of the hero. The very elements of the plot, which pre-date the novelistic experience, facilitate its operation and provide it with its symbolic framework. This operation is at once less visible than with Proust and less self-aware. It is further removed from the positive anecdotal elements of the novel. Only spontaneously, almost without the creator's knowing it, does the conclusion become charged with novelistic symbolism.

Novels that metamorphose their creator into a novelist always allude, indirectly if not directly, to the spiritual adventure that made them possible. Their genesis is inscribed in the very structure of the work, and in particular in the itinerary of the hero. This itinerary is analogous, moreover, to that of *Remembrance*. Warned of the fate that awaits him by a portentous event, the hero sinks deep into a world of illusion and deceit. This downward movement is finally reversed through death and resurrection in a tragic dénouement.

That is the Stendhalian itinerary, and Gilbert Durand traces it admirably in his *Décor Mythique de la Chartreuse de Parme*.[3] Following the hero, it is the work as a whole that moves, as the critic shows, from the *epic register* to the *novelistic register*. But the word *décor* strikes us as inadequate. A number of uncertainties vanish as soon as we take seriously the terminology proposed by Gilbert Durand, as soon as we render operational, for example, that reversal of signs that characterizes, in his eyes, the novelistic register. Since Julien's itinerary is "ascensional," *The Red and the Black* would constitute an exception to the Stendhalian norm. But this itinerary is only ascensional from the worldly, that is to say "epic," point of view. If the reversal of signs is carried out, everything that is ascent in the first register will become descent in the second and vice-versa. Prison, an awful fate in the eyes of the world, turns out to be a boon in the novelistic perspective. In the same way, *Time Regained* reveals the worldly ascent that precedes a descent into the hell of desire.

The novelistic always comes after the epic because it is the *truth* of the latter. Otherwise, why assign it the name novelistic, especially if it is not the monopoly of a single literary genre? It is already the novelistic, Gilbert Durand remarks, which provides *The Odyssey* with its dominant note, that of the return to Ithaca. It is not necessary to resort to the notion of a collective unconscious to explain the presence of *myth* in writers who have never given myth a thought. Myth is not the trace of an immemorial past, it is not a vestigial presence, it is the living witness of the novelistic experience. The work is the site, the instrument, the product and, indirectly at least, the account of this experience.

Myth is the glimpse of a structure linked to the genesis of truth. The archetypes identified by Gilbert Durand are not imaginary since they give us access to true realism. Over and above the tragic anecdote, henceforth pervaded with symbolism, the work defines itself as the inauguration of this realism. The notion of an archetype is not useless insofar as it takes us beyond thematic subjectivism. The two registers are not themes but matrices of themes. They are even, in our eyes, two visions of the world that are at once successive and simultaneous since the second overlays and explains the first. To increase still further the fecundity of these notions, we must call on a myth whose privileged status may be affirmed without fear. The Oedipal myth crowned by the two tragedies, *Oedipus the King* and *Oedipus at Colonus*, will allow us to assemble and to articulate all the results of the novelistic analysis.

Oedipus sits on the throne of Thebes. He delivered the people from the sphinx; he believes himself to be safe from the dangers foretold by the oracle of Apollo. The only shadow in the picture is the plague lingering over the city. An unclean creature must be attracting the wrath of the god. Oedipus vows to punish the monster. He begins hunting for him after uttering solemn curses against him. The shortest path from the non-guilty to the guilty is a straight line, and so our champion of justice marches straight ahead. He does not notice when the path begins to curve—yet it proves to be a circular path in the end. The investigator turns back towards the Self he believes he has left safely in the distance behind him.

If, somewhere in the world, evil exists, somebody else must be responsible. At first Oedipus is certain of one thing only: he is not himself implicated in the business. Such is the imperious stance of natural subjectivity. But this imperious stance is secretly undermined. The hero would not condemn the Other so precipitously if he were not acting for the Self's benefit. He himself tells us as much. Oedipus's excessive indignation, his zeal to track down the culprit, are revealing. They are reminiscent of the passion with which Jean Santeuil/Legrandin condemns snobs.

Reading the signs of the Other and misapprehending one's own are but two sides of the same coin. The perspicacity that Oedipus displays with the sphinx only regards man in general, meaning the Other; it is blind where self is concerned. Later, the hero accuses Creon and Tiresias of the crime he himself committed. Creon, the enemy brother, and Tiresias, the blind prophet, are the *doubles* of Oedipus, blind and a prophet himself. Each episode goes a little further in revealing Oedipus's adversary to be an alter ego. It is this alter ego that Oedipus accuses with ever more violence and ever more impotence in his blind, and prophetic, march towards the truth.

Like *Oedipus the King*, the genesis of the novel is a struggle against the *double*, and it culminates in the novelist's defeat. The eternal duel between Self and Other is present in his work but the writer, at first, does not see it. He takes this work to be the pure, shining emanation of an incomparable Self. The assurance he displays is equal to that of Oedipus. He believes he is tossing our way an abundance of beauty, wisdom and, of course, justice. Like the reassuring hypotheses rigged up by Oedipus, the drafts of the work based on the Other's guilt and the Self's innocence collapse one by one. The novelist recognizes the poverty of dualist schemas. Oedipus discovers the inadequacy of his judicial positivism. The curse hurled at the Other boomerangs back against the Self.

The egotistic liturgies of which Baudelaire provided the model dissimulate the true meaning of Flaubert's exclamation "*Madame Bovary c'est moi.*" Stendhal, in a letter, makes a statement that would be as famous as Flaubert's if it were not so clear: "Seeing that Julien is a rogue and that it's my own portrait, I've had a falling-out with myself." Stendhal attributes to himself, not without humor but without ambiguity, the experience that is Julien's at the end of the novel. Here, again, is the identification with the double hunted by Oedipus. And here again, it is the conclusion that delivers the founding truth, invisible to those eyes of flesh that Oedipus wants no more of. Just as prison frees the Stendhalian hero, Oedipus blind becomes the wise man of Colonus, the seer. In the latter work, a further amplification upon the tragic dénouement, we see the signs reverse themselves once more. It is not a curse but a blessing that the dread oracles bring in the end.

The Oedipal myth presents us successively with the reflection of desire—the illusion of the initial subjectivity—and the experience which, revealing the desire, destroys this illusion. Thus it shows us the transition from the initial subjectivity to the secondary subjectivity. The myth in the strict sense is the idea that the initial subjectivity is master of itself and master of its relations with the Other, meaning, in the first instance, its father and mother. Everything that contradicts this dogma is presented to us, in the early episodes, as an accident or as the result of a "fatality." These early episodes are mythical *stricto sensu* because they mask the truth behind an anecdotal plot. Oedipus is unaware of his victim's identity, and . . . etc. Not being the product of a conscious design, this masquerade does not omit any element of the structure. Its extreme transparence makes it hard to see.

In the light of Freud, and also of the novelistic experience, all the episodes of the myth can be understood as representing the progressive externalization of a relationship to Self and Other that is founded first of all upon the father. Oedipal desire and novelistic desire are one and the same. The son desires mastery. He desires his father's *being*, meaning that which his father possesses and seemingly never ceases to desire in the midst of the blissful autonomy that he enjoys. The son imitates his father's desire. The double reference to Self and Other is present in *hubris*. The modern formulations, pride, self-love, etc. do not do justice to the *hybrid* nature of desire.

Nothing could be more explicit than the murder scene. The father and the son set out on the same path. Each is an obstacle for the other. The son desires to replace his father on the throne of Thebes and in his mother's bed. But the elimination of the obstacle cannot satisfy desire. Mastery proves disappointing and, above all, ill assured. The usurper constantly feels threatened. The veiled hostility between the son and the father, that primordial Other, the first model and first rival, is succeeded by an intersubjective struggle in which the truth is unveiled little by little, even though the increasingly rigid initial subjectivity first sees this truth as the truth of the Other, even though the growing lucidity is also a more extreme blindness. Laius is already the double of Oedipus: the more one advances toward the ending, the more the Other and the Self render themselves identical through accusation and counter-accusation.

The idea of *catharsis*, at least as it is usually interpreted, does not do justice to the conclusion of *Oedipus the King*. Catharsis is fabricated in view of the spectator; it presupposes an artist concerned only with the effects he produces. Without speculating about the experience of Sophocles or his predecessors, we may recognize that the conclusion of *Oedipus the King* and its further amplification in *Oedipus at Colonus* are not merely tacked onto the myth; the two tragedies are an integral part of it. Freud and the novel should lead us to a more complete, more "totalizing" reading. Indeed, in the psychoanalytic and, above all, the novelistic experience, we encounter once more the intersubjective content and even the form of Sophocles' conclusion. More importantly yet, Oedipus's anguished quest has its parallels in the genesis of each experience (the dualist drafts of the novel and, in psychoanalysis, the transference). The conclusion is thus inseparable from what precedes it; it is its ultimate, if not its necessary, development. Already, the conclusion affirms obscurely what we are reaffirming here.

We should note, however, a crucial difference between the myth and the novel. In *Oedipus the King* the mythical material is not restructured in the light of the dénouement. Freud put it well: "*Oedipus the King* unfolds *like* a psychoanalysis." *Oedipus the King* is therefore not a psychoanalysis; it is not a novel either. The ending has no retroactive effect on the beginning. *Oedipus at Colonus* is a perpetual return backwards but the reversal of the signs is more symbolized than signified. The content of the revelation remains undecided.

A first reason for this difference is obvious. The tragedy uses traditional materials; the artist cannot modify them as he pleases. The plot of *Oedipus the King* rests on the most "mythical" elements of the myth, the circumstances of Laius's murder, for example. The conclusion must be adapted to these time-honored givens. This means it must present itself in a form that remains partially mythical. The de-mythification, inseparable from the myth, is itself mythical. But there is more to the question of the mythical tragedy than the traditional nature of the materials used by Sophocles. The tragedy can help us better grasp the mythical element that subsists in the de-mythifying conclusion of the classical novel.

Freudian thought, for its part, is interested only in restructuring the myth in a perspective that is still that of the dénouement. It wants to be radically de-mythifying. And it constitutes, as such, a new variant of the myth. Lévi-Strauss is right. Psychoanalysis is Oedipal. That is no reason to conclude that it is intellectually sterile, or even inferior to a theory that would be uncontaminated by the myth and that would judge it from the outside. Such a theory does not exist. The myth expresses both the illusions of the initial subjectivity and their transcendence, without omitting the intermediate stages. One may therefore believe that no form of thought is foreign to it. Every intellectual attitude will have its counterpart at a given point along the mythical trajectory. Every true innovation will be rooted in the revelatory conclusion, the only opening onto de-mythification. The value of a form of thought should therefore be assessed by its position within the myth, in other words by the Oedipus that, implicitly or explicitly, it chooses. A literary example will make clearer this status of universal paradigm.

An analysis of Camus's *Stranger* reveals the real function of the murder of the Arab.[4] The author wants to prove that, in our world, an innocent man is doomed to persecution. But he wants to prove this about an innocent man of a peculiar sort and in a peculiar context inimical to his design. The character of the hero, his lack of ambition, his radical solipsism rule out any possibility of a significant conflict between him and society. That is the problem that is resolved, in appearance, by the involuntary murder of the Arab. To find the mythical model of the first part of *The Stranger*, one must go back to the murder of Laius. Just as Oedipus kills his father "without knowing it, " Meursault kills the Arab "without meaning it." A psychoanalysis would no doubt show that the murder of the Arab is rooted in Oedipal resentment. But a literary analysis has no need for testimony external to the work, however authoritative. It can show the author forcing situations, biasing his own data and employing procedures analogous to those of the myth in order to reach the goal he has assigned himself, namely the persecution of the angelic double by the evil Other. The structure is always intelligible since it is organized without conscious calculation on the author's part. Thanks to the involuntary murder, the hero is *guilty enough* for his punishment to be plausible but *innocent enough* to remain the victim of a cruel injustice. The involuntary murder contains and conceals a contradiction that has no rational solution precisely because it embodies desire and the illusions of the initial subjectivity.

The Stranger is thus far from coinciding with the conclusion of the myth. *The Plague* is not very different. The good doctor Rieux uncannily calls to mind the first scene of *Oedipus the King*. He puts his *lucidity* to the service of the benighted. He presents himself as a man of good will, moved by a disaster which, at bottom, hardly touches him. His "*engagement*" is only conceived against the backdrop of a prerequisite disengagement, alone essential. Oedipus believes he was born outside the city. He considers himself to be external to this kingdom which he oversees paternally, from far above. He is certainly not sick with the plague, and neither is Doctor Rieux.

With *The Fall*, everything changes. Clamence, the generous lawyer, is an allegory of the writer himself, as Doctor Rieux was, but the meaning is no longer the same. On the pretext of defending widows and orphans, the generous lawyer had sought to place the accusers in the position of the accused. In sum, he had forged an Oedipal myth for his own personal use. The last Camus reveals implacably the symbolic meaning of his earlier creations. And he defines them as attempts at personal justification. He recognizes his Double in the ferocious judge, that culprit, unknown and known, that he cursed in each of his writings. The generous lawyer is a judge in disguise, a superior judge who sets himself up as judge of the judges. The Oedipal circle has closed back in on him. *The sentence that you pronounce on others ends up flying straight back into your face, where it manages to do some damage.*

The Fall is to *The Stranger* and *The Plague* what *Remembrance* is to *Jean Santeuil*. But this "novelistic" experience is a little too distant from its object. The works that it seeks to restructure were published long ago. They have an independent history, they are in some sense out of reach. The experience is decisive but the restructuring that it initiates is only a game, confined to the level of ironic allusion and parody. For this reason the work does not attain a universal mode of expression. One may imagine a novel—Camus did not write it but he could have written it—that would accomplish a synthesis of *The Stranger*, *The Plague*, etc., in the final perspective of *The Fall*. The author's various books would be no more than episodes in the life of a single hero. The early works would be revised in the light of *The Fall*. Their distinctive perspective would survive only in the vision of this hero marching toward the novelistic experience.

Our conception of the Oedipal myth will be clearer, perhaps, if we compare the mythical structure to what would be yielded, not by a synthesis of Camus's works, but by a chronological juxtaposition, still crowned by *The Fall*. As in the preceding operation, one must eliminate *The Fall*'s ironic allusions to the earlier works and reassemble all the heroes in a single figure thanks to modifications in the plots. Between the imaginary novel and the imaginary myth, only one difference remains but it is decisive in its consequences. Since the first episodes have not been revised in the light of the conclusion, it is this conclusion itself that must be revised. The revelation can no longer bear directly on desire, it will only attain the mythical materials brought forth by this desire. Such a work would no doubt give us, a little like the Oedipal myth itself, a dual impression of superficial disparity and deep-seated unity.

~

It is not by denying the relevance of the Oedipal myth that we will succeed in transcending the limitations of a certain literary Freudianism, it is by showing that the relations between literature and the myth include the famous "complex" but are not always limited to it. The more profound the works are, the longer and more faithfully they follow the myth. Freud does not grasp the most profound aspects of the literary experience, but he sees the truth as an intersubjective conquest, the difficult revelation of a mythical content long confused with immediate perception. He prepares us to see that this conquest is at the far end of misunderstanding, the whole being signified by the "complete" trajectory of the myth. Freud and the novel are located at the same point on this trajectory. The reciprocal attempts at reduction should therefore be replaced by dialogue.

If Freud is only in appearance the enemy of literature, Jung or at least Jungianism is perhaps only in appearance its friend. Jungian nostalgia treats myth as an object external to the overly lucid beings that science has made of us. "Reality" is not enough for us, we need to complete it with "myth." If literature is bound up with myth thus understood, it no longer has anything to do, at whatever level it is situated, with truth in the strong sense of the term. It is this secret indifference, this defeatism of the truth—an indirect homage to the positivism it denounces—that produces criticism with a doubtless incomparable ability to navigate the twists and turns of the initial subjectivity, but also criticism devoid of criteria, and closed to the deeper history of the works, criticism for which no book is mediocre because none is truly great either.

What is most significant in a work may not always be what is most singular. All the structural elements of *Oedipus the King* turn up again in the novelistic masterpieces. They all need to be interpreted in the light of a process of transcendence internal to the work of art. The most noteworthy of these elements, apart from the conclusion, are the *oracles*, much in evidence in Stendhal where they have given rise to numerous commentaries.

Before going to visit the Rênals for the first time, Julien stops at the church in Verrières. At his feet, a scrap of newspaper attracts his attention; he deciphers it: it announces the execution of Louis Jenrel. A little later he thinks he sees blood in a basin of holy water. The oracle foretells the breach of the alliance between the hero and the world. It cannot spring up in the world's midst without provoking confusion, anxiety, disarray. There is thus a maleficent aspect to the oracle which is also its immediate aspect, the only one that we noticed in *Oedipus the King*.

The oracle points to the dénouement. It therefore has a hidden meaning, a secondary meaning. It announces prison and death, which is to say that it also announces freedom and life. To understand properly the nature of the oracle we must compare the works with each other. The famous scene of the *madeleine* occupies in *Remembrance* the same relative position as the Stendhalian oracles. Without being absolutely first, it is located at the beginning of the chronological sequence. It is the oracle pointing to *Time Regained.* Here the maleficent aspect has completely disappeared, and it is not hard to grasp the reason for its absence. Proust has understood the relationship between the oracle and the conclusion. He therefore interprets the oracle solely in view of the conclusion. He retains only the beneficent aspect, which is in fact the essential one even though it is generally dissimulated. Proust deciphers certain aspects of the structure that elude his predecessors. He organizes his work very consciously in accordance with these aspects, illuminating them in remarkable fashion to the exclusion of certain others.

The meaning of the *madeleine* is clear: it is a revelation that fails as a result of its beneficiary's inability to receive it as it deserves. A first brief glimmer of novelistic grace, the *madeleine* makes its appearance, like the final experience, in an atmosphere of lassitude and discouragement. The narrator is weary of the world but he cannot yet detach himself from it. He has not exhausted all of its desires. The internal emptiness is lacking that alone would make plenitude possible. The feeling that dominates Marcel at the moment of the revelation is a stultifying curiosity. There is thus a failure at the level of the event itself. The revelation is still sketchy. It cannot be integrated into the world. The world cannot be restructured around it. The revelation is therefore denied by the desire that it denies. And this desire triumphs, temporarily at least; the beneficent sensation remains isolated, detached from everything, derisory in the eyes of the world and soon half-forgotten.

The failed revelation's full significance only becomes clear in the light of the successful revelation. Then it can be perceived as a harbinger of the conclusion, an oracle properly speaking. This is evident in Proust. *Time Regained* abolishes the naiveties of the empirical perspective, the only one accessible to the initial subjectivity. The failed revelation is integrated, as an annunciatory sign, into a reality restructured by the definitive revelation. The failure only appears in all its magnitude at the moment when its consequences have at last been conjured, at the moment when the restructuring confers a positive meaning on the negative itself.

In Stendhal, more profoundly perhaps than in Proust, because more obscurely, the oracle is the failure of a revelation. It is understood neither by the hero, nor by the reader, nor even perhaps by the author himself, still immersed too deeply in the world to be able to interpret his own signs. The Stendhalian oracle still bears the imprint of the artist's original intention. The maleficent aspect reflects, up to a certain point, the novelist's initial error concerning the meaning of the conclusion, his incapacity to reach the novelistic register. The maleficent side is not, however, all there is in

Stendhal. The oracle is frightening but it has a secret sweetness. It is always in churches that it makes its appearance. In *The Charterhouse* it emanates from Father Blanès, an eminently beneficent character. A quick glimpse at the other side of the world, a sudden flash from a swiftly turned mirror, the oracle presents us with a shorthand version of the reversal of signs that defines the conclusion and the novel itself, except that the relationship between the two meanings is reversed. In the dénouement, the positive wins out, the resurrection has definitively triumphed over death. In the oracle, by contrast, it is the sinister aspect that dominates.

One can show that the oracle is bound up with the creative dynamism. It is always from the conclusion, we saw, that the novelist sets out to rectify his work in a novelistic direction. In the round of successive drafts, the omega immediately precedes the alpha. Nothing in the order of creation is closer to the conclusion, therefore, than the beginning, understood henceforth as a new beginning. If the inspiration is born at one extremity of the work it is at the other extremity that its effects are felt the most quickly and directly. From another point of view, however, the beginning of the work remains the place that is furthest from the novelistic experience. The point of departure is still permeated with the spirit of the origin. Even if, unlike in myth, the beginning is revised from the perspective of the ending, this revision is never complete enough to eradicate the opening perspective. That comes down to saying that the novel is a spiritual passage or transition; it is never the fruit of a fully accomplished transcendence, of a transcendence that has inventoried and organized all its effects, of a transcendence itself transcended. It is transcendence in the act. It is the snapshot of an esthetic and spiritual movement.

The creative process must not be conceived as if it simply followed the chronology of the story unfolding before the reader—as if the novelist moved along a straight line leading from the beginning to the end. This linear schema must be abandoned. The straight line curves back on itself, and its two extremities tend, not to meet, but to be superimposed. The creative process is not a circle but a spiral. A perfect circle would lead literally nowhere, there would be no internal transcendence. The oracle embodies precisely the novelist's inability to close the circle, to produce a work whose perspective would remain constant from one end of the story to the other. The oracle represents the gap between the two extremities of the novel, the opposition between the epic register and a novelistic register suddenly made concrete by irrational allusions to creation itself and its mysteries. The shadow of the Kierkegaardian paradox falls momentarily across the work.

If, in the ultimate order of the narrative, the oracle prefigures the catastrophic transcendence of an illusory world, the truth that can establish itself definitively only at the other extremity of the work, in the genetic order it constitutes the first glimmer of authentically novelistic inspiration and its quasi-thematization in a place where it is as difficult to express this inspiration as to pass over it in silence. The oracle thus testifies to a certain hesitation and even confusion. The creator is not master of the shifts in perspective that he finds in his work. The moment of the conclusion and the moment of the oracle are therefore very close to each other. In a sense they are one and the same. To convince oneself of this, one need only reread the quotations from *Contre Sainte-Beuve* at the beginning of this essay. They can be interpreted equally well from the oracular perspective or from the perspective of the conclusion. Proust is torn between two opposite and irreconcilable modes of the work of art. He does not know which he should prefer. The artist is at a crossroads, contemplating his literary *future*. The tiniest incidents then acquire the status of *signs*.

The opposition between the two perspectives, the two registers, should not, in theory, pose any special problem. If the *epic* does not include the *novelistic*, the *novelistic* for its part quite readily includes the *epic*, and it is as a function of the novelistic that the work must be structured. But the novelist lives through the novelistic experience before he thinks it through, if indeed he ever does think it through. He is not sufficiently detached to be able to arrange and rearrange the elements so as to organize them systematically. He still looks somewhat fearfully at *the boy inside him who plays among the ruins*. The oracle is the place where the gap between the work's two perspectives is greatest; it is also the place where this gap appears for the first time. Not yet having grasped the possibilities for articulation that will reveal themselves little by little, the artist manages the best he can, sometimes using, in the manner of Stendhal, procedures condemned by *realism*. And that is doubtless what explains the curious awkwardness of certain opening gambits.

The oracle plays an essential role in the novelistic structure. A fragment of the conclusion uprooted from its place of origin, it has its place in the esthetic economy of the work, it contributes to the balance between its parts. More importantly yet, it orients the reader; without taking anything away—quite the contrary—from the dramatic impact of the conclusion, it provides a mysterious foretaste of its effects. Since the oracle is never correctly interpreted, the oracular structure overcomes the traditional opposition between didacticism and divertissement. It suggests that events have a hidden meaning, more essential than the apparent meaning. It tells us that the work has two levels to it. The simultaneous duality and unity of the novel's perspective makes the oracle necessary from the reader's standpoint.

The Divine Comedy is structured like a novel. The work flows from the ending and is organized as a function of this ending. Dante the pilgrim must pass through hell and purgatory to arrive in paradise, in other words to become the visionary Dante, the author of *The Divine Comedy*. To read Dante properly, Charles S. Singleton remarks, one must read him twice, the first time starting from the beginning, the second time starting from the end. This observation is justified from a practical and even theoretical viewpoint. Ideally, however, the second reading is not necessary, thanks to the oracles also present in Dante. They let us glimpse a fragment of the future truth, the minimum indispensable for an understanding of the work; they put the reader on guard.

It is the writer's confusion, we said, that opens up the specifically novelistic possibility of the oracle. This must be taken as confirmation of the fact that the novelistic structure is transcendence in the act. Confusion itself is an opportunity that must be seized. The perfect oracle, the fully realized oracle, is Stendhal's double oracle, the oracle whose ambiguity confirms the uncertainty of the creator and the authenticity of the novelistic experience. To understand the oracle is to understand that the work is forged through the transcendence of the original intention.

The necessary imperfection of the novelistic circle shows us that the most unified works, the ones that triumph over previous dualisms, are nonetheless not "autonomous worlds," separate and closed upon an inaccessible perfection. From the vantage point of the definitive work, the opening pages culminating in the oracle, that minor conclusion, represent a microcosm of the novel at the threshold of the novel itself; in the order of creation they constitute an umbilical suture, so to speak, and a bridge linking the novelistic structure to its creator and to the outside world. Nothing reveals this aspect better than the express mention, in the oracle of *The Red and the Black*, of Louis Jenrel, that is to say of the real, historical individual who also has his role to play in the conception of the novelistic work.

One may also compare the conclusion to a volcano whose lava spreads outward into the surroundings. The oracle is a cooled-down fragment of this lava. It appears to be remote from its source because the definitive work locks us into an irreversible temporal succession.

Calm block that some unseen disaster sent,[5]

the oracle makes such a sharp contrast with the landscape around it that reason renounces any attempt to account for its presence. Either reason avows its impotence, bowing before the mystery, and the oracle is then pervaded with the sacred, or else reason refuses to bow down, and it treats the oracle with disdain. These two ways of fleeing the oracle are at bottom very close to each other. Following Oedipus himself, Stendhal confirms this for us by combining them both in rather remarkable fashion. He answers the summons that comes from the novelistic experience, but he has ideological scruples. He senses that he is not being completely faithful to the dogma of "small true facts." Each time he uses anecdotal elements to bring the "Oedipal" articulations of his work into play, he feels the need to justify himself. He does not know what demon impels him to include bits of "German mysticism" in his work. Indeed, he chalks these up to his hero. He insists on the irrationality of the oracles in order to make clear that he is no dupe.

The ambiguity of the Stendhalian oracle is halfway between the oracle in *Oedipus the King* and Proust's *madeleine*. In the myth it is the maleficent connotation which dominates, in other words the connotation *for* the world, *for* the initial subjectivity. It cannot be otherwise since the myth has not been restructured from the perspective of the conclusion. In Proust, on the other hand, the restructuring is so thorough that the initial meanings have nearly disappeared: the beneficent connotation alone is present. Stendhalian ambiguity may well embody the novelistic norm, if there is one, as opposed to the myth on one hand, and on the other, to the deciphering of the structure, already begun by Proust and pushed much further by Freud although in a quite different spirit. The deciphering of the myth represents, moreover, a modern resurrection after the rationalist and positivist phase during which the Oedipal structure was hardly present except in works of art. The progressive unveiling of the structure has its model in the myth itself; the history of art and of thought conforms to this model, as does the history of each thinker taken individually. In *The Charterhouse of Parma*, for example, the beneficent aspect of the oracle is more pronounced than in *The Red and the Black*. As the novelist progresses in the use of novelistic structures, the link between the oracle and the conclusion asserts itself with greater precision. The last Stendhalian oracle comes close to the Proustian one.

The oracle in *Oedipus the King* is not exclusively maleficent either. The allusions to a positive religious value are all the more interesting in that they appear difficult to integrate into the tragic context. The chorus sees in the scorning of oracles the cause of the city's ills: "They are nothing now, the oracles rendered to Laius, they are disdained, Apollo is no longer honored with splendor anywhere; the worship of the gods is on the wane" [906–10]. The presence of a double oracle in the higher regions of the myth seems to contradict the foregoing theses. We see in these higher regions the expression of the mythic in the strict sense, as opposed to the lower regions which express the degradation and revelation of the initial subjectivity. Is the mythic in the strict sense compatible with the oracle?

The oracle, remember, is not revelation; it is the failure of a revelation. But the verification of the oracle can no longer be defined by this failure. Even if it does not correspond to a "complete" revelation, with a reversal of signs, it nonetheless shows that the Oedipal subjectivity, as deeply mythified as it may be, is always oriented towards its own revelation. The mechanism that triggers this revelation is never lacking but the revelation's first stage is embryonic, a purely oracular stage that might define primitive Greek religion.

These speculations are useless anyhow. The nature and degree of the revelation signified by the verification of primitive oracles is of scant importance. One may affirm that this revelation had ceased to be understood by the time of *Oedipus the King*. But little is gained by maintaining that its substance had evaporated. The message of the secondary subjectivity falling into the grip of the initial subjectivity will necessarily be misconstrued, distorted, ridiculed. To say this is to reiterate that the oracle is an evanescent revelation, slipping more or less slowly into oblivion. The literature of antiquity is proof of that. Reading Oedipal and novelistic oracles as a function of the transcendence they embody or symbolize may be a way of shedding some light on that *ambiguity* of oracles often mocked by ancient authors. They treat the oracles as absurd riddles, evasive ploys dreamed up by greedy priests anxious to conceal their ignorance. This is already Voltaire's *Oedipus*. The oracle is ambiguous because it encodes the very act of transcendence: no stable perspective can account for it. Judging by *Oedipus the King*, scorn for the ancient oracles is not justified, in its principle at least. But rationalism, ancient and modern, marks the triumph of the initial subjectivity, in other words the oblivion, in appearance definitive, of oracles . . .

In his art, Sophocles revives and reactivates the forgotten oracles. This idea appears less absurd in the light of modern interpretations of *Oedipus the King*. Most exegetes see nothing in the myth but "fatality," meaning the strictly mythical element. They miss the intersubjective struggle and the de-mythification because they suppress the oracles and the conclusion, which is to say the most essential part of the structure. The dénouement becomes nothing but a *catharsis*, increasingly pallid and tacked onto the myth from the outside. As purists of myth, mythologists often regard with some suspicion the crowning episodes which are also, it seems, the most recent. Explanation for Oedipus's self-punishment is sought in Sophocles' political opinions, in his hostility toward tyrants. In short, there is always an attempt to eliminate the revelatory dénouement. Literary criticism, whether idealistic or realistic, treats the conclusions of the great novelistic works no differently.

It is this myth reduced to "fatality" which anthropologists discover everywhere. The presence, within the myth itself, of the formidable and fertile mechanism that always leads to intersubjective struggle and that *can* lead to demythification is no doubt peculiar to the Oedipal myth proper and to the Western world. In this privileged myth, the order of the episodes is not indifferent; it is linked to the process of unveiling—that indeed is what defines it as *historical*.

Rationalism postulates, in the last analysis, that Oedipus has *nothing to learn about himself*. And that is exactly what the first Oedipus thinks. Rationalism chooses the first Oedipus and defines itself by this choice. We all know the academic Oedipus. He is a very respectable gentleman. He passed his exams with flying colors and rose to a high position in society. Quite obviously, he does not deserve the troubles besetting him. His story remains perfectly unintelligible.

Like the first Oedipus, proud of a wisdom obtained without the help of oracles, rationalism locates all lucidity in a static relationship between subject and object. It rules out any possibility of transcendence. It sees nothing in the myth but "fatality," and "fatality" returns the favor. It nails Oedipus to his misfortune and that is the image of its own destiny. Nor does it see in fatality anything but an absurd chimera; it empties it of all content. This abstract negation is not true knowledge; it does not totalize the myth. And soon we find "fatality" acquiring a content. Rationalist assurance culminates in the absurd and in nihilism, meaning the struggle of consciousnesses. That is what the last two centuries of thought have demonstrated once again. The Oedipus who stubbornly refuses to question his own certainties ends up like Camus's Sisyphus. To choose this first Oedipus is to resemble him to the extent of sharing his supreme illusion, which is not to choose at all. The interpretations that nullify the dénouement of *Oedipus the King* justify their inability to totalize the myth by an appeal to "scientific caution." They pose as "Greek" in the face of Freud and modern manipulations. But the myth was never, for the Greeks, a naturalist slice of life, "full of sound and fury, signifying nothing." Demystification is poles apart from de-mythification, for which it nonetheless lays the groundwork. Its model is the vain lucidity of Oedipus before the sphinx. Both the understanding and the misunderstanding of the myth are interpretable within the terms of the myth itself.

Freud in a sense does nothing but repeat and decipher Sophocles. Freud tells the Oedipal subjectivity its future and interprets its past. He, too, brings the oracles of Laius back to life. Only those modes of thought which encompass the *conclusion* can attempt to follow the writer in his essential journey. They do not possess, for all that, any jurisdiction over the work of art.

Translated by Mark R. Anspach

CHAPTER 2

Oedipus Analyzed

Father and son meet on the same road, and this road is too narrow for the both of them. One must yield his place to the other. At no time can the city have more than one king, at no time can Jocasta have more than one husband. To want to be Oedipus is to desire what Laius desires, it is to imitate Laius at the fundamental level of desire, it is to desire *to be* Laius. Driven by the *same* desire, the two men are constantly headed towards the *same* violence.

The son is a faithful copy of the father, his mirror-image. The conflict between the two men does not feed on *differences*, as all thinking in line with common sense would have it, but on *resemblances* continually elicited by the identity of aims and the convergence of desires. The logic of desire must be distinguished from the logic of ideas. Two contradictory ideas are always, of course, two different ideas. By contrast, for two desires to oppose and to contradict one another, they must be *identical*.

To possess the throne and to possess Jocasta are two things that always go together in the myth. We must therefore associate them with each other and refer them back to the father. Desiring what the latter desires, soon to possess what he possesses, always and everywhere, the son wants to conquer the father's being. The modern idea that the individual does not come already made but needing to be made, that existence is not given but constructed, remains an abstract proposition as long as it is conceived without breaking out of the solipsistic framework of philosophy. To choose to be *oneself* is to choose to be the *Other*. And the Other here is the father and, at first, he alone.

The father blocks the son's path to a throne and a wife that he does not want to relinquish. Why look any further? Instead of reading the myth in the light of a certain anthropology, we might ask ourselves about the anthropology implicit in the myth. This approach has only its own obviousness to recommend it. It always opts for the simplest solutions, those that invoke, if possible, no element foreign to the myth, those that neglect, if possible, none that is a part of it.

To imitate the father is to heed the deepest and most sacred summons. It means seeking fulfillment in the father's tradition, it means wanting to be at the center of a familial and social universe that is the same as his. Filial piety and revolt thus have the same origin.

The father and son are competitors, *concurrentes*: they *run together* on the same road.[1] The father is not superhuman as the son imagines. He is neither transcendent nor perfect. If he rules, it is in the same world as the son. It is the best son and not the worst who makes the most dangerous rival. Stopped short by the paternal obstacle, the son will believe himself to have been judged and condemned; he will believe himself to be unworthy of replicating his father's being.

The object that lies behind an obstacle is only the more desirable for being forbidden. The obsession with forbidden fruit is not primary, it is not the cause but the consequence of the rivalry. It is with the model and not the obstacle that the dialectic begins. But this hierarchy will soon reverse itself, dissimulating the true genesis of desire. The appearance of a mechanical obstacle in the form of a competing intention—perhaps this stranger who insists on passing ahead of Oedipus on the road to Thebes, provoking a quarrel over *priority* in the most trivial sense of the term—is enough for the hero once more to hear the sentence condemning him. The moment he detects an obstacle, he thinks he is on the track of the supremely desirable, the secret path of paternal being. The possessions of this man who chances to stand in the way—his throne and his wife—acquire a sacramental value.

Oedipus's sphinx is the Greek sphinx, which has received quite diverse interpretations. But the Egyptian sphinx is the common ancestor, it seems, of all the later variants. This original sphinx is the image of the deceased king engraved on a stone lion, an imposing statue that bars violators of the crypt from entering the royal tomb. One could not imagine a clearer or more direct representation of the paternal obstacle, that essential obstacle that rears its head anew behind every accidental obstacle. Oedipus puts the sphinx out of the way; violently removing this new obstacle from his path, he loots the treasures stored in the royal tomb. The throne and the wife are his. He lacks no attribute of paternal power. The sphinx is originally male but one can easily see what tends to feminize it.

Oedipus has long lived away from Thebes, in Corinth where Polybus and Merope raise him "like a son." Heeding the oracle, Oedipus resolves to flee this second father and this second mother. The dialectic of desire governs this flight. There is nothing in the myth that is not governed by it. Oedipus does not want to break through the obstacle that wounds him, he wants to heal the wound; he intends to found, far from the father, a desire with neither obstacle nor model. This first repudiation of the paternal model, this declaration of independence is sincere but superficial. In the manner of nearly all the readers of his myth, Oedipus confuses the interchangeable individuals with the relationships which alone are permanent. He mistakes the imprint for the mold. It is from the imprint that he distances himself, not knowing that he carries the mold with him.

The drama averted with Polybus and Merope plays itself out with Laius and Jocasta. Does the role of the "adoptive" family here belong to the first couple or the second? Oedipus fled Polybus and Merope; they must therefore embody, from a certain standpoint, the paternal essence and the maternal essence. To reverse the immediate data of the myth, substituting Laius for Polybus and Polybus for Laius, is already to identify certain aspects of the structure. But this reversal is not sufficient. It constitutes the first moment in a dialectic that must be carried through to the end. Reversing the roles does not yet mean recognizing that they are wholly interchangeable. It means imposing a new distribution of parts, just as rigidly fixed as the first. It is this fixity that must be abandoned, it is this rigidity that must be transcended to arrive at the identity of the father and son and, beyond that, the equivalence of all the roles.

Every man, when he leaves his father and mother, goes towards his father whom he will kill and towards his mother whom he will marry. We must therefore renounce clearcut identities and stable points of reference. To demand individual differences from the myth, breaches of symmetry that are not there, is to flee the vertigo of undifferentiation and to succumb to the same mistake as Oedipus when he thinks he has escaped his parents by running away from his childhood home. Oedipus lives on within us; that is why we misapprehend the structure and its mirror play. We delude ourselves about the father to the precise extent that we think we know who he is.

The double movement from Thebes to Corinth and from Corinth to Thebes suggests a double reciprocity in which identities are confused. In the midst of this confusion which needs to be rendered systematic, certain distinctions remain and even become sharper, but they are always relative and reversible. The distance between Corinth and Thebes is the deep peace of childhood, it is remoteness from the father, as happy as it is unhappy. The father and son live in different places. They think, act and, above all, desire in two separate regions of being. Their paths temporarily diverge.

As fundamental as it is, the conflict with the father is initially glimpsed only in fleeting instants, far removed from one another. There is a father of everyday life, Polybus, and a father of desire and prohibition, Laius. The names hardly matter here; it hardly matters, in truth, whether there are two men or only one. The structure reverses itself at the moment the son flees. The circularity of the myth turns on perpetual reversals.

In psychoanalytic terms, Corinth represents the "latency period." And that is essentially what the hero tells us at the dénouement of *Oedipus the King*: "O Polybus, Corinth, old palace I called paternal, what shameful things did you cause to grow in me concealed beneath the beauty" [1394–96].

~

Oedipus is now king of Thebes; he is the husband of Jocasta. The dialectic of the model and the obstacle no longer has, in a reasonable view of things, any reason to exist. It is in spite of all reason that it perpetuates itself and even comes precipitously to a head. This dialectic is easy to detect behind the political significations of *Oedipus the King*. Heeding the oracle, the tyrant contemplates the undoing of a man, the murderer of Laius, who may dream of taking his place:

It is not for the sake of distant friends that I shall wipe out this stain, but for my own sake. Whoever killed Laius may well also wish, with a like hand, to take vengeance on myself. By coming to the aid of that king, I serve my own cause [137–41].

Oedipus treats this Other who killed or might kill the King in the same way that he was himself treated by Laius and for the same reasons. Each seeing in the Other a real or potential rival, each takes refuge in the same violence. To understand Oedipus's motives is to understand the circularity of the myth. The father who does violence to his son, the king who does violence to the Other, always believes he is drawing the lesson from a previous conflict, vaguely recollected. The oracle is the voice of the father, the father of Laius, the father of Oedipus, addressing the son and reminding him of the danger that at all times and in all places sons represent for fathers. The son turned father thinks he can escape from the circle by redoubling the violence that was first directed against himself. It is in order to break with the past that each time a new cycle of misfortune is set in motion.

Oedipus himself declares that he is acting as Laius's son, without grasping the profound irony of his words: "Today, since I have the power that Laius had before me, since I have his bed and his wife as my own . . . for all these reasons, as if he were my father, I will fight for him" [258–60, 264–65].

The father is never anything but a first accursed son. He himself seized the paternal inheritance by force and by ruse. Nobody is truly legitimate. There is no true king, there are only tyrants. *There is no true father.* That is no doubt the deepest, most hidden meaning of the myth. And this meaning is none other than the identity of all the characters, the equivalence of all the roles. The desire for the father is never transcended, for nothing can satisfy it. There is no true father but, through a paradox as stupefying as it is fundamental, the son always succeeds—over and above the misunderstandings which, always reciprocal, end up canceling each other out—in replicating that being which, always wrongly, he takes to be the true father's. Perpetual failure and the panicked reactions that it engenders insure, unbeknownst to the disciple, the very precise reproduction of the being that is sought for—that of a model which the disciple believes to have been repudiated long ago and which he really would repudiate if he knew its true nature. What is perpetuated from father to son is the injury and the distancing, it is the violence and the usurpation, it is that wound to the foot that runs from father to son in the family of Labdacus.

Bruised by the obstacle and ruled by that bruise, the son heads straight for the father he thinks he left behind. What we have here is, once more, that flight from the father that is an ironic return to the father. To be mistaken about the real identity of the model is the sole means of equaling him, for the model's own being is founded on an analogous error.

It is Creon, this time, who transmits to Oedipus the oracle of Apollo. Creon, brother to Jocasta, passes for the closest male relative of the late king, his presumptive heir. At first a bit abstract, Oedipus's anger quickly fixes upon this brother-in-law who in "reality" is an uncle, that is to say a quasi-father, but who is not recognized as such, just as, a little earlier, Laius was not recognized as father.

Oedipus treats Creon as inferior and guilty out of fear that he is superior and innocent. He is afraid Creon is the legitimate heir that he himself is without knowing it. He has broken through the obstacle and taken his father's place; he is therefore infinitely close to him but also infinitely far away. He is more unworthy than ever. He is at once above and below other men: above inasmuch as he occupies the place of the father, below inasmuch as he ought not occupy it. Official holder of title to the kingdom, Oedipus remains eternally excluded from it. Political usurpation perfectly expresses the relation to the father.

Just before the conclusion to *Oedipus the King*, the chorus wonders aloud about the hero's origin. A god must have sired him, they think. Oedipus expects to learn, on the contrary, that he is of servile birth. Like Laius before him, he is at once the father and the accursed son, the king and the slave, the victim and the sacred executioner. He describes himself as "now humbled, now exalted." He is split in two, "divided against himself." Sophocles emphasizes the dual character of the Theban universe. Here every living creature, everything that aspires to unity, succumbs to duality. Laius's herdsman has two flocks, the one from Corinth only one. Jocasta gives birth to a *double progeny, a husband from her husband, and children from her child.* The duality of Thebes and Corinth is but a particular expression of this doubling. Everything that comes from Laius is double. Internal division is matched by the emergence of external doubles. Oedipus's partners act more and more like Oedipus himself; the resemblance is ever more perfect, rendered so by the illusion of a difference ever more profound.

Never does Oedipus recognize the Same, the Alter Ego at his side. He does not see, in other words, the truth of the myth, the equivalence of all roles, the double structure, at every level, of his own history. Oedipus limps and it is the paternal wound that makes him lame. His asymmetrical gait carries him, and his myth along with him, towards an ever more perfect symmetry.

Oedipus accuses Creon of having killed the king. He accuses him of his own crime, he denounces in him his own desire. Oedipus, it will be said, *projects* his desire onto the Other. No doubt, but the Other's desire is no less real for being projected. No one will deny that Creon covets the throne. He occupied it not long before and he will soon occupy it again. No more than the conflict between Oedipus and Laius, the conflict between Oedipus and Creon does not spring from concrete differences. It is rooted in the same desire, always directed towards the same objects.

The dialectic of the model and the obstacle is double, reciprocal. Each plays, for the Other, the double role of obstacle and model. Each contemplates in the Other the truth of his own desire. The anger of Oedipus, the anger of his partners, constitutes the overwhelming and ever denied evidence of the competing desire. This truth is also the most egregious of lies since each makes it out to be the Other's truth and his alone. Oedipus does not want to see his own inclusion in the structure that gradually reveals itself. Believing he was born away from Thebes, he volunteers his services as a disinterested redeemer. "Uninvolved" by divine right, he condescends, he thinks, to get "involved."

The conflict between generations gives way to a conflict between contemporaries. Like each of us, it will be said, Oedipus must make the transition from childhood to adulthood. That is true, but before being part of the natural order, this transition belongs to the mythical order; it can only truly be read in the language of desire. Creon demonstrates this, and Jocasta too, by not growing old when they should. Jocasta remains forever the wife of the King. Creon becomes a quasi-brother to Oedipus. Between the mythical partners, the difference in age is abolished. Their identity becomes all the more perfect. This identity, in the Laius episode, is less immediate, less manifest than it will be later. The first conflict unfolds through the intermediary of other people, or monsters, and on the basis of thoroughly mistaken identities. The conflict is made up of moments that are isolated in space and time. This double distance must be bridged if the reciprocity is to be grasped. The shift must be made from Thebes to Corinth and from Corinth to Thebes; the hero's early childhood and his young adulthood must be juxtaposed. It is not without difficulty that we perceive equivalences which, at every stage of the myth, are alone essential, since they structure even the earliest episodes.

Identity is the only thing that counts, and it is what we perceive with increasing clarity, since it never ceases to become more perfect and more precise. The myth continually produces identity out of evanescent differences. The very notion of brother signifies identity. The story of Oedipus's sons, Eteocles and Polynices, the "enemy brothers," is the sequel to the story of Oedipus, which is essentially the story of the father/son relationship. That is what we find in the Oedipus cycle considered as a whole. If we limit our perspective now to the story of Oedipus alone, we see that here, too, the relationship between the two "brothers," Oedipus and Creon, succeeds the father/son relationship. In Genesis, Cain and Abel come after the Fall. Some mythical accounts redouble the quality of brother, carrying it to the second power. Romulus and Remus are twins; their identity is signified twice.

Eliminating the differences that subsist means bringing the ego closer to the alter ego and bringing the conflict out into the open; it means eliminating the distance that still separates the adversaries and superimposing two symmetrical violences. Oedipus and Creon, Oedipus and Tiresias come face to face. The myth advances towards its own revelation. Mythical repetition is not repetition pure and simple; it traces the trajectory of desire. The truth, ever more fully unveiled, is ever more fully veiled as well, for it is ever more violently denied.

In both time and space, the structure is reduced and concentrated. The guiding lines show up in sharp relief as each seeks to accuse the other of having killed the father. The truth that is coming to light is everyone's truth, the truth of the myth itself.

And the truth that emerges is the reader's own truth, a truth always denied and shunted onto the Other, a truth understood as if it pertained to the hero alone, that "doomed" figure marked by "destiny" for a fate of no concern to us.

The partners still listen to the impersonal oracle of the god but more and more they are listening to each other. Together they are thrashing out the primordial question, the question of the father. From now on this question is itself the object of conflict as well as the chief, if not sole weapon in the hands of the combatants. The structure eliminates what is inessential and closes in on the essential nakedness of the relationship to the Other.

The earlier rivalries culminated, at least apparently, in the physical destruction of the rival through physical violence. Oedipus, Laius, the sphinx, each is eliminated in turn if only to reappear a little later in the same or a different guise. In the Creon and Tiresias episodes, the only ones where we do not know to what extent they are Sophocles' alone, the rivalry is expressed and embodied in language. These episodes are therefore eminently dependent upon their transcription in tragic form. At the same time, there is a continuity between the mythic account and the tragic discourse. The sphinx episode acts as a pivot between the two modalities of the mythic narrative demanded by the myth itself. The sphinx is still eliminated physically, but already by means of a word, which thus stands revealed as violence.

To try to convince the Other that he killed the father is to repeat, in all its plenitude, the murderous gesture. Hölderlin tells us that the essence of Greek tragedy lies in the murderous Word, deadly to the Other, *der wirkliche Mord aus Worten.* In *Oedipus the King,* however, the word "tends to wound rather than to kill outright." The physical violence of Laius against his son already fits this pattern: *mehr tödtenfaktisches als tödtlichfaktisches.* It does not destroy its victim, it cripples him, it makes Oedipus lame.[2]

The words uttered later are perfectly analogous to the acts of violence committed earlier. If the rivals are no longer able, even in appearance, to eliminate each other, that is not because a curse is more innocuous than a gesture, it is because the same words pronounced at the same moment on both sides balance out. The parry is as potent as the thrust. Identity and symmetry triumph, the "fearful symmetry" of a hate ever more hollow and ever more vain, the never-perceived identity of hostile relationships within the terrible mythic vortex.

~

Tiresias is the seer, an inspired creature who deciphers oracles. In the eyes of Thebes, the city that his word delivered from the sphinx and may yet deliver from the plague, Oedipus, too, is a seer. The spiritual brotherhood of the two prophets is no less close than the brotherhood through marriage of Oedipus and Creon. To understand this is to recognize, once again, the identity of the partners. Tiresias replies to Oedipus's accusation with a like accusation. The curse always returns to its point of departure. The two men swat back and forth like a volleyball the truth that nobody wants to accept. Insults and threats, always symmetrical, follow one another in rapid succession. The two characters correspond perfectly to the mirror image metaphor employed above in a less evocative context. Which is the original, which the reflection? Here again it is not important, or rather it is important to dismiss the question so as not to arouse hope of an answer.

Nothing could be clearer, therefore, than the identity of the two prophets, and yet nothing is more obscure. Whether we are assiduous or inattentive readers of Sophocles, we all identify Tiresias with *lucidity* and Oedipus with *blindness*. We want true and false to be solidly anchored in a world without surprises. Good and evil must be embodied once and for all by infallible champions.

This division conceals from us the underlying meaning of the myth. Yet unlike so many modern works that are unreadable when stripped of the "Manichean" differences they seek to suggest, the tragedy remains close to the myth and, behind the structural asymmetry that we are tempted to impose on it, the symmetry can be discerned. The signifiers of good and evil superimposed on the tragic relationships are always unstable, always ready to reverse themselves. Oedipus limps and the myth, which knows this, does not. In *Oedipus the King*, a modest and measured Creon seems to be the very embodiment of decency and innocence next to an enraged Oedipus; already this is no longer the case in *Oedipus at Colonus*, where the hero's complaints against his uncle appear to have a sounder basis. An arrogant Oedipus irritates us, an audacious Oedipus arouses our sympathy. Western man recognizes himself in this child of *Fortune*, in this passionate hero of knowledge and experience, in this skeptic who rejects the oracles. The rationalist exegesis is one long plea *pro Œdipo* that is barely disconcerted by the luminous simplicity of its own arguments. This Oedipus who has nothing to learn about himself, this Oedipus in whom his defenders think they recognize their own innocence and their own clairvoyance, is assuredly the victim of some malicious god. Malicious or absurd gods, especially absurdly malicious ones, do not remain plausible for long. Soon they will be seen as having been purely and simply invented by the priests, ever "scheming and greedy." Oedipus is right, no doubt, to tell off old Tiresias. From the traditional Oedipus to the Enlightenment Oedipus—why in heaven's name tear out those eyes of light?—the meanings are reversed. The true prophet and the false have traded roles. The myth, here again, is the mirror of its own exegesis. The opposing points of view on Oedipus and Tiresias curiously reproduce the quarrel of the two sages. The history of the Oedipal signifier recalls the about-faces of Sartre's hero in *The Devil and the Good Lord*. The interpretation is never firmly grounded on both sides of the myth. It perches first on one foot, then on the other. Like Oedipus himself, it limps, and, limping along, it too makes its way towards the truth of the myth.

Every ideological, "Manichean" reading posits an essential difference between Oedipus and Tiresias and, more generally, between Oedipus and the other characters. Oedipus is sometimes "superior," sometimes "inferior" to them. That, we have seen, is how he conceives of himself. He always thinks of himself as *standing apart* when in fact he shares with us what is most essential, as we share it with him without knowing it either. The error of the ideological readings is therefore the error of Oedipus himself, or of Tiresias; it is the illusion of difference, which secretly fuels an ever more perfect identity.

Are there no real differences between Oedipus and Tiresias? The two characters come from different places, but they head down convergent paths towards competition and identity. Their differences will gradually cancel themselves out. Oedipus owes his glory to the solution of an objective riddle, external in principle to what he is. His answer to the sphinx applies only to man in general. The hero believes himself to be detached, scientific, positive. But reality constantly gives him the lie; hence the anger and fear of conspiracies which lead him to set himself up as an oracle. Confronting Tiresias, presumptive incarnation of the oracle, Oedipus poses as a rival incarnation. He identifies himself with the refusal of authority, with the spirit of enterprise and of free investigation. This *intellectual* spirit is a new absolute, a truer wisdom that claims to supersede the outmoded wisdom of Tiresias:

Come now, tell me, when have you been a clairvoyant soothsayer? How is it that when the She-dog sang her verses, you did not speak the word needed to deliver the Thebans? Yet the riddle could not be solved by the first person to come along, divination was required. You clearly proved that you had none to offer, whether learned from birds or from gods. Then I came along, the man who knew nothing, Oedipus, and I silenced the Sphinx: my intellect showed me the way, and no birds had instructed me [390–98].

As for Tiresias, he does not at first speak in his own name, he speaks in the name of the god. But he is quick to cloak himself in the oracles, making them his property. He hardens them, he "reifies" them. In his hands, religion becomes what reason and experience already are for Oedipus: a club used to beat the adversary over the head. The two attitudes are equivalent; they both destroy the living relationship to ideas. The oppositions of desire dissimulate their own vacuity behind ideological differences which in truth grow more tenuous the more they are inflamed.

Each episode, we said, brings a "heightened awareness." This awareness broadens and intensifies without cease. Oedipus did not know, at the moment he struck him, who Laius was. He does not fully realize, at the moment he curses him, who Creon is; on the other hand, Oedipus and

Tiresias know very well with whom they are dealing when they destroy each other with words. The truth, a product of the myth itself, emerges *between* the two men; it is not the property of Tiresias alone. And the lie that also emerges is not the property of Oedipus alone, it is the lie of the myth, the effort of all men to shunt their truth onto the Other.

I, Tiresias, see it clearly: the Other is guilty of this crime of which he accuses me; I see the "projective" character of his accusation. I therefore see, this time, the whole truth of desire, but this truth is more deceptive than ever if I do not make it *my* truth. Each person, at this level, plumbs the other's "unconscious," each congratulates himself on his own extraordinary perspicacity. The more real this perspicacity is, and it is real, the more it focuses us on the Other. It conceals from us essential aspects of the structure, the role that we personally play in it.

I, Tiresias, do not hesitate to recognize as my own, if I must, that desire of which I have made myself the historian and exegete, that desire which I cannot stop sifting over again and again, but this avowal does not constitute true self-scrutiny. It does not realize in me the truth of the myth. The desire confessed remains, in my eyes, a desire "transcended."

The blind prophet has already accomplished the trajectory that the Other, Oedipus, is undertaking now, the trajectory that leads, through the loss of corporeal eyes, to authentic vision. He is thus akin to the psychoanalyst who boasts of but one superiority: that of having been psychoanalyzed himself. This superiority is in principle quite unlike previous superiorities, those already rejected and dethroned by the leveling and undifferentiating movement of the myth. This claim to superiority is no longer based on an essence possessed from the outset but on an experience, a hard-won victory. It is in history, in human time that wisdom incarnates itself.

All of that is well and good, but to interpret in this way the wisdom of Tiresias—and this is indeed the way it must be interpreted—is to bring it closer than ever to the wisdom of which Oedipus boasts. It is Oedipus, after all, who proffered the idea of a knowledge founded on experience and not on birth. Always preceded by the same history, always driven by the same desire, the two partners arrive together at the same pseudo-solutions. They display, when attacking and when riposting, a subtlety always more acute and always just as vain.

There is a mysterious exchange in *Oedipus the King* whose mystery evaporates within the framework of the present reading. Oedipus questions Tiresias: "Where did you learn the truth, in your profession no doubt?" And Tiresias replies, "It is you who taught it to me, for you forced me to speak against my will" [357–58].

How should Tiresias's wisdom be defined, what is the foundation of his truth? Here is the problem that Oedipus raises and that he resolves, not without irony, by alluding to the prophet's profession. That is indeed the type of wisdom that is always attributed to Tiresias, a wisdom of experience perhaps, but a wisdom always already made, not to say ready-made, a pre-existing wisdom external to the hostile dialogue that it shapes from without, that it overwhelms with its almighty power. To confer on Tiresias this type of wisdom is to admit that the myth is not a totality, that it is not always governed by its own dialectic. But it is Tiresias himself who refutes this interpretation. He does not claim to hold some secret, some truth long possessed and capitalized. It is from the conflict itself that the truth emerges and it is the conflict that makes it a lie by feeding upon it. The prophet is drawn into the vortex *against his will.*

Sophocles seems to emphasize Oedipus's "flaws." He shows him to be aggressive and hot-tempered. The tragedy veers into psychological drama but it is the modern reader, perhaps, who tips it in that direction. Always eager to *take sides,* the modern reader misses something essential that is said: "It is anger, I think, that inspires Tiresias's words, and yours too, Oedipus" [404–405]. The chorus is not merely expressing its naive desire for compromise here. Nothing is without significance or even of little significance in *Oedipus the King.*

Nothing in this dialogue is more significant than the interplay between images of light and darkness, vision and blindness. Each asserts his own clairvoyance and accuses the Other of failing to see. It is generally at the level of a pure and simple *reversal* of traditional metaphors that the symbolism of the blind prophet is interpreted. The true prophet is not Oedipus, whose eyes are open, but Tiresias, whose eyes are closed. The light is a lie, the darkness is light. This reversal is possible, even necessary, but it is no more than a first step towards the dialectic of symbols. By itself it only spells the failure of this dialectic, for its static distribution of mythic roles and functions keeps the symbols' meaning fixed. In a sense, the reversal is more deceptive than the initial order. The reversal *is* the sagacity and blindness of Tiresias. At the Tiresias stage it is almost incorporated into the story's plot; it appears self-evident since the myth is always the mirror of its own exegesis and of the traps it sets for us. The reversal of symbols offers a reading so immediate and so unremarkable that we no longer see the choice behind it; we do not see any alternative. The unfolding of the myth is one with the gradual and, paradoxically, ever more misleading revelation of its meaning. At the most advanced stages of the myth, the reversal of symbols is a *fait accompli*; in modern poetry, it appears as natural as can be. Entirely based on the reversal and dispersal of metaphors, this poetry lays claim to a wisdom analogous to that of Tiresias. From Hugo's mage to contemporary poetry:

> The blind in shadows see a world of light,
> When dims the body's eye, the mind's shines bright.

But blindness—who could deny it?—is a highly ambiguous symbol of light. Ambiguity always suggests a non-explicit meaning, a dialectic still folded in on itself, waiting to be unfolded. The true symbolism of the blind prophet, and also the richest, lies beyond the reversal and renders it explicable.

Every man is Oedipus, the guilty party, *to the Other*, and Tiresias, the misjudged prophet, *to himself.* Every man is a blind prophet, a prophet in his very blindness, blind to the truth of his own prophecy. We all speak the truth while remaining blind, none of us recognizing in what we say the truth about ourselves. Each accuses the Other of having killed the father. The accusation is mendacious as long as it distracts us from ourselves, veracious when it comes back to us, like a boomerang, with redoubled force. The myth is constructed so as to produce this boomerang. But the partners do not see it; they are the playthings of a desire still striving to prevail over the Other's desire. *Lucidity* is a supreme effort to eliminate the competing desire that in fact it generates. It is always *identical* to this desire that obsesses it. The thing is obvious, from whatever angle one approaches it. Where would lucidity acquire its science of desire if it did not find it within itself? Thus, the degree of lucidity exactly matches the degree of blindness.

The truth resides in the overall structure, not in either "half." Oedipus and Tiresias believe themselves to be exterior to the Other, and uniquely endowed with an essential quality—here, clairvoyance—which in reality they share with their adversary. The overall structure which assures the full dialectic of symbols is, in a sense, a restoration of the original order. Light is light once more, darkness no longer anything but darkness. But light and darkness are no longer the object of an exclusive and definitive division. All light in this world "supposes a mournful shadow half."[3] The more intense this light is, the more the darkness accompanying it thickens.

~

   The conflict of the protagonists in *Oedipus the King* is located in a context that must be specified if the ultimate stages of the myth are to be defined properly. The picture at first appears confused. The plague has been bringing Thebes endless devastation. The unhappy consequences of Oedipus's investigation are seemingly added on top of this already long-lasting calamity. The idea of bringing these two series of events together and making a totality out of them does not occur to us. How could we put the doctor, bad as he may be, on the same level as his patients? Yet that is exactly what we must do. If the judge and the defendant are identical to each other, the doctor and his patients are no less so. As the disease progresses it manifests itself as a determination to cure others. As the rivalry spreads, as the rivals succeed one another, they come closer to the Self; the father's murderer, the usurper *par excellence*, seeks to eliminate them by denouncing their own desire for usurpation; he is seeking, he thinks, to purge the city of its "crime." The mythic conflict should appear to us as the essential element, even as the sole cause of the country's misfortune. The plague is not a mere backdrop to the front-stage quarrels of princes and sages. The foreground and background are inseparable from each other.

   What do Oedipus and Creon, Oedipus and Tiresias, do in their fratricidal struggle? They mutually destroy each other's prestige as sage and hero. Each wrests from the Other his emblems, titles and decorations. Each flails away at the Other's prestige, that *paternal* prestige overtly denied, covertly envied and imitated. The mythic conflict weakens and even destroys the paternal values on which the city rests. To understand the nature of the danger threatening Thebes, we must free ourselves of our overly absolute respect for the wisdom of Tiresias, the wisdom of antiquity. The chorus, following the oracle, ascribes all the misfortunes of Thebes to impiety. This in spite of the religious ceremonies which take place on the play's periphery and which suggest a perfectly normal religious life. If the religious and paternal values embodied in the eyes of everyone by Tiresias had emerged intact from the terrible debate with Oedipus, nothing could justify the chorus's lamentations, nothing could justify the description of a state of anarchy so profound as to make us speak of nihilism. The city, the hero tells us himself, *is perishing in sterility, abandoned by the gods.*

The tragic conflict, in *Oedipus the King*, presents itself at first as a consequence of the plague; to get to the bottom of the question we must reverse, as always, the order of causes and consequences but, more profoundly yet, we must grasp the unity of the plague and the tragic conflict; to reveal this unity is to reveal the unity of the tragedy which itself rests on the unity of the myth. Tiresias enters into the Oedipal dialectic of model and obstacle *against his will.* He "catches" Oedipus's hate the way one catches a contagious disease. The mythic plague is the passive contagion of desire and hatred which, spreading from one person to the next, shakes the very foundations of society. The plague is the indefinite extension of the mythic conflict, an extension whose principle has already been laid down: the myth is a process of universal identification; it transforms each of us into a new Oedipus, and it is when this process has come to its conclusion, or nearly so, that a Freud can identify all men with Oedipus. If Freud is right and if the myth is the mirror of our condition, which is historical, each person, within the myth itself, is not Oedipus but ceaselessly becomes him, in a frenetic imitation always analogous to that of the son before the father, but ever more negative, ever more intent on denying itself. Within us and outside of us, in external reality and in the myth itself, the myth becomes ever more universal.

Metaphors borrowed from nature signify the intersubjective dialectic. Along with the plague there are bad harvests and women dying in childbirth. Everything here is a metaphor of sterility. And every metaphor hews to the requirements of intersubjective truth. Any attempt to cure these collective ills feeds them and aggravates them.

Alas!... I endure countless ills: the contagion has attained the whole population, and the mind can invent no weapon capable of bringing help to anyone; the fruits born of the glorious earth no longer grow; women do not recover from the howling torments of childbirth; one after another victims are seen, like some swift bird, and with more force than invincible fire, hurling themselves from the shore of the western god [168–78].

But those are not yet the only consequences of the mythic conflict, and certainly not the most striking. Oedipus himself underscores, at the dénouement, the scandalous scrambling of kinship, the total confusion reigning in his double family:

O Hymen, Hymen, you gave me life, and after giving it to me, you made the same seed germinate a second time; you brought to light fathers who are brothers of their children, children brothers of their father, brides at once wives and mothers of their husbands, and all the greatest horrors that can exist among men [1403–1408].

If the plague and the anarchy of values are easily tied to the conflicts staged in *Oedipus the King*, the scrambling of kinship goes back, for its part, to more distant episodes, to the murder of Laius and the marriage of Jocasta with her son. These distinctions are not essential, however. All the episodes are both a repetition of Laius's murder and an ambiguous elucidation of it. Tying the plague and subversion of values to the conflict between Oedipus and Tiresias means tying them to the original murder of the father. The collapse of social hierarchies and the collapse of the kinship system are one and the same phenomenon. The defining unity of the myth recurs in its most distant consequences. The distinction between the conflict of the protagonists and its consequences corresponds to the needs of dramatic exposition rather than to a structural imperative. The oracle confirms this. Does the oracle say that Laius's murderer must be punished to save the city? That is how it is interpreted, but it would not suggest this interpretation if it did not proclaim, at a more essential and original level, the close, direct relationship between the family quarrel and the collective misfortunes.

~

The kinship system determines the relative position of each individual with respect to all the others. The Western world distinguishes itself from many primitive cultures by the fact that this position is not determined once and for all. Each individual must assume, not without anxiety, several roles, successively and even simultaneously. The son is destined to become a father. The system is not a rigid chart, a genealogical tree projected into the future, but a dialectic. With a small number of rigorous prohibitions replacing the immense variety of positive prescriptions, the exchanges display a degree of mobility never before attained.[4] The appearance of an Ego transcending all the roles and functions that the individual may assume in the culture is obviously linked to this system. But we must be aware that the familial relativity is never complete. The son never knows that he is, for his son, exactly what his father was for him. The system is no longer mechanical but it is not fully dialectical.

The mechanical system stops short of the opposition between father and son. A dialectical system would go beyond it. The sphere of this opposition is the transition from the mechanical to the dialectical. To institute the dialectical order, to see in this order if not a reality, at least a fundamental requirement of the cultural order, to lay down the principle of a reciprocity without limits, would be to doom men to the most terrible conflicts. To love a son as son is to see in him a possible rival. To venerate a father as father is already to contemplate his undoing. The system is not conceivable, especially in the beginning, without some form of palliative. There is a need for religious and social institutions capable of dissimulating and moderating the convergence of desires, the fundamental contradiction between father and son.

This institution is perhaps animal sacrifice. One may see in the sacrifice performed by Abraham the essential moment in the founding of a patriarchal culture. Abraham is not another Laius. It is God, it is the sacred oracle who suggests that he put his son to death. But God, at the last moment, substitutes an animal so that the child will live. To sacrifice an animal is to have recourse to a means of purification that may originally not be simply ritual, since it substitutes, for the fathers and sons pitted against each other, for those *guilty parties* of whom the interminable pursuit would lead to a terrible familial vendetta, a living creature, a victim still but a "neutral" one, intermediate between a man and an inanimate object, a victim that can be put to death without aggravating the divisions within the city. To sacrifice an animal is to make allowance for a desire for violence incapable of being entirely sublimated. The fathers' and sons' hatred is drained and spent in this destruction without consequence.

The idea of the scapegoat provides us with perhaps the original meaning of animal sacrifice. The goat takes upon itself the sins of the fathers, of the sons, of the brothers, indeed of all the citizens. It carries away, into death or into the desert that closes around it, the seeds of those conflicts that the convergence of desires, which is to say the very unity of the culture, its internal cohesiveness, cannot fail to provoke.

Tragedy, in Greek, is the ode of the goat. Is there a link between animal sacrifice and the performance of tragedy? The pre-Sophoclean Oedipus is pursued by the Erinyes. If the Erinyes go after the hero alone, they leave the city behind. The plague retreats. Like the scapegoat, the tragic hero is sacrificed. He dies or gets chased out of town, taking with him the evil that lingered on as long as he did.

The myth is religious tragedy; far from bringing the spectators closer to the hero, it distances them from him. The Greek Oedipus is outside the norm, sacred, transcendent, unique. When they discover the patricide on their territory, the citizens of Colonus recoil in horror. The scapegoat must be kept at a distance, he must be excluded from the community, like a leper, so as to escape the contagion of his evil. The Greek spectator is therefore far from perceiving the equivalence of all the roles, the always-symmetrical structure of the myth. The Oedipus of antiquity is not our own. Far from minimizing these differences, we must emphasize them, for our reading is based on them. If the myth is symmetrical, if all the roles in it are always equivalent, if it illustrates perfectly the reciprocity that all of us demand, that is not because those from whom it emanates and to whom it is addressed have the slightest suspicion that it displays these properties— rather, it is precisely because these properties are unsuspected that nothing has been done to conceal them. Oedipus is the absolute Other. None of the spectators thinks he has anything in common with him. So ingenuously is the reciprocity denied by the myth that it is indelibly etched into it, albeit in reverse form, like an image frozen in a mirror. The reciprocity is marvelously reflected in the narrative designed to keep people from getting to it.

The scapegoat is responsible for all guilty desires. He is the only one to commit the crimes these desires suggest. If the myth is a perfect mirror, if it is purely and simply the projection onto a single mythical figure of a reality common to all men, the choice of this figure, the choice of the scapegoat, is completely arbitrary. Nothing concrete distinguishes Oedipus from other men. The choice will not be arbitrary if, at any point along the mythic trajectory, Oedipus acts differently from other men. This difference, minuscule perhaps, but real, structural, must be barely visible; it will be shielded from our eyes by the apparently formidable but actually specious difference constituted by murder of the father and marriage with the mother.

Does Oedipus set the fatal mechanism in motion himself? At the gates of madness, Hölderlin reflects upon Sophocles' play and puts his finger on the essential point. Oedipus, he tells us, interprets "too infinitely" (*zu unendlich deutet*) the oracle's words:

> Clearly he commanded us, Phoebus, the King,
> To purge the land of the impurity nurtured on this soil
> And not to lend vigor to the incurable [96–98].

And here is Hölderlin's commentary: "That could mean: Apply yourself, in general, to establishing clear, strict justice; maintain proper civil order."[5] Oedipus could avoid the worst, perhaps, by conducting himself prudently.

It is not the riddle of the sphinx that makes Oedipus a hero of knowledge; it is instead, as we see here, the irascible curiosity regarding Laius, the suspicion-laden investigation, the mad curse. At the crucial moment, Oedipus does not content himself with half-measures and soothing words; he does not resort to *ritual.* He demands absolute justice. A clearly-designated culprit is what he requires. He wants to get to the bottom of a certain affair and nothing will stop him. Here Hölderlin expresses what is secretly the Greeks' point of view. One must turn away from the terrifying riddle. Oedipus is impious. He does not order a purification. As a result, he seemingly attracts the divinity's wrath onto himself . . . One thinks of all those individuals and societies who turn away from their monstrosities. France during the Dreyfus Affair, America with the death of Kennedy. Rather than a new Affair, or maybe something worse, isn't a reassuring Warren Report to be preferred?

The city is the scene of disturbing phenomena. It is time either to launch a vigorous investigation, letting the chips fall where they may, or else to order a nice expiatory ceremony. In the ancient world, such a ceremony always includes an animal sacrifice. Oedipus, at the decisive moment, abstains from sacrificing. And he ends up taking the place of the unsacrificed goat.

Just as an animal was first substituted for man, so the hero substitutes for the animal. The hubris does not consist in supplanting his father and desiring his mother, but in disclosing these two things, in revealing the primordial contradiction and thereby unloosing it on the city as a whole. *Oedipus the King* shows us what would befall the city if men were to cease sacrificing—if they were no longer able to conceal and contain the conflict between fathers and sons.

~

If the mythic narrative is more than a scattered mass of events, if it is not ultimately governed by an absurd Destiny, then the conclusion is still more significant than what precedes it. The Myth depicts the Other closing in ever closer upon the Self until the two are finally superimposed in the Tiresias episode. Self and Other appear at this point as a symmetrical pair of inverse figures. This is where opposition is most radical and difference non-existent. Perfect identity passes for maximum divergence at this place where discord is always at its noisiest and vainest. The conclusion lies beyond this paroxysm but clearly arises out of it. Oedipus recognizes himself in that Other, that culprit he was looking for everywhere far from himself. Oedipus discovers the truth of the myth by discovering his own truth. The conclusion is thus a resolution. It refers back to the entire structure, it enunciates the meaning of the whole, which is to say the meaning of each of the episodes. The anecdotal link assuredly fails to do justice to this enormous truth. . . . It was towards this conclusion that the structured dynamism was carrying us. In this terminal point, the coherence of the myth, already manifest, asserts itself anew in its purest and most dazzling form. For it is no longer a question of anything but the identity of Self and Other.

The revelation is dazzling but ambiguous. Hölderlin suggests a first reading of it, as necessary as it is frightening. Oedipus has been wholly overrun by the oracular utterance. He no longer resists the transcendence of the Other as it slowly envelops and kills him. This total absorption in the Other renders the individual foreign to himself, it alienates him irremediably. It is at the price of its integrity that the Self eliminates the Oedipal obstacle; it no longer resists the fascination. This eclipse of the Self in the face of the Other is well in line with the implications of the myth. And it is in the light of his mounting madness that Hölderlin arrives at this reading. The poet's letters contain phrases that correspond to it. Hölderlin foresees the day when "all that is Other will have become ours."

Hölderlin abstracts out the murder of the father. He turns away from this essential point. Blind to what is essential, blinder than any of us could be, he is also the most lucid. He goes straight to the only thing that counts, at bottom, for those less blind than he, and indicates it to us: how to perfect our blindness, how to insure its permanence and to render it more total yet. He does not see that the incurable has already gained vigor everywhere. He wants to recover the origin and his innocence in a world that has left it behind. He is *modern* since he identifies with Oedipus. But it is from the viewpoint of the ancient Greek city that he identifies with the scapegoat. His radical alienation internalizes the Erinyes of the pre-Sophoclean Oedipus.

Sophocles cannot conclude the myth without expressing, in that conclusion, his experience of the myth, the truth he reads in it, his truth. To interpret the conclusion is therefore to make a judgment about Sophocles' experience. Does the absence of the Erinyes in *Oedipus the King* signify for Sophocles what it signifies for Hölderlin? The very fact of the tragedy, its structural coherence, contradicts this interpretation. The playwright does not turn away from the essential point; he does not pass over the murder of the father in silence. What the dénouement expresses is not a dispossession, but an achievement of hard-won mastery. The Self that recognizes its own guilt, the Self no longer opposed to the Other, is Sophocles himself discovering the truth of the myth and identifying with Oedipus, but in a very different sense from Hölderlin.

Hölderlin's conclusion opens onto a transcendent Other, which means a deceptive Other. Sophocles' conclusion opens onto the truth of the Self and the Other, meaning their identity in a common non-transcendence.

Must Sophocles' dénouement therefore be ranged with modern forms of knowledge resolved to tackle the father's murder and the intersubjective struggle? In a sense, it must be. Yet nothing could be further from Sophocles than these *demystifying* theories, inimical to any hint of the sacred. Freud understood that, since he preserved nothing of the dénouement to *Oedipus the King* even though he recognized the structural analogy with psychoanalysis. In order to make this analogy more precise, must the "religious" element be relegated to the background and regarded as a mere survival? Is there nothing there but the last sentimental and emotional harmonics of an already essentially outmoded form of thought?

To think about the sacred in *Oedipus the King* is to reflect upon the oracles, their real significance, their structural value. If the thesis proposed is correct, the oracle is nothing else but the voice of the Other. It does not possess the independent reality that the first episodes of the myth attribute to it. In these early episodes, the Other is only the oracle's messenger, the intermediary with the sacred. As Self and Other draw closer together, the oracle also draws closer; it ends up merging with the messenger in the person of Tiresias. It is Tiresias's oracle that is identical with the Other. Like all the other aspects of the myth, the incarnation of the oracle is the outcome of the mythical process. But the meaning of this history of the oracle is indeterminate. If the oracle and the Other were really one, as we have supposed, the truth of the myth would be that of their union; their original dissociation would be a doubling analogous to those we have already noted, and destined to return to unity through the mythical process.

This thesis, apparently congruent with all the foregoing analyses and seeming to follow from them, is on the contrary unacceptable. The murderous gesture of the first episodes, analogous to the murderous words of the last ones, is never a direct extension of the oracle that came before. It is not in a spirit of obedience to the oracle, but rather in an effort to thwart it, that Laius wounds his son and Oedipus kills his father. The flight from the oracle continues in hidden form in the last episodes. Tiresias's murderous words are not faithful to the oracle either. That indeed is why the prophet regrets having uttered them.

Tiresias is not the authentic incarnation of the oracle. Behind the apparent unity of the Word and the Other a negative relationship is concealed. And to this internal division there corresponds, as always, an external division. Tiresias is not the only one to embody the oracle. Oedipus, too, embodies his own oracle which he believes to be the only true one and which, violently denying the opposing oracle, is in return denied by it. Tiresias and Oedipus each embody "half" an oracle pitted against another "half." The original oracle is to them what the chaste Suzanne is to the lie at once single and double of the two lecherous old men. Hölderlin's Word of death is none other than this oracle split in two. The original oracle is one, it is the Word of life. Laius, Oedipus, Creon, Tiresias all mutilate this oracle in their struggles, they divide it, they corrupt it, they turn it into a dead thing and a carrier of death, like the child in Solomon's judgment that the spiteful woman would cut in two if the wisdom of the true King were to permit it.

The original oracle is truth, even for us. It is the expression of the totality, the authentic enunciation of human relations. And that indeed is what explains its history. The truth always appears so redoubtable that everyone wants to escape it; everyone busies themselves disfiguring the oracle, whether they know it or not. The inadequacy of the messenger distorts the original message, turning it into the voice of the Other, ever more negative, ever more deceptive. The initial error is amplified with each new transmission so that the oracle metamorphoses into a destructive force. We ourselves, after so many others, we too deform the Oedipal oracle, we sever it from its roots when we see in it the intrusion of a superstitious imagination, of a "religious" element empty of any deeper meaning.

Not only is the foregoing schema true at the level of the operations that take place within the myth, not only is it true of our own relationship to the myth, it is also true of the mythical givens themselves, of the state in which they reach first Sophocles and then us. Who knows if the Oedipal oracle is not a mangled, mutilated, disfigured document? Creon's oracle first appears to us as exclusively negating and punitive when it links the plague to the presence of Laius's murderer in the city, but if it appears that way to us it is perhaps because it provokes a negating response from Oedipus and also because this negating response is the most "natural" in the face of any expression of the totality. We associate ourselves instinctively with it and no longer exercise our critical faculties. Each person tends to read a personal threat into the oracle that links the father's murder to the Theban apocalypse. The oracle is not, however, aimed at anybody in particular. The proof is that it says exactly the same thing to everybody. The original oracle is a succinct but sovereign expression of the totality.

In certain versions of the Oedipus story, the link between the hero's actions and the city's fate is not mentioned, the relationship between the individual and the collective is omitted. The structure is mutilated. The last traces of the totality have disappeared. It is impossible to guess the truth behind the negating version of the oracle. The oracle itself is therefore the object of a degradation, and this degradation is the product of a history analogous to the one structured by the myth.

Earlier, we conceived of the myth as the product of a form of thought that constantly displaces its truth towards the Other. Any thinking that closes itself in this way to the Other ends up in a delirium of exclusion and expulsion. Any thinking that does not accept the original *messenger* ends up in a vain and terrible quest for a *scapegoat*. It is a form of thought that banishes and denies, that curses, executes and proscribes. The frozen mirror of a lost reciprocity, such thinking is cruel but naive, for the moment it believes itself strongest and most "radical" it is blown over by a puff of air. If we understand such thinking, we may account for the displacements, inversions, divisions and fragmentations. We may even account for the myth's ability to express the reciprocity after having denied it. But how can we account for what is, at the origin, displaced, inverted, divided and fragmented, how can we account for what subsists, in the degenerated myth, of the oracle and in particular of its marvelous totalizing circularity? Just as we must seek out the model behind the obstacle, so, behind the divided oracles and death instincts, we must seek out unity and life. Scapegoat thinking distorts the meaning of an original Logos of which all the known variants of the myth are the grotesque failure. The very concept of the oracle isolates from the profane a derisory sacred and testifies to a degradation. In the last instance, it is this Logos, itself always deformed and mutilated, always disfigured and betrayed, which will appear to us as the first and ultimate figure of the scapegoat: the lamb of God. It is the latter, in the last analysis, that one always wants to be rid of, that one always wants to escape.

This logos must not be confused with the religious in a narrow sense that is the object of a sterile debate, pro and con, at the Tiresias stage. The religious, at this stage, is necessarily confused with the institutions that dissimulate and moderate the primordial competition, or rather that no longer succeed in fulfilling this function. But these institutions, and notably animal sacrifice, are inseparable from what makes them necessary, namely the opening of the kinship system onto the familial dialectic, onto the relativity of all roles. What limits this opening is inseparable from what founds it. To grasp this dialectical totality is to grasp the Logos, inconceivable conception of the totality, which apprehends from every angle that which it founds. The dialectic that insures the widening of the system is in place from the beginning. It is present in animal sacrifice; it is one with the relative closure of the system, with the very thing that seemingly dooms it to stagnation. The myth and the mythic tragedy perpetuate, we said, the cathartic effect of animal sacrifice. The transition from an animal to the mythic or tragic hero betrays a certain degeneration of the "religious." Sacrifice has lost its efficacy; men must resort to more extreme means to attain the same end, namely the dissimulation of the primordial conflict. But these means are one with the unleashing of that conflict. The culture is in crisis. It is obliged to open up further or to perish in a vain attempt to close itself up again.

Oedipus is the man of this crisis. He no longer sees in ritual the panacea, the solution to all the conflicts that are convulsing the city. It is he who substitutes man for animal in a futile effort to radicalize the catharsis and bring the process to a halt. Oedipus is thus indeed the mirror of the Greek spectator who is likewise seeking a radicalized catharsis and who seeks it in tragedy itself. The art of tragedy replaces the animal with the hero and the ritual gesture with the word; it is thus a "humanizing" interpretation of the ritual function. It is this art that reveals to us, as in a sense it reveals to the Greeks, the significance of animal sacrifice. It tends to repeat the latter at a heightened level of understanding and, therefore, of dissimulation insofar as the Other, the scapegoat, the hero himself, is declared solely responsible for the suddenly revealed conflict. If the tragedy plays the role assigned to it, if the revelatory word succeeds in perpetuating the rite, there is closure, this time, of what was not open at the stage of animal sacrifice, to be sure, but was not expressly closed either. The truth that men did not formally deny since they were not yet aware of it is henceforth denied in its very revelation; it is displaced onto the Other. The dialectic that leads from animal sacrifice to myth and tragedy is not new to us; it is, once more, the myth that is unfolding before our eyes.

The closure that is sought for never comes. From now on the priest seeks his victim among human beings. But, for the very reason that this victim is human, it is no longer neutral, it must be *guilty;* the rite becomes a trial and nobody agrees any more on the choice of the scapegoat. The remedy so desperately sought for, the remedy that needs to be ever more effective, is one with the scourge that is blighting the city. The always-contradictory efforts to surmount it are what define the anarchy. Everybody, in the last analysis, wants to make the Other the scapegoat whose death or banishment will save the collectivity.

Antigone illustrates this dialectic. The heroine does not acquiesce in making one of her dead brothers play the scapegoat's part. Creon, who believes he is being "pragmatic" in choosing this scapegoat dispassionately and in upholding his choice against any and all opposition, is himself the plaything of the circle he thinks he is breaking. The incurable has gained vigor in the city. The monarch's "political" choice is no less a symptom of it than Antigone's intransigence. The two attitudes are intertwined; each reveals the hubris of the other. The efforts to re-establish unity perpetuate and exacerbate the dividing into doubles. But Sophocles does not get to the bottom of things until *Oedipus the King,* where he studies the struggle with the father, which is to say the original hubris, the earliest engine of intersubjective struggle, the primordial desire to be oneself that loses itself in the headlong imitation of the Other, the original will to be One from which springs the original division into doubles.

The consequences of this primordial struggle make up the tragic material chosen by Sophocles. To take the myth's final episodes as a subject for tragedy is to treat once more this same uniquely familiar material, but while juxtaposing it, and soon linking it, with the detritus of a discourse that at once reveals and negates the original meaning, the remnants of a tradition corrupted by the very thing of which it at first offered an account. Oedipus is not a tragic subject like any other, not for the Greeks and not for us. The mythical data and Sophocles' material are superficially heterogeneous but the poet senses their underlying unity. The mutilated fragments arrange themselves into unity as they come into contact with one another.

The tragedy is an exegesis of the myth, the most profound that we possess. The creative experience of which it is the fruit follows the mythic trajectory. The tragedy is rooted in its own conclusion. It is not the immediate, intuitive apprehension of its object, an apprehension all the more necessarily mystified in that the very facts of the myth are distorted, but a reapprehension, a recomposition of the myth in the light of an experience analogous to that of Oedipus, namely the identification with a long-rejected Other, the Other in this case being quite obviously Oedipus himself, the tragic hero. It is therefore the poet, before anyone else, who verifies in his conclusion Laius's oracles, or rather who gives them new life. But this prodigious verification reveals the original significance of the oracle. The verified oracle is not what it appeared to be; it brings not a curse but a blessing; it is not the sinister echo of an implacable destiny but the ambiguous sign of a hard-won salvation. That indeed is why all the symbols have changed meanings. Sophocles does not restore the oracle's original meaning—how could he?—but he approaches it, he senses it, he conveys to us its flavor. He intuits that the word of death is in reality the word of life; the totality represents the transcendence of the conflicts that it renders, in appearance, irremediable. But the dénouement will not be distinguishable for us from the one the degenerated myth calls forth if we do not perceive the degeneration of the oracle, if we know only this degenerated version of it, the oracle of ill-tiding. If, on the contrary, we divine the original oracle, we also divine that it is itself divined in the conclusion of *Oedipus the King* and in *Oedipus at Colonus*. If the Erinyes have fled, it is because they have lost their *raison d'être*. A new relationship to the Other has appeared: after turning away from Oedipus in horror, the people of Colonus accept the pariah; the sacred itself accepts him. Chosen and no longer cursed, chosen in his very malediction, Oedipus goes to join the divinity who calls him.

Sophocles recovers something of the myth's original significance, which the word "initiatory" fails to capture. Initiations always entail a predetermined itinerary, a clearly marked path. Yet that is precisely what the poet lacks and what every reader of the myth lacks. All the signs have shifted position. The itinerary has not been erased but its meaning has changed. It will be objected that this makes the *ordeal* all the more real. One could regard the very disorder of the myth, the damage that it has suffered, as but additional obstacles on the path of the new "initiate."

The idea of initiation must be rejected for more fundamental reasons. What is entailed by the apprehension of the totality defies the categories of ancient religious thought. The totality exists only for the individual who recovers that half of himself that scapegoat thinking strives to make him lose. The totality exists only in *identification with the scapegoat.* If the accent is placed on the discovery of the truth in *Oedipus the King,* on the confession by the hero of a guilt long reserved to the Other, that is because it informs this identification. We said this identification must be distinguished from Hölderlin's. It is not absorption in the Other. Far from maintaining and radicalizing the previous determinations, it reverses them, it reorganizes the structure from top to bottom. Does psychoanalysis provide us with an adequate analogy? No, for psychoanalysis, far from verifying the oracles, goes all out to prove that the oracular claims are deceptive.

Are we obliged, then, to return to Aristotle? Less than ever, for catharsis belongs to closed thinking, to scapegoat thinking, even if it softens the contours. It reinforces the structural bonds of the spectators at the sole expense of the hero. If the tragic emotions are "terror" and "pity," the hero has been reduced to an object and the Erinyes are never far away. Modern estheticism harks back to catharsis and is equally incapable of seeing the reversal of signs at the tragic dénouement.

The experience of the creator is as far removed as possible from catharsis. It does not respect those values which catharsis reinforces, it discloses what lies hidden behind the protection of catharsis; it is "on the side" of the scapegoat, outside the bounds of closed thought, radically subversive. Plato is right to expel the poet from his Republic. He speaks as a poet, as a man threatened by poetry, while Aristotle speaks as a spectator and a man of prose. The banishment of the poet is a logical consequence of his identification with the scapegoat. It is the poet himself who chooses to play this role; he is the ready-made scapegoat of the "perfect" city, meaning the city where what was once religious, having become civic, takes on distinctly "totalitarian" shades; in other words, where the absence of the totality becomes an ever more obstinate refusal.

Sophocles is in a place where the ancient wisdom, the wisdom of Tiresias, is summoned to surpass itself or perish. Even if he approaches the brink, he does not fall into the abysses of unreason, and he arrives obscurely at a domain that is closed to Greek thought. Only the prophets of Israel penetrate within this domain, and the dialectic of this penetration moves through their works, that of the second Isaiah in particular. The Songs of the Servant of Yahveh render fully explicit an identification with the scapegoat that we believe to be implicit in Sophocles. It does not define a superior form of religion, or something beyond religion, but rather a deepened relationship to religion. Before its religious meaning is revealed, the identification with the scapegoat looks like the ultimate in irreligiosity. This misconception concerning the victim, terrible but necessary, is an added ordeal to be undergone; it even ends up becoming the essential ordeal, the one that defines the essence of the prophetic condition.

> Surely he hath borne our griefs, and carried our sorrows:
> yet we did esteem him stricken, smitten of God, and afflicted.
> But he was wounded for our transgressions . . . [Isaiah 53:4–5].

It is not an innocuous "reconciliation," an agreeable *dépassement* or any other such intellectual game that the prophet announces to us. The identification with the scapegoat appears in an historical setting analogous to the one that may be surmised from the text and context of *Oedipus the King*. The outlines, however, are more clearly drawn, the structure is fully visible. God no longer accepts the sacrifices. Traditions are falling into ruin. Hierarchies are collapsing, no legitimate authority remains in place. But all these events are the throes of birth. Idolatry, defeat and exile, the very destruction of the holy city, herald a new relationship to God, henceforth conceived as the one and only true father. Nothing distinguishes this new relationship to God from a new relationship to the Other, no longer experienced as immanent or transcendent, slave or master, scapegoat or sacrificer, but as neighbor, *proximus*.

What lies beyond nihilism, barely hinted at in Sophocles, is constantly held up to us here as the very goal of history. Synchrony and diachrony are always perceived as functions of each other, grasped dialectically. Amidst a totality always in movement, the levelling process that we identified in the myth is present once more. And it is not implicit either, this time, but explicit. Its presence and its structural, functional value are formally recognized in terms that, while exclusively metaphorical, possess extraordinary evocative power. So that God may be revealed, the reign of discord, injustice and vanity must be fulfilled. It is an unheard summons that engenders the universal flatness, the fascinating identity, the desolate geometry of doubles and, because it is unheard, this summons becomes ever more pressing, ever more exhausting, a summons to the only *identification* that counts, the identification with the scapegoat.

The voice of him that crieth in the wilderness, Prepare ye the way of the Lord, make straight in the desert a highway for our God. Every valley shall be exalted, and every mountain and hill shall be made low: and the crooked shall be made straight, and the rough places plain: And the glory of the Lord shall be revealed, and all flesh shall see it together [Isaiah 40:3–5; cf. Luke 3:4–6].

Two types of thought in the modern world conclude or appear to conclude the myth, the oracular type of which Hölderlin is the supreme expression, and the anti-oracular type exemplified by psychoanalysis. The first type embraces and the second rejects the oracle *in the guise its history presents it to us.* Which is to say that in both cases this history is misapprehended. If the entire truth of the structure were present, the relationship to the original oracle would be perceived, or at least intuited. If, moreover, the myth is a microcosm and a mirror of our own situation, this loss of the oracle is significant—it is the promise of a rediscovery. Anti-oracular thought, ever more lucid and ever more blind, draws ever nearer the totality but the latter still eludes it. It cannot help setting itself up as an oracle; it is the other "half" of the oracular thought that it combats. It relives the self-evidence of Oedipus as he faces Tiresias or the self-evidence of Tiresias as he faces Oedipus. And it is indeed in a new nihilism, in a new reversal and an extreme dispersal of values that all modern thought is rooted. Contemporary nihilism must be placed in the context of a history of the "oracle." Heidegger saw this, and that is, without any doubt, what distinguishes his thought from all contemporary thought. However, to exclude from this meditation the Judeo-Christian contribution is to eliminate perhaps what is most foundational, the "oracle" specific to the Western world, external in a sense to the process it sets in motion, literally grafted onto the Greco-Western body, but, in the first and last instance, always determinant. As revelatory as it may be, here Greek thought is not the most explicit, and it is assuredly not alone essential. Those who, in our day, believe themselves thinkers of the oracle, are they not still, as always, thought by it? We who haunt the shores of the "Western god," do we not resemble that *unknown criminal,* that Oedipus, one last time, of whom the chorus imagines the flight even though in truth everything takes place before its eyes?

Unhappy wretch, his unhappy flight isolates him from men. He seeks to escape the oracles arriving from the center of the world, but they, ever alive, hover about him still [479–82].

Translated by Mark R. Anspach

CHAPTER 3

Symmetry and Dissymmetry in the Myth of Oedipus

Taken as a whole, the Oedipus myth and *Oedipus the King* display a persistent contradiction:

Oedipus is unique; he is guilty of the greatest crimes; everything about him is exceptional. Oedipus is the very epitome of *difference*.

Oedipus is *identical* to everybody and first of all to his father. In every episode of the myth, the actions of the characters are symmetrical, reciprocal:

—Laius, heeding the oracle, puts Oedipus violently out of the way for fear that this son will take his place on the throne of Thebes and in Jocasta's bed.

—Oedipus, heeding the oracle, puts Laius violently out of the way and takes his place on the throne of Thebes and in Jocasta's bed.

—Oedipus, heeding the oracle, contemplates, at the opening of *Oedipus the King*, the undoing of a man who may dream of taking his place on the throne of Thebes and in Jocasta's bed.

The violence is always reciprocal, allowing for the fact that the reprisals can be directed against a newcomer. Everybody is equally guilty of violence. When Jocasta asks if Oedipus and Creon are both responsible for the quarrel between them, the chorus answers simply, "Yes." If the chorus refuses to take sides, it is less out of fear, or desire for compromise, than out of recognition of the "equal weight" on either side, that *Gleichgewicht* of which Hölderlin speaks.

Tiresias himself, before designating Oedipus as, and perhaps *making* him into the man of absolute difference, suggests the symmetry of the oppositions, the reciprocity of the relations between himself and this hero, the deep-seated identity of their two destinies:

Send me home: we shall have, if you heed me, less trouble bearing, I my fate, you yours [320–21].

Never will I reveal my misfortunes, or rather yours . . . I do not want to afflict either you or me [328–29, 332].

The play concludes with belated obedience to the orders of the oracle as they are interpreted, following Tiresias, by the collectivity and the hero himself. It is a religious event, a ritual expulsion. The hero gathers upon himself all the impurities circulating in the city. His departure from Thebes cures the citizens of the "plague." He is an object of horror that must be gotten rid of in a hurry to avoid contamination:

Quick, in the name of the gods, hide me somewhere far from here; kill me or throw me in the ocean, in a place where you will never see me.

Throw me out of this country as soon as you can, into places where no one will ever talk to me again.

Ah! Believe me, have no fear: my ills are mine, no other mortal was made to bear them [1409–15, 1436–37].

These words are well calculated to calm the collective anxiety of the Thebans. It is the archaic function of the scapegoat that finds definition here.

The scapegoat is already present, it seems, at the beginning of the myth. The violence that Oedipus undergoes at the hands of his parents can be interpreted in terms of the custom of exposing newborn babies that are monstrous, deformed or otherwise exceptional.

This presence of the scapegoat could be understood as an historical survival. The myths and legends reinterpreted by the tragic poet might have conserved traces of an earlier institution whose meaning is more or less forgotten or transfigured in the classical era. These traces would therefore be indecipherable, for us even more than for Sophocles. Sometimes this fact is used as an argument to assert the futility and vanity of all modern speculations about the myth. What can the desire for coherence do in the face of the heterogeneous elements that coexist in Sophocles' play?

To refer to forgetfulness or misrecognition in the context of a custom such as ritual expulsion is already to introduce a certain ambiguity. If it is anything but a rite emptied of its meaning, this expulsion may aim first to ensure its own misrecognition. It is likely that a ritual expulsion would not fulfill its purpose, whatever that purpose might be, if it could be defined by what in our eyes is its essential feature, namely its arbitrariness.

We may lay down the principle of a certain incompatibility between the *theme* of the scapegoat and the very *fact* of expulsion. If the Oedipus myth and *Oedipus the King* rest on this fact, we may expect that they will not broach the theme or will do so only partially.

This hypothesis, it must be noted, accounts for the contradiction between the baleful singularity of Oedipus and the reciprocity of the acts of violence in the myth and the tragedy. It is the function of the scapegoat's expulsion to deny the reciprocity, and it denies it by imposing on the myth itself the image of an absolutely exceptional Oedipus.

The scapegoat's expulsion would thus impose on the myth a non-reciprocal reading of the reciprocity. But, to account for this myth, the hypothesis must also suppose that the dissymmetrical reading, the message of the expulsion, reacts back upon the structural symmetry, that it contaminates it in some essential points, notably the patricide and incest, which have no immediate counterparts among the other characters.

We are familiar with this kind of tension, within a single work, between a symmetry and a dissymmetry that reciprocally deny each other. Mass culture offers us something quite analogous and even more remarkable, in a sense, since the dissymmetrical reading in no way affects the structural symmetry. On the sheriff's side and the outlaws', the violence, the passion, and the galloping horses are all the same. The spectators' thrills depend on their not perceiving the symmetry. They attend exclusively to the differential signs, at once minuscule and formidable, that justify triumph and life for one side, defeat and death for the other. Often the decision hinges on the hair, a little longer here, a little shorter there, or a little less dark. Or else the choice of a church rather than a saloon as command post. It is not accurate to call these works *Manichean*: they don't make it an equal fight between "good" and "evil" since "good" always triumphs and "evil" is always expelled. The equality is present, on the contrary, in everything unrelated to the arbitrary dichotomy between life and death—meaning it is everywhere, or just about. The indicators of good and evil prepare the way for the ritual expulsion, and it is this expulsion which, in return, confers their value on them. The violence of the content reflects the very genius of the work, its inspiration, its *daimon* which is a violence done to the structural symmetry.

This symmetrical/dissymmetrical form accommodates contemporary subjects as well as traditional ones that have been treated a thousand times, from the Greek legends themselves to *The Three Musketeers*. An historical figure can thus reappear in a new work after having played the role of the scapegoat in an older work. (In the modern world, the scapegoat function is most often carried out through the intermediary of a "psychology" which dissimulates it from us.) The earlier use does not preclude, it facilitates the modern re-use for ends at once different and quite analogous. The modifications of the earlier work can be insignificant even though the individual or collective tensions animating the re-use may have completely changed. One may imagine that the same is true for the different layers of the myth.

Literary criticism focuses on differences, meaning the differential signs that make up a limited if not negligible part of the work in quantitative terms. It therefore defines itself as a search for quality. The domination exercised by this quality is waning but it perpetuates itself through such notions as ambiguity, semantic tension, etc. This domination rests, in the last analysis, on the expulsion of the Other that it dissimulates from us. It embraces the myth such as it has always appeared to us. It is closed to the relationship between symmetry and dissymmetry, between difference and non-difference. It rests, like the myth, on the elimination of non-difference, which is the outcome of the ritual expulsion.

All critical rigor presupposes grasping the relationship between symmetry and dissymmetry. Take for example the *chansons de geste*. Located a third of the way from Sophocles to us, these works well illustrate the perennial nature of a problem that is of eminent interest to, let us say, the myth and its tragic sequel. Medievalists periodically puzzle over the attitude of the *chansons de geste* vis-à-vis the Muslim adversary. Some stick to the indicators of good and evil, always much in evidence, and they see nothing anywhere but fierce hostility toward the heathen. Others are beguiled by the parallelism of the descriptive features, by the striking non-difference of the mores, the passions, the chivalric ideal. They yield, in sum, to the structural symmetry, which whispers to them that the vision of the enemy is perhaps "not so negative as all that," or even "more positive than it seems." This debate is rooted in a contradiction internal to the texts. The failure to apprehend the contradiction endows the debate with nearly the same longevity as the myth.

~

To verify the foregoing hypothesis, we must look everywhere for the symmetry that lies beneath the message negating it.

The fact that the tragedy presents Oedipus to us as an investigator and hunter much more than as a victim and prey does not point, all things considered, to an initial distortion of the structure. If the collective decision designating the scapegoat is arbitrary, that is because only this decision can put an end to the hunt of all against each and of each against all. If the scapegoat is first of all a hunter, that is precisely because he is identical to everyone. The investigation that ends badly for Oedipus is not his alone, it is that of all the Thebans. But the investigation conducted by Oedipus appears to us, thanks to the expulsion that concludes it, in an unfavorable light, whereas Tiresias's quite similar investigation becomes, from the standpoint of the dissymmetry, a legitimate case of clairvoyance, a designation of the culprit that brings salvation. Behind this always very conspicuous dissymmetry, the symmetry asserts itself, not only in the dialogue between Oedipus and Tiresias that we cited above, but in even more direct statements where the struggle of the protagonists is presented to us as a selfsame effort to convince the people that the only salvation lies in the death of the adversary. When the chorus asks him to spare Creon, Oedipus answers that there is no way for him to accede to this request without risking death or expulsion himself.

The scapegoat is always at the center of the tragic work but we must not regard this perpetual presence as an obstacle to interpretation. It is from Oedipus himself, sacrificer before being sacrificed, that we must seek the how and why of ritual expulsion.

In the myth, Oedipus is essentially the rival of the father, first elbowed out, then victorious. The father and son both desire the throne and wife. The myth relates their competition. In the tragedy, the competition continues, with Oedipus pitted against his brother-in-law Creon, whose rights over Thebes are real: it was he who transferred the throne to Oedipus and it is he who will occupy it after the death of Oedipus and his sons.

It is easy, it is all too easy, to grasp the relationship between father and son at the level of a competition provoked by the son. The son is then defined by the will to usurpation. In this perspective, which, despite certain indications to the contrary on Freud's part, is generally that of psychoanalysis, the desire for the father's objects is authentically original; it comes before the relationship with the father, which it ensures will be one of rivalry.

It must be noted, however, that if the myth succeeds in maintaining right up to the end the positive and permanent nature of the goods in dispute, namely Thebes and Jocasta, it is only thanks to the patricide. Now, the patricide seems to constitute one of those points in the myth where dissymmetry is substituted for symmetry. It is not a question here of abstracting out the patricide but of grasping it at the level of the symmetry we have postulated. And this symmetry is not absent here, it is even because it is too much present, in a sense, present in too condensed and spectacular a form, that there is a patricide at all. The violence is always reciprocal, we said, allowing for the fact that the reprisals can be carried out against a newcomer. Creon and Tiresias are such newcomers. The reciprocal violence comes full circle with them, to be sure, but the first term of the reciprocity lies elsewhere, with the father. In the case of the patricide, the circle opens and closes with Laius.

Oedipus is typified by extreme susceptibility to suspicion and anger; he strikes back rashly against anything resembling a threat or an obstacle. This characteristic attitude strongly marks the tragic dialogues with Creon and Tiresias, just as it marked the initial decision to get to the bottom of the murder of Laius. But it marks more originally still the "patricide." Oedipus is seized by anger—he tells us so himself—when his way is blocked. It is in the heat of this anger that he massacres the entire royal convoy.

That this particular *temperament* is the tragic temperament, more or less common to all heroes, is quite evident. The fact is hardly calculated to discourage us, since it brings us back to the non-difference and symmetry that we saw as critical. But to speak of a "stereotype" in this regard is a way of recognizing the non-difference while devaluing it in the name of an individual difference which, even absent, remains alone essential. Why does Sophocles associate the patricide in *Oedipus the King* with the "stereotype" of the "tragic temperament"?

The structure of reprisals is universal in the myth. The patricide merely affirms this structure by closing the reciprocity back upon the individual who opened the circle. The tragedy perpetuates the structure of reprisals, but it extends it to individuals other than the father. In a sense, then, the tragedy situates itself in the same zone of interpretation as its modern exegesis. It suggests, in other words, that the patricide, behind its exceptional appearance, defines a type of relationship that is constantly repeated in the Oedipal tragedy. The patricide is the dissymmetry accomplished at the expense of the scapegoat, but this dissymmetry is but an extreme form of symmetry.

The type of relations defined by the patricide may be equated with the heroic, hubristic and tragic temperament, except that the atomistic individualism of this temperament conceals from us what is most essential: the reciprocity, the structural identity. When this identity wends its way into the consciousness of the critic, it is relegated to the background and its scope is limited by treating it as a stereotype. This estheticizing psychology is less advanced than Sophocles; it respects more strictly than he does the dissymmetry imposed on the myth by the expulsion of the scapegoat.

Sophocles always shows us Oedipus acting with the same angry haste. Behind the tragedy we detect something other than banal competition or blind fate. Oedipus has seized the throne and Jocasta. All his desires have been realized; and yet the circle of violence is going to open once again. The throne does not wobble of its own accord; Oedipus sets it wobbling.

Oedipus, it will be said, has positive, concrete reasons to fear the loss of goods acquired through violence and ruse. The usurper must beware of future usurpations. The absence of legitimacy is a real dimension of the myth but it does not suffice in and of itself. That is obvious even at the level of the dynastic quarrel. If usurpation and tyranny had only a political meaning, they would be incompatible with their opposite: legitimate succession. But Oedipus, a tyrant come from abroad, is at the same time the son and legitimate heir. To forget this truth, to fail to take it into account, is quite simply to share in the hero's own misapprehension.

What does this juxtaposition of legitimacy and illegitimacy signify? To understand it, we believe that the son's desire must be given an original object other than the paternal objects; in the myth that whispers not a word of it there must be heard the supreme summons, the one law given to sons in the Western world: "Be like the father, do as the father does." To want to be Oedipus is to desire to be at the center of the same familial and social universe as Laius. To desire the father's being means taking the father as model on the plane of desire. Such a desire can only become concrete at the level of objects. Behind *imago* there is *imitari*. Identifying with the father means desiring what he desires, it means coveting Thebes and Jocasta.

The son does what the father does, he desires what the father desires, without any inkling of how he is threatening the father's world. Nothing prepares the son for the father's violence. The son cannot suspect what the desire, not the law, of the father holds in store for him.

The stark and for us unmysterious fact of competition does constitute the positive basis for the conflict with the father, but this competition is the inaccessible truth of the relationship. The prohibition laid on the son is incomprehensible; that is why it carves out an infinite distance between the father and him. The son is literally de-ported [*dé-porté*] by the father's violence. This original difference, from *dis fere*, to put at a distance, disperse, disseminate, defer, is the matrix of all "value." Forced by the paternal obstacle to choose between the father and himself, the son cannot help choosing the father. He excludes himself from the kingdom. He judges himself unfit to succeed the father, forever disinherited. He sets himself up as the original scapegoat.

The son cannot renounce the paternal legacy which alone could cleanse him of his indignity, solve the riddle of his destiny, and convey to him his father's power. But the son seeks in vain the law that would spell out this indignity, the precise text that would condemn him. Lacking any positive clue, he must fall back on the unvaryingly negative signs that he is able to deduce from harrowing experience. The silence surrounding the son, the serenity of everyone else and in particular of the father, all this must conspire not so much to provoke a delirious interpretation of the obstacle as to make the latter the cornerstone of the shadowy world in which the son has taken refuge, the key to all knowledge, the end of every enterprise, the signifier of what is desirable.

As soon as Oedipus detects an obstacle—for example, this stranger absurdly blocking his way—he thinks he hears the mysterious sentence condemning him, he thinks he perceives, behind the obstacle, the secret path of paternal being. The possessions of the man who chances to stand in the way—his throne and his wife—acquire sacramental status. They become the one and only throne, the one and only wife, Thebes and Jocasta.

Removing the obstacle is useless for fresh obstacles will present themselves, and the paternal difference, the difference that the conquest of

Thebes and Jocasta was meant to eliminate, will gape anew beneath the feet of the son of Laius.

Oedipus constantly runs up against the obstacle. He fears and pursues a competition that he is incapable of reducing to its true proportions. He does not perceive in the rival the *riverain* by his side, simply parallel to him; he does not perceive, in short, the symmetry of the myth. He sees difference everywhere when everywhere identity reigns.

The Tiresias episode shows us clearly that something is at stake in the tragedy other than Thebes and Jocasta. The paternal inheritance cannot be reduced to the objects that symbolize it. To be sure, Oedipus claims to see Tiresias as nothing but a vulgar "accomplice" in Creon's plot against the throne. But this insult does not do justice to the centrality of the debate between the two seers. What is at stake is the sacred prestige of the priest and thaumaturge. And that too is part of the "paternal inheritance." In the presence of Creon, Oedipus already sees himself deprived of the throne, and the hostile silence of Tiresias threatens him with an analogous dispossession. The vanquisher of the sphinx, the savior of Thebes, strives to hold onto this clairvoyance and omniscience which he believed were his forever and which are in the process of getting away from him. At every moment, Oedipus feels the paternal inheritance slipping between his fingers and it is always the Other who holds onto or seizes it, it is Creon, it is Tiresias, it is always that Other who blocks his path, hence it is always Laius.

The obstacle is, first, physical violence, and then it is the curse, the word that foretells expulsion, the menacing and violent word from just about anyone. It is Creon conveying an alarming oracle, it is Tiresias, it is all the messengers of misfortune and bearers of bad news who deprive Oedipus of his "inheritance," who cause to fall from his hands a scepter that he immediately sees gleaming in theirs. Oedipus does not belong to himself: he belongs to that Other whose word or gesture is an obstacle to him. Jocasta puts it superlatively:

Oedipus belongs to any man who speaks to him when that man speaks to him of misfortune [917].

The notion of the obstacle that emerges little by little is elucidated by the symbolism of limping. The first to limp is Labdacus, the hero's grandfather, whose name means "lame one." Following Lévi-Strauss here, we see in the impossibility of walking straight the common denominator of all the masculine names in the family of Labdacus. It is the father who dooms the son to his crippled gait by violently casting him back far from himself, by standing as an obstacle to him. To limp is not to trip accidentally over a chance obstacle, it is to repeat indefinitely the same false step. The distension of the feet is the inability to avoid the obstacle and the inclination to conjure it up. To limp is to trip once over the obstacle of paternal desire and then to seek out this same obstacle, to come back stumbling against it in a tireless quest to pry its secret out of it.

These suggestions are valuable but limited. The aphoristic character of the symbolism encourages speculation but does not provide the necessary basis for more rigorous development. Nothing is more common, however, outside the French language, than the figurative broadening of terms implying at once the idea of limping and that of obstacle. The English "stumble" yields the term "stumbling-block." The Old Testament makes constant use of this symbolism. The New Testament gathers up and develops the wealth of meaning latent in this usage with a rigor that illuminates the myth and is illuminated in turn by it.

In Greek, the root *skal,* to limp, yields the noun *skandalon,* obstacle, trap, or scandal in the sense of Paul and the evangelists. Scandal signifies the closure of the obstacle as opposed to the openness of welcome. Scandal in the strict sense exists only in the event of a welcome refused, an ardor quelled, a call unheard. Scandal is the perpetual barrier of the false sacred, the deceptive prestige which, created by one obstacle, finds or creates others in order to superimpose itself on them or to transfigure them. In the Gospel, not to believe always means to believe in the scandal, it means to go looking for openness in the direction of the obstacle. Not to believe is to be scandalized. To cause a scandal is to divert towards the obstacle, in particular towards oneself, the power of worship that is in the other. The scandal-monger is therefore always an *underling* of Satan, who is the quintessence of scandal, always seeking to be worshipped in God's stead.

Childhood is mentioned insistently in connection with scandal. Those who expose children to scandal bear a terrible responsibility. Scandal is a permanent structuring of human relations. A social, political, and economic dimension suggests itself, as well as a sexual dimension, Freudian "castration." Many great modern intuitions come together in the notion of *skandalon,* except that the gospel concept is subordinate to openness and reception. It is free of the impasses of negative thought and of the primacy of revolt.

Scandal is everywhere. The disciples are scandalized, dispersed, deported by the arrest and execution of Christ. And those who no longer believe in any but a dead Christ, the holy women, are no less scandalized when they wonder how to remove the rock, the obstacle closing the tomb. At the announcement of the crucifixion, Peter is scandalized; he endows Christ with a purely earth-bound prestige that would divert him, were he to embrace this obstacle, from the only open path. That is why Christ accuses Peter of scandalizing him, and the *Vade retro Satanas* signifies to the apostle that he must fall behind Christ. That indeed is the place of a Satan already beaten who cannot pose an obstacle to redemption. The cross has triumphed over scandal, even if it is destined to create scandal and to multiply initially the scandals around it.

The symbolism of limping, the sphinx, and, as we shall soon see, the "enemy brothers," none of these things can be read at the level of scapegoat dissymmetry, nor even at the level of symmetry. These elements shine with all their brilliance only once it has been discovered how these readings are opposed and intertwined. They introduce a mediation between the symmetry and the dissymmetry. The same is true of the doubleness always attributed in the tragedy to Oedipus, to Laius, to Thebes and to the entire legacy of Labdacus's lineage.

The extraordinary relevance of this symbolism at once complicates and simplifies the task for the exegete. It simplifies it because this relevance lends support at every moment to the principles of the double reading and confirms its results. It complicates it because it has been transcending forever, or nearly so—its extreme antiquity does not seem to be in doubt—the misrecognition to which the myth never ceases to give rise, in periods less ancient and certainly down to the present day.

~

Oedipus the King illustrates the propagation of the *skandalon*, its contagious character. Creon initially appears as a man with no interest in acquiring the mantle of kingship. Proximity to the throne is enough for him: it offers truly concrete advantages, without any risks or worries. Oedipus's prestige does not pose an *obstacle* to Creon. If Creon and Tiresias are slower to anger than Oedipus, that is because when they enter the scene they are still outside the vicious circle of the *skandalon*. Oedipus pulls them into it by his arrogant and suspicious attitude, by the living scandal that he himself constitutes, and all the tragic characters soon reach the same pitch of violence. When Tiresias arrives before Oedipus, his complaints are prompted by the extreme degree of contagion which he perceives. To engage the tyrant in debate, or simply to speak to him in the state that he is in, means exposing oneself to the *skandalon*, it means catching the disease which Oedipus wants to cure, that *plague* from which he thinks he alone is exempt:

Alas! Alas! To know is a terrible thing when knowledge is useless to its possessor! I was not ignorant of that, but I forgot it. Otherwise I would never have come [316–18].

To be sure, it is Oedipus's anger which is *contagious*. But the very idea of contagion belies the unilateral character of a purely "psychological" reading. "Psychology" does not see that as the scandals come face to face, they reinforce and embitter each other, provoking an ever more perfect convergence of passions, which is to say ever more scandal. Each sees the sacred difference radiating from the other and strives to wrest it from him.

Sophocles' tragedy describes—in unilateral fashion, certainly, but less unilaterally than many modern readings—the type of relationship, born of the *skandalon*, that unites and separates the face-to-face antagonists.

Oedipus is the *child of Fortune*, the man of spectacular highs and lows. At every moment his destiny takes an unforeseen turn. Sophocles preserves this religious symbolism; he interprets it and enriches it with "psychological" notations. His Oedipus displays a "cyclical" temperament: sometimes the hero recalls his epic feats, praising himself to the skies; at other times he becomes discouraged and plunges into the darkest pessimism. The two themes of Fortune and of cyclothymia converge in the hero's anxiety about his birth. Oedipus is forever wanting to know whether he is the son of a king or a slave. This is such an exclusive concern with him that he perceives its reflection everywhere, even in the terror displayed by Jocasta when the truth begins to emerge:

Hah! Let any misfortunes come that will! But however humble my origin may be, I intend to discover it. In her woman's pride, she is blushing no doubt at my lowly ancestry: as for me, I deem myself to be the son of Fortune, generous Fortune, and I feel no shame at that. Fortune was my mother, and the years of my life have made me small and great by turn [1076–83].

Oedipus does not know if he was born a king or a beggar, a master or a slave, a superman or a nobody. Behind all this will be found his double status as father and accursed son. Both the Fortune of antiquity and modern cyclothymia must be interpreted as functions of "belonging to the Other who speaks of misfortune"—as functions of a relationship to the Other that is governed by sacred difference. We are in a universe where mastery and slavery are the two extremes of a difference perpetually swinging between the one and the other to the rhythm of the tragic dialogue. All hierarchies human and divine are caught up in a back-and-forth movement, all relative positions are ceaselessly interchanged. There is an Oedipus full of majesty, serenity, and generosity: this is the Oedipus assured of his "difference." At the slightest obstacle, this assurance gives way to anxiety and fury. But that is not true of Oedipus alone: everyone in the tragedy is radically deprived of stability and repose.

Each is turn by turn the all-powerful father and the accursed son. The truth of this unstable double relationship, this perpetual oscillation of difference, is obviously equality, that symmetry of the myth itself that Oedipus is incapable of perceiving since he is incapable of seeing anyone as anything other than a master or a slave, a god or a nobody, a tyrannical father or an accursed son.

Alongside the symbolism and the psychology, always suggestive but always limited by their unilateral character, there are numerous indications at the level of structural symmetry that hint at the adversaries' inability to perceive their identity. Oedipus and Creon are brothers-in-law. To understand their relationship, it must be grasped as identical to that of all the *enemy brothers* of Greek tragedy, in particular Oedipus's sons, Eteocles and Polynices, those *Sames* whom nothing separates but the mythical *difference* which provokes and transfigures the convergence of desires. Each of them sees himself turn by turn as sole heir or as disinherited depending on the position of the Other. Eteocles and Polynices attempt for a while to stabilize the instability; they give up trying to divide the indivisible difference and decide to occupy the highest office by turns, with each assigned an equal length of time. This telling compromise fails, naturally, and the two brothers end up killing each other.

If the conflict involved tangible goods, a solution would be conceivable. It is the nullity of the difference that renders the conflict inexpiable. This is a truth frequently expressed in Greek mythology. Cadmos, like Jason, tosses into the midst of terrifying warriors, all born of the same dragon's teeth, a stone that sets them at one another's throats, each suspecting the other of having thrown it.

Here once more, as at the origin, parallelism, symmetry, identity—in other words, vulgar rivalry—is the inaccessible truth of the relationship. The enemy brothers never perceive this identity insofar as they experience it, from one moment to the next, as an oscillating difference in the life-or-death struggle in which they are pitted against each other. But they perceive it better and better as identity, ever contagious, rapidly spreads and propagates. The loss of differences is not limited to the scapegoat alone, nor even to only one family. To re-establish the symmetry is to see that nothing is unilateral. The loss of difference affects the entire community. It translates into a multitude of particular conflicts. The *plague* is merely a euphemism for this state of things that condemns men to the deadly strife of enemy brothers. Nothing yet can halt a contagion ever analogous to that whose effects we have seen on Tiresias and Creon.

No one recognizes the non-difference of the brother with whom he himself struggles, but everyone recognizes this same non-difference, everyone observes it with serene and satisfied perspicacity outside of his own struggle, which is to say in the immense majority, the near-totality of cases.

The illusion of difference, always present between the enemy brothers even though it oscillates without cease, combines with the real exteriority of each individual vis-à-vis most of the conflicts caused by this same oscillating difference to produce the attitude that is so characteristic of Oedipus at the beginning of the tragedy. The monarch's somewhat condescending superiority stems from his illusory detachment, his exteriority at once genuine and deceptive.

The always-fleeting difference gives rise not only to a "problem of identity"—the hero's anxiety about his birth, his alternation between enthusiasm and despair—but also to his lofty impassiveness, his quasi-scientific detachment in the face of an enigma to be solved. All of which is as unstable as ever, and gives way with no transition to the hate-filled obsession with the Other. Oedipus thinks he was born outside Thebes, the latest arrival among the town's citizens; he takes himself to be a doctor diagnosing with complete objectivity the illness of others, a judge settling impartially a conflict in which he is not himself involved. And these ostentatious claims to knowledge must be compared, of course, to the nobly inspired attitude of Tiresias. These two ways of believing oneself above the fray, opposite but at bottom identical, quickly yield, at the first contact, to blind fury and murderous rage.

Here indeed is the *exasperation of the prophetic spirit* that Hölderlin's genius presents to us as a universal phenomenon linked to that strange "moderation," that "mediocrity" of tragic eras that we are calling non-difference or identity here. The prophetic spirit perceives this non-difference to the extent that it is not essential to the prophet, that is, to the extent that it structures all the conflicts in which the prophet is not himself mixed up. The prophetic spirit always displays a blind spot. Nobody recognizes identity where it is essential, at the level of the particular struggle engaging the enemy brothers. The two perspectives—serenity for what is distant, wrath for what is close at hand—are correlative. The myth perceives this unity split in two and presents it in the case of Oedipus as extremely sudden anger, as anger bursting forth out of a perfectly calm sky.

Looming in the background of *Oedipus the King* is the vast social and religious crisis whose echoes will gradually be heard more distinctly. The first conflict with the father, as we saw, opens up a difference between the father and the son. *Dis fere* means to transport far away, to remove, to put at a distance. This distancing finds expression in the myth; it is even expressed twice. The first time, Oedipus is carried far from the father, towards Corinth. The second time, it is Oedipus who flees the father by fleeing Corinth. The son always wants to avoid a new encounter with the father. Far from plotting the destruction of this obstacle that bruises him, the son dreams only of fleeing, escaping, and forgetting. This will to flight, escape, and oblivion ends up failing, but it fails only belatedly. The distance between Thebes and Corinth is the deep peace of childhood. The father and son act and desire in two different regions of being. Their paths temporarily diverge. For quite a long period of time, the son is safe from the father, separated from him by the prohibition itself, always productive of distance and difference.

If Corinth evokes what in an individual existence is called a "latency" period, it also corresponds to what in collective existence is a first type of society, or else a first stage in the *historical* development of a second type of society. This use of the myth as a universal model rests on a preliminary postulate: all cultural creation is the fruit of the *skandalon* in the sense that it aims at preventing its repetition. The difference produced by the *skandalon* gives rise to separations and fire-breaks that prevent or neutralize rivalry; this difference materializes in the form of taboos, hierarchical distinctions and institutions that block the convergence of desires and eliminate the possibility of confrontation.

Thus, a moiety system that divides society in two, or in an even number of parts, is nothing but the inscription in cultural reality of the split vision of the *skandalon*. The Same is perceived as Difference and this difference is guaranteed by the sacred; it is the sacred itself. One moiety is therefore to the other what Thebes is to Corinth in Oedipus's childhood. They are actually one and the same from many standpoints, but the distance that separates them is no less real; never do they meet from the essential standpoint of rivalry. They break the Oedipal triangle.

Every society effectively structured by the sacred horror of the *skandalon* prevents the latter from becoming a living relationship. The *skandalon* is crystallized into institutional *obstacles*, into religious or other barriers that keep people from turning into fascinating *obstacles* for one another. Never do father and son meet at the fatal crossroads.

The societies termed "primitive" are those where the institutions born of the *skandalon* succeed or appear to succeed in definitively preventing the latter from constituting a real threat. In other societies, the descent of the *skandalon* into everyday life is preceded by long periods of religious and social stability, the "primitive" periods. This double usage of the term "primitive" is rightly condemned by enthnological rigor. In their very principle, and particularly in their religious foundations, the societies that are bound for the *skandalon* and for history assuredly differ from those that are not. But it is understandable that this double usage remains invincibly present in Western conciousness. The word "primitive" is applied to everything that evades, temporarily or more or less permanently, the reactivation of the *skandalon*, which is a very particular mode of destruction and revelation of everything built by the *skandalon* itself.

Anthropologists often point to societies where the confrontation of father and son is unknown. Psychoanalysts have no trouble answering that misapprehension of the "Oedipus complex" is the first condition for having one. The anthropologists' objection may be poorly formulated but it conceals an essential intuition. One must distinguish societies that inscribe the ignorance of the Oedipus *in their institutions* from those that do not. It is only in the latter that one can truly speak of "misapprehension"—that one can measure and judge everything in the light of an "apprehension" that perhaps remains faultier than is realized, but which in any case could not come into being without the effective presence of the *skandalon*; that is, of the transfigured rivalry.

In the present perspective, the "Oedipus" can be considered universal in the sense that the *skandalon* is the never-apprehended foundation of every society. The Oedipus is not universal, however, in the sense of the Oedipal tragedy, in the sense of the loss, indefinitely eluded, of this misapprehension. History is the ceaseless re-plastering of symbolic forms at which the *skandalon* is forever chipping away. The universal Oedipus is the non-historical Oedipus, the still-innocent Oedipus for whom Western society is nostalgic. What is specifically Western, on the other hand, is the halting progress of the enemy brothers towards the ambiguous knowledge of the sunset god.

The tragedy presents itself as an investigation into the "murder of Laius." But the real theme is the universal impurity which, thanks to the expulsion of the scapegoat, passes for a consequence of this one murder. The origin of the crisis affecting the whole society is unknown. To seek a scapegoat is to seek the person responsible for the crisis. Difference always seems to come from the father, the king, the dispenser of sacred oracles. The scapegoat will therefore be the assassin of difference. We saw that everyone fears having to recognize in the other that authentic incarnation of paternal power that he fails to become himself. Everyone suspects the other of having made off with the paternal inheritance, of having stolen the celestial fire. That is why the accusation of having "killed the father," of having succeeded him through violence and hubris, will be reciprocally exchanged by the enemy brothers. Each will see in the Other the original source of conflictual identity, the universal fomenter of disorder, the person responsible for the collective ills. The accusation amounts to a covert confession, to the very extent that it concerns the undue appropriation of difference, and that it imputes this enormity to a single man, the enemy brother.

The "murder of Laius" is thus the reduction of the crisis to a single man and a single act, Oedipus's "patricide." The symbolic operation is in no way a premeditated camouflage. Premeditation would ensure its failure. The Other is eliminated, but this elimination proceeds in logical fashion: it is always possible to re-establish the underlying symmetry. Moreover, elements of symmetry still persist here, highlighted, even, by Sophocles' tragic art. With Tiresias, the accusation of having killed the king becomes reciprocal.

It is important to see that the sacred does not retreat here, it does not disappear, or at least not yet, but it detaches and separates itself from that which is ordered, regulated and moderated by it, and which, in turn, moderates the sacred itself. The transition from the primitive mythic to the "individualism" of the tragic oppositions always looks like a pure and simple loss of the sacred, for individuals become capable of observing in the abstract the withering of religion. Difference has not disappeared but it has come loose and broken away; it wanders panic-stricken through the city; it is no longer the ordering and regulating power of yore. Incapable from now on of durably fitting in anywhere, it renders *impure* the relations it once purified. The nascent individualism is not a true ebbing of the sacred, it is the alternating sacralization of an Other and a Self always defined as functions of the illusory difference that constitutes them both without ever assigning them a fixed position in the structure thus constituted.

Piety kept man within the limits prescribed by the gods; it respected the differences that defined the traditional order. The tragic chorus laments the growing impiety of the Thebans:

They are nothing now, the oracles rendered to Laius, they are disdained, Apollo is no longer honored with splendor anywhere; the worship of the gods is on the wane [906–910].

These definitions of impiety are too narrow; tied to the expulsion of the scapegoat, they perceive above all the insolent joy of Oedipus and Jocasta at the idea of having thwarted the oracles of Laius. Here again, one must re-establish the symmetry that has been broken at the scapegoat's expense. Impiety in action, the impiety that never ceases to occur in the tragedy, is, once more, the conflict of the enemy brothers and, as a result of this conflict, the dwindling of institutional difference, of difference incarnate. Each strives to prove that the Other is unworthy and unfit to succeed the father. The targets are individuals, but institutions are hit. Oedipus strives, for example, to destroy the authority of the prophet Tiresias in the minds of the Thebans:

When have you been a clairvoyant soothsayer? How is it that when the She-dog sang her verses, you did not speak the word needed to deliver the Thebans? [390–92].

The determination to maintain or restore order is but one with the impiety that horrifies the chorus. Each would not accuse the Other with such violence if he did not secretly exalt him as the possessor of the difference coveted by all. To battle the temptation of divinizing the obstacle is at the same time to attack what's left of the former order. We see this when Tiresias in his turn heaps sarcasm on his antagonist's impotence, asking

Oedipus, "Where is your skill at solving riddles now?" [440]. It is no use to pose as the defender of religion and oracles if one is going to raise an impious hand against the dignity of the king. Tiresias behaves no differently, in short, from Oedipus himself. Together the enemy brothers destroy this city they all aspire to cure. The prestige of the monarch, the hero, the priest, the sage, gradually crumble away. It is significant that the chorus compares the *plague* ravaging Thebes to the discord among the elite. We must go further still; we must recognize that the two ills are indistinguishable. Or rather, only the expulsion of the scapegoat operates a distinction that the tragic art of Sophocles tends to abolish without entirely succeeding:

But this land that is dying grieves my soul, if I must now see added to yesterday's ills new ills that come from you two [665–67].

To understand *hubris* is, once more, to refrain from treating the scapegoat any differently from his tragic partners; we must put *hubris* back into the context of the enemy brothers and stop seeing it as an exclusive property of one or the other of them. *Hubris madly lays its hands on what is inviolable*, that is, on difference itself. If it is Laius's killer who is guilty here, if it is he who murders difference, then it is Tiresias too, since every new accusation makes the murder more complete.

The sacred—the original source of all peace, of all fixity, of all eternity—turns little by little into an infinite turmoil that penetrates and poisons the life of each individual. While the institutions die whose being rested solely on its invisible support, difference unloosened wanders hither and yon at the whim of the obstacles that individuals constitute for it; their hold on it becomes ever more ephemeral; it whirls about faster and faster, bringing with it discord instead of serenity.

The elements of the structure are mutually reinforcing. Conflict feeds on symmetry and it renders symmetry ever more exact. As the identity between the partners in conflict becomes more perfect, the illusory difference never ceases to widen. One ends up with a line-by-line and point-by-point opposition between the object and its mirror image. Accusations become ever more obstinate and ever more earnest at the same time that non-difference and uniformity become more glaring at the level of the collectivity. Henceforth everyone perceives non-difference as the truth of the structure. Impiety grows bolder. It will even go so far as to proclaim that there is no difference and that the gods are dead. Competition, spreading everywhere and everywhere openly displayed, except where it involves the enemy brothers, appears, with the retreat of all previous significations, as the ultimate meaning of collective life. Knowledge becomes sophisticated and demystifying. It is bent on destroying the illusory prestige that the "naive" attribute to the obstacle. It exposes the obstacle's true rationality, economic or sexual.

It is towards the truth of the myth itself that the partners in conflict are heading. Even a superficial reading reveals this: Oedipus did not know, before striking him, who his adversary was. He little knows, at the moment he curses him, who Creon is. By contrast, Oedipus and Tiresias know very well with whom they are dealing when they destroy each other with words.

The impious adversaries are heading at full speed towards the knowledge of the father himself, which is to say towards the pure and simple nullity of this father. If there is no longer any difference between men, that is because in truth there never was. The truth of the myth is absolute symmetry. There is no true father, and that indeed is the knowledge that the expulsion of the scapegoat obscures.

The transition from the myth to the tragedy must be defined, we said, as a transition from the paternal to the fraternal relationship. One finds this same transition (although it does not always have the same meaning) in all the great texts of the Judeo-Greek West. One finds it in the Bible where Cain and Abel come after the Fall; one finds it twice in the Oedipal myth, first with Oedipus and Creon, then with Eteocles and Polynices. The slide from one relationship into the other signifies nothing else but the loss of difference. This significance is particularly visible in *Oedipus the King*. As a result of that "hypostasis" of the structural relations that is also responsible for the patricide and incest, the slide from the paternal to the fraternal relationship with respect to Oedipus is realized in the person of a single character and thereby revealed as essential: the psychological and biographical coherence of the character is sacrificed to the modification of the structural relationship. It is in the character of Creon, who is first an uncle, which is to say a quasi-father, and who turns into a quasi-brother after the marriage of Oedipus and Jocasta, that this slide is made manifest. It becomes manifest at the level of the "realist" objection that reproaches Sophocles for not giving us a more mature Creon, just as he fails to show Jocasta more advanced in years. It is the fraternal status assumed by Creon that determines his relative age. Creon talks like a young man and a rival of Oedipus, for the fraternal status is defined by the abolition of all differences, including the difference in age. The Creon of *Oedipus the King* needs to be essentially identical to Oedipus.

The fraternal relationship cannot triumph without imposing itself as universal, even retrospectively. The irresistible contagion goes back in time as it spreads through space; it turns into a demystifying investigation of the past, the history of historians. Fraternal non-difference is discovered to be the truth of the paternal relationship itself. Thanks to the full advent of this identity, we are able to decipher ourselves, latecomers that we are, the symmetry of the paternal relationship, more difficult to see in the earlier episodes of the myth.

The first mythic conflict was characterized by completely mistaken identities. It was composed of episodes isolated in space and time. To grasp the reciprocity, it was necessary to recognize and overcome a distance at once double and single, to shift from Thebes to Corinth and from Corinth to Thebes, to put together the hero's earliest childhood and his young manhood. At the myth's opening, it is not easy to perceive equivalences which, at every stage, are alone essential, but which become more and more visible as the myth progresses, precisely because the differences and the distances, particularly those in time and space, are gradually abolished. That comes down to saying that the acts of violence occur in ever more rapid succession, until they literally hurtle into each other in the tragic dialogue, in the curses exchanged by Oedipus, Creon and Tiresias. This extreme proximity, this juxtaposition makes it possible to put these acts of violence together intellectually, it makes it easier and easier to perceive the "bad" symmetry, meaning the structure of reprisals. By moving towards ever greater symmetry and identity, the myth thus homes in on its own truth. It is this abbreviated, "foreshortened" reciprocity which, projected onto the past, becomes the "patricide" and the "incest" of the Other, the enemy brother.

There is no true father; there are only enemy brothers, those double beings, one-part ferocious fathers and one-part accursed sons, who spread their own duality everywhere. Laius is not a well-assured possessor of the paternal inheritance either. It is the usurper and the tyrant in him that fears the threat coming from his son. He scandalizes his son because he is himself scandalized. The father/son relationship thus participates in an initial contagion. That indeed is what the familial symbolism of limping tells us. The uneven gait that Laius passes on to his son is common to Labdacus's entire male line.

Bruised by the obstacle and still constrained in his gait by this bruise, the son walks right back into the father he thought he had left behind. The escape far from the father is an ironic return towards the father. To delude oneself about the model's identity, to endow the obstacle with an undeserved prestige, is in truth the only way of equalling him, of making oneself identical to him. For this same error characterizes the father.

There is no true father, but, through a fundamental paradox, the son always succeeds—beyond the misunderstandings that, always reciprocal, always end up cancelling each other out—in replicating that being whom he imitates by completely mistaking his identity. Brotherhood is the truth of fatherhood.

The interpretation of the Other is always true, indeed it is truer and truer, but never does the interpreter give up trying to recover that difference of which he henceforth proclaims the emptiness. It is of this very emptiness, frantic perspicacity, devoid of all respect and all pity, that the enemy brothers now boast. They make a royal scepter out of nothing, then rush to whack each other with it in a manner that is hardly regal. Oedipus makes a show of a wholly profane clairvoyance in order to bring down Tiresias and his oracles.

The tragic investigation therefore veils at the same time that it unveils, for it remains unilateral. The modifications of the structure delineate a solicitation that is ever more insistent, ever more urgent. Every nuance is now erased, every placating meaning is abolished, every inequality eliminated, every valley exalted, every mountain and hill made low. Nothing is left but the fierce opposition of enemy brothers while all around, in Hölderlin's expression, "the desert grows."

This schematization reduces the structure to its essential lines, which the hardening of oppositions throws into sharp relief. Thus simplified, the structure cries out to be deciphered, and it will be, again and again. Yet it never really is, for, always partial in both senses, the readings themselves mesh with the structure of reprisals, perpetuating the very thing they are meant to abolish.

This elimination of what is inessential, this ceaseless heightening of what is essential, this whole maturing of the structure is summed up quite nicely by the different meanings of the French verb *accuser* ["to show up" or "to accuse"]. The features of the structure *show up* in the sense that features *show up* more sharply in a caricature or on an aging face. The truth showing up ever more clearly is none other than the loss of differences and everyone's identical responsibility for this loss. Inside the structure, the complete truth is never perceived. Here, each symmetrical element *shows up* the symmetry of the other without recognizing its own reflection, without recognizing that the symmetry of all the elements is the only thing truly *shown up*. Oedipus tries to *show up* Creon and Tiresias as the real villains; Tiresias seeks to *show up* Oedipus as the guilty party; each throws the accusation back at the other. It is by turning themselves into living lies that the characters in the tragedy make the whole truth shine out.

This truth that keeps on coming and that each tosses back at the other without ever accepting it, this truth that the lack of acceptance turns into a purely scandalous lie, is the word that curses, offspring of the earlier violence of gestures. Here the word is nothing more than the increasingly precipitate rhythm of the violence exchanged between the two men. This accelerating pace, the source of all structural comparison, is the revelation itself and its violent re-utilization against the other; it is the dialogue that is characterized, according to Hölderlin, by an "excessively mechanical interplay, each drumming out the other." That is the ultimate, most manifest form of the "bad symmetry" that has defined the myth from the beginning, but which even the most obtuse can now perceive and turn back against the adversary. Words are the double speech of expulsion and death; *der wirkliche Mord*, the veritable death which, as Hölderlin tells us, comes from words. They alone may accomplish, with the unleashing of *hubris*, what physical violence had only prepared, the destruction of the city.

Truth and falsehood emerge together, equally divided between the adversaries. The further one advances into the myth, the more glaring is the symmetry and the more irresistible the need to deny it. All the readers of the myth and all its interpreters experience this need. Sooner or later, good and evil, truth and falsehood must be embodied in infallible champions. The temptation to eliminate the symmetry by expelling the scapegoat is irresistible. Lévi-Strauss is right to think that each reading of the myth is a continuation of it. One must go further. There is no human relationship, there is no reading of human relationships, whether it is called literature, psychology, psychoanalysis or ethnological observation, that is not situated with respect to the myth, that is not decipherable as a function of the place where, the symmetry becoming intolerable, a dissymmetry of some sort is substituted for it, the necessary and unrecognized product of an expulsion of the Other.

That indeed is what is revealed by our intolerance for the identity between Oedipus and Tiresias. Whether careful or cursory readers of Sophocles, we see in Tiresias the lucidity of truth and in Oedipus delusion. We require the true and the false to be solidly anchored in a universe with no surprises. The scandal here is the destruction of all wisdom to which the absolute reciprocity between Oedipus and Tiresias threatens to lead. It is here that we must rigorously maintain the principle at the basis of our reading and deny Tiresias the possession of a ready-made truth that might weigh on the myth from the outside, doing violence to it and destroying its balance. But this rigor is difficult since it is unfaithful to the tragedy's most apparent meanings. Is it not said, upon Tiresias's arrival:

Now they are bringing in the venerable soothsayer, he who alone among men bears the truth in his breast! [297–99].

Must it be denied that Tiresias perceives a truth which eludes Oedipus? It must. Certainly, Tiresias is the first to perceive the identity of the accuser and the accused; he perceives the pattern of retorts that defines the myth. The guilty one is the one who accuses the others, who sees guilty parties everywhere. This truth is not of a different order from the previous truths, from the truth pronounced by Oedipus himself against Tiresias. It is merely more complete. The interpretation is an accusation; it has only to become a counter-accusation by redoubling itself so as to turn into a re-interpretation that includes the preceding interpretation. Here we confirm that the structure of interpretation and the structure of reprisals are one and the same: the advances of knowledge and of discord are defined by the ever more rapid exchange of curses.

Tiresias answers Oedipus's "You are guilty" with an identical "You are guilty." But, for the counter-accusation to be as effective as the accusation, or even more effective, the paradox on which it is based must not be dissimulated, it must be underscored. One must say, with Tiresias: "You who accuse me, and who think yourself innocent, the wonder of it is that you are the guilty one. This difference which you believe you have discovered between the two of us and of which you boast, this difference which, in your blind eyes, justifies your hostility towards me, this difference indeed exists where you have placed it, except that it does not work to your advantage, but to mine. The one you are hunting down is none other than yourself."

There is no truth external to the structure, no *veritas ex machina* in authentic tragedy. If Tiresias speaks the truth of Oedipus, it is because Oedipus "poses an obstacle" for him, scandalizing him and obliging him to strike back in reprisal. It is thanks to Tiresias, therefore, that the accusation

will come back to the place where it belongs, its place of origin, but anyone at all would have sent it back. The prophetic gift is one with participation in the tragic dialogue, with the insertion of the "prophet" in the structure of reprisals, the quite literally *apocalyptic* structure of a revelation that
only the breakup of the city could bring to completion.

If Tiresias takes the revelation further than Oedipus, this "further"
consists in reflecting back the previous truth and in thereby adding a new
dimension to it. Tiresias is one step removed along the spiral constituted by
the ambiguous self-revelation of the *skandalon*. This type of separation reappears and disappears without cease; it is what gives each person the illusion
of gaining firm possession of difference and then of losing it once again.
Oedipus will soon catch up with Tiresias. The myth's limping gait does not
compromise the symmetry: in the last analysis, it is what guarantees it.

The counter-accusation is superior to the accusation precisely to the
degree that it challenges the implicit *cogito* of innocence on which the latter is founded. It raises the question of the "subject." It reduces to nothing
the "individualism" of the previous stages, the splendid self-assurance and
scientific detachment of the hero. Individualism occupies an intermediate
position between the myth and the tragedy properly speaking. The
counter-accusation is more negative, more subtle, more "modern" than the
accusation. In Tiresias, certain forms of thought that are ours and certain
methods of analysis find a "model" of astonishing richness. Tiresias opens
perspectives on the "sciences of man" that connect up perhaps, though by
an unexpected path, with certain of Michel Foucault's intuitions.

It is not without reason that Tiresias has been seen as the symbol of
the psychoanalyst. The blind prophet gives us a preview of that seer deprived of bodily eyes into which Oedipus will also be transformed by self-
reflection. Tiresias speaks as a man who has preceded us all on the road of
the myth and who, having reached the destination, proposes to guide our
steps on this journey fraught with pitfalls. At this advanced stage of the
myth, nobody will lay claim to a difference in essence, to a "paternity" too
conspicuous and too easily contested.

But to interpret in this manner the wisdom of Tiresias is to bring out
more clearly than ever its affinity to the wisdom which Oedipus prides
himself on possessing. It is from Oedipus that the idea comes of a knowledge based on experience and not on birth. Oedipus, too, is the man of
trick conclusions. His victory over the sphinx is nothing else. He, too,
poses as the demolisher of false essences, of abusive titles, of undeserved

distinctions. At this level, each deciphers the unconscious of the other, each congratulating himself on his extraordinary perspicacity. The more real this perspicacity is, and it is quite evident that it *is* real, the more it fixates the interpreter on the Other, the better it conceals from him the most essential thing about the structure: the role he plays in it himself.

Always preceded by the same history, always driven by the same desire, the two partners arrive together at the same pseudo-solutions. Everything that Tiresias, spurred on by Oedipus, thinks by himself, Oedipus, spurred on by Tiresias, also attributes to himself. It matters little if one of them identifies himself with tradition and the other with progress. Tiresias, cloaked in his oracles, and Oedipus, proud of his skepticism, both bellow the same dead truths.

~

The myth adopts Tiresias's unilateral accusation. Oedipus becomes "the assassin of difference"; here he is, alone responsible for all the conflictual symmetry brewing in the city, the single point where difference is most completely and scandalously lost—a veritable cesspit of all identity.

The incest is nothing else. Oedipus is the man who abolishes every difference between father and son, mother and wife, brothers and children. Patricide and incest converge if they are both grasped in terms of the meaning given above to the problem posed by the mythic tragedy. To inquire about the king's murder is to inquire about the loss of difference. We saw that each accuses the Other of monopolizing difference and propagating identity, of causing all the Thebans to be "plague-stricken." The structural symmetry is ever more obvious and ever more loudly affirmed, but it is also denied by all the enemy brothers when it comes to their own particular quarrels, to the precise extent that it represents for each of them not so much the objective destruction of the sacred as the renunciation of desire itself. The "why" of the scapegoat and the "how" of its expulsion are contained in these definitions. To choose a scapegoat is to choose the universal Other who will put an end to the universal discord. Each can play this role for all the others since the enemy brothers are all; interchangeable. To expel a single one of them means expelling them all, it therefore means imposing on the myth as a whole the vision, now fixed and solidified, of those same enemy brothers. That is why the myth's split vision, its insistence on seeing the Different in the Same, on always inserting an illusory difference in the midst of the identical, is always, as we have seen,

Oedipus's own vision, it is the splitting into two that Sophocles' text presents as characteristic of Laius and of Labdacus's entire line. If the myth incessantly produces identity out of evanescent differences, it never ceases rendering this identity unrecognizable in turn through the use of unbalancing violence.

In Oedipus, difference is so radically destroyed that all men shrink back in horror. And this shrinking back, this putting at a distance, is the restoration of the lost difference. This restoration repeats and completes all the acts of violence of which the memory survives in the myth itself and which are always violence done, through the other, to balance and truth. From now on, the myth sees Oedipus alone as violent. He seizes through violence (patricide) a difference that recoils in his hands, toppling him to the nethermost depths of incestuous non-difference.

There is patricide and incest, we saw, because the homology of the structural relationships experienced by the scapegoat turns into an identity between the individuals who figure in those relationships. The father becomes the hypostasis of the paternal relationship. The myth's message is either "beyond" the structure, in the paranoiac perspicacity concerning Oedipus, in the blind lucidity of Tiresias, or, on the contrary, "beneath" it, in the evasive and obdurate narrowness of a quasi-scientism and an objectivism closed to the homology of the relationships, seeing in them nothing more than the phenomenon of "contagion."

All through *Oedipus the King*, we hear echoes of a religious and social crisis that we never fully grasp, for that would mean nothing less than grasping the structure itself. We are able to apprehend directly only divergent metaphors of this crisis: the plague that exonerates the Thebans, the patricide and incest that condemn the scapegoat. Only the notion of the scapegoat and the role played by his expulsion in the relationship between the myth's message and its structure make it possible for us to understand the patricide, the incest and the plague as a dissymmetrical reading of the structural symmetry, itself a function of the struggle of enemy brothers.

The patricide and incest culminate in disorder and sterility in marriage and kinship, in all the fundamental processes of human existence. This is, we know, the very definition of the plague in the mythical and religious sense of the term. Everything is identical in either direction, except that Oedipus is a criminal, whereas the plague introduces us into the climate of passivity and irresponsibility which is already that of microbial medicine in the modern world.

What the myth never wants to face is the truth of its own genesis, and it is the free play of symmetrical elements, the unlimited exchange of terms that would reveal the emptiness of the oppositions and of the "individual" perspectives based on them.

It is always the expulsion of the scapegoat, in one form or another, which resolves, in the Western world, the conflict between Same and Same. But the operation is often disguised under some flattering name: *dépassement*, synthesis, progress, science, humanism, religion, etc. Hegel's greatness lies in having read in history the ineluctable dilemma of Oedipus and Creon: kill or be killed, expel or be expelled. But this dilemma was then conjured away by Hegel. He thought that two desires must behave like two concepts that cannot fail to agree once *nothing* separates them any longer. But in the realm of desire, this nothing is everything, since two perfectly identical desires are two desires for the same object: they pose an obstacle for each other. They are, for each other, an irreconcilable *scandal.*

At the ultimate stage of the conflict, there is no way out, no possibility of compromise. If Oedipus does not destroy Creon, Creon will destroy him. All that is left are sacrificers and victims. "Wisdom" cannot venture that far. Wisdom is willing to meet the other "half way"; it even consents to take "the first step." But do not suppose that the enemy brother will fall into step. He will doubtless see nothing coming but an iron boot. And the noble attempt at conciliation will soon slide into legitimate defense. Molière's philosophy teacher never succeeds in reconciling the music teacher and the dance teacher.

Any demand for reciprocal recognition leads to reciprocal violence. The only way left to escape the bad kind of reciprocity is to stop demanding the good kind. But to do that means putting one's life on the line, it means accepting the role of the victim. Indeed, only the consenting victim is pure of any participation in the expulsion of the scapegoat. As relevant as it may be in as many special cases as one likes, the objection of masochism is of absolutely no avail against the theoretical conclusion that emerges from the foregoing analyses. If Oedipus's detachment is false, if the prophets are blind, if every superior vantage point is illusory, if the exteriority of indifference is deceptive, since it escapes the showdown of enemy brothers, this showdown itself limits our choice tremendously. If there is a place from which the truth of the structure is revealed, it is not the one occupied by the sacrificer. All that remains therefore is the victim's.

But the desire for knowledge cannot, by itself, freely reach this place where all knowledge is in peril. The desire to know is in any event rooted in the struggle of enemy brothers. Only the desire *not to kill his brother* can lead the brother to this extremity.

These remarks bring us closer, perhaps, to the properly Sophoclean dimension of *Oedipus the King*. The tragedy respects the legend: it therefore cannot rid itself of certain elements directly derived from the expulsion of Oedipus. Within this rigid framework, Sophocles, as we have seen, brings out the structural symmetries and underscores them in extraordinary fashion. That indeed is what Hölderlin grasps when he speaks of that balance, that equal weighting—*Gleichgewicht*—which characterizes the tragic art. Sophocles revives, perhaps, that archaic symbolism which, at certain points in the myth, affirms the rupture of the symmetry and thereby transcends the dissymmetry of the scapegoat.

Sophocles' tragedy renders the myth truer and straighter; it *rectifies* it. The poet, an interpreter of the myth like any of us, or just about, is animated by a spirit which cannot flow from the expulsion of the scapegoat, understood in the sense of the symbolic operation analyzed up to here. The conclusion of *Oedipus the King*, whose impulse continues on through *Oedipus at Colonus*, reveals a dimension that is original and utterly irreducible to the violence of enemy brothers.

Already in *Oedipus the King* and more clearly yet in *Oedipus at Colonus*, the focus of attention slowly shifts away from the city, which the expulsion of the scapegoat will close up again, and towards the scapegoat himself. This tragic shift, properly ineffable, is nothing other than the "march beneath the unthinkable" of which Hölderlin speaks. Outside the ancient city, outside every closed city, the only road is the one that *follows the scapegoat*. The poet of Oedipus no longer belongs entirely to the city, and that indeed is what Plato senses in his loyalty to the latter. Plato himself has no choice: he must either renounce his perfect city or expel the poet from it.

Modern thought likewise rejects, with splendid unanimity, this conclusion to *Oedipus the King*. It finds in it the absurd verdict of "destiny," the "return of the repressed," or sometimes even a pure and simple falsification of the myth. Were our own reading not to be properly understood, one could see it as leading us to a yet more negative vision. What is Oedipus's acceptance if not the final mystification of the individual who, called upon to pay for everyone else, still adopts his executioners' perspective as his own? What is the furthest removed from scapegoating if not the modern mind-set of revolt, the mind-set that rebels against so odious an expulsion? In reality, this kind of thinking merely changes scapegoats. Voltaire demonstrates this with his rationalist version of the play: he would expel Tiresias, if he were able, the better to justify Oedipus.

The mind-set of revolt perpetually changes scapegoats in order to persuade itself that it is expelling nobody; it follows the very movement of the difference between the enemy brothers. Modern thought does not want to see that Oedipus is guilty, even if he did not kill his father and marry his mother. The violence to which he falls victim in the end is no different from that which he contemplated against his brother. His responsibility for everybody's misfortune is real: it is exactly the same as the responsibility of anybody else.

The tragic art orients itself towards the scapegoat whose fate is henceforth less horrifying to it than mystified existence. The shift from the grimacing divisions and disequilibrium of the enemy brothers to the simplicity and beauty of the tragic art is but one with this new orientation. It is the shift that Sophocles himself makes. Oedipus's gesture of tearing out his eyes is compelling because, through it, tragic creation signifies itself.

A work that freed itself completely from the dissymmetry of the scapegoat would still maintain the form of the expulsion and justify it. The shift from murder to the acceptance of death, from misrecognition to recognition, is inscribed *in advance* in the myth founded on an expulsion that it dissimulates *and nowhere else.* The collective choice that designates the scapegoat necessarily seizes on an individual who is convinced of being innocent, since this choice is arbitrary in its essential dimension. But it never has to appear as a glaring injustice committed by a collectivity gone mad. It conceals a more vital possibility: it can turn into the terrible incursion of truth succeeding the deceptive illusions of "wisdom" and "detachment" and permitting the accusation to fall back onto the reckless accuser.

Only the consent of the scapegoat makes possible the advent of the truth—a minuscule event, an almost imperceptible displacement at the level of the structure. To say that is to say that this event is called forth, solicited by the structure. And the confirmation of this fact, meaning the answer to this call, an answer at last clear and distinct, is not to be sought from the Greeks but from Jewish prophetism.

In the period before and during the exile, the prophetic books of the Bible describe, overtly this time, a religious and social crisis analogous to the one that can be discerned behind *Oedipus the King.* Fathers and sons are pitted against one another. Everywhere familial and social discord rages.

Hierarchical differences are no longer respected. God no longer accepts the sacrifices. The rites of worship have lost all efficacy. Here, too, the universal investigation, the passionate search for those responsible, assumes an ambiguous meaning. The effort to restore the sacred is but one with its loss, or rather its shift into hate-filled idolatry of the other. The struggle of enemy brothers can be defined in religious terms as the tendency to slide from animal sacrifice into sacrifice of the brother, in a movement opposite to that which once substituted an animal for the son threatened by the father (sacrifice of Abraham, paschal lamb). Animal sacrifice brings individuals closer together; it allows them to escape from the circle of mythic violence. But they fall back into this circle when the sacrifices are no longer accepted, in other words when the mechanism of religious sublimation has worn out. The attempt to reinforce this mechanism orients men towards a less "neutral" victim, towards a more "robust" sacrifice, which is to say towards man himself. But that means slipping little by little, in the name of religion itself, into the gratification of desire and hate; it means renouncing all sublimation.

Instead of trying to patch up these mechanisms of sublimation, the Jewish prophets devote themselves to revealing and eliminating them. At the crisis's nadir there appears, in the second Isaiah, the essential figure of the Servant of Yahveh. Two themes converge here: that of animal sacrifice and that of the human scapegoat. But the scapegoat voluntarily substitutes himself for the deficient object of the previous sacrifices; he consents to suffer for everybody.

. . . he was wounded for our transgressions, he was bruised for our iniquities: the chastisement of our peace was upon him; and with his stripes we are healed. . . . He was oppressed, and he was afflicted, yet he opened not his mouth: he is brought as a lamb to the slaughter, and as a sheep before her shearers is dumb. . . [Isaiah 53: 5, 7].

Christianity rests in its turn on the idea of the consenting scapegoat, which it deems to be fully incarnate in the passion of Christ. Whatever may be the essence of Christianity, no misinterpretation could be more complete than to assimilate it to the religions of difference. The way of thinking that believes it has thus understood Christianity is in fact always understood by it, for this way of thinking is located inside the city and perceives poorly or not at all how the latter's closure is achieved through constant recourse to the expulsion of the Other.

Christianity breaks free of the ancient city whose closure it rejects. If the first Christians were accused, in the Roman empire, of infanticide and incest, it was perhaps not without reason, in the sense in which myths reason. The fact that Christianity subsequently and very rapidly became a new but always quite precarious religion of difference is something which may not pose an insurmountable problem for interpretation and which in any case cannot justify classing the great Judeo-Christian texts with the myths that are the most opposite, if not the most foreign to them, the myths of the scapegoat.

To be sure, the original Christianity may appear to be lost and forgotten in later Christendom. Heidegger asserts that no sooner does Christianity encounter philosophy than it is absorbed by it. The destiny of the Western world can then be conceived without any reference to a distinct entity that would be *Christianity*. This elimination is more profound, certainly, than many abusive assimilations, but it is no less strange at the moment when the world of "Christian" difference likewise culminates in the mediocrity of a tragic age. Once again, in the infinite turmoil of difference cast adrift, the old dilemma of Oedipus and Creon, the absurd and terrible "him or me," hangs suspended, in plain sight of everyone, over all individual and collective life. If we seem to have been granted an indefinite reprieve, we cannot assign the credit for this to the "wisdoms" that solicit us but rather to monstrosity alone, to its planetary domination, to the overly decisive means at its disposal, to everything that ensures we can no longer hope to destroy our brother without equally destroying ourselves.

One may ask whether the original Christianity, the Johannine *logos*, misunderstood, disfigured, rejected and finally almost forgotten in the world it brought into being—like those oracles in the myth which the chorus's lamentations and the relevance of the surrounding symbols suggest were once distinct from Hölderlin's Word of death—one may ask whether that original Christianity, too, does not play, in the purity of its letter, intact this time, at the roots of this world of which it is, in the last analysis, the scapegoat, a role utterly unrelated to the pale "ideals" and trifling "humanism" with which it is believed possible in our day to identify its most "authentic" legacy, a role in strict conformity with the unsurpassable radicalism of its essence.

∼

To conceive, even implicitly, the original relationship to the father as the infraction of a law, the disobedience to an order actually received, is to succumb to a vision inspired by the expulsion, thus keeping oneself from seeing the mechanism which, in the myth, ensures repetition.

Freud himself is on the track of this mechanism when he insists on the primacy of an identification with the father *prior to any object choice.*

A little boy will exhibit a special interest in his father; he would like to grow like and be like him, and take his place everywhere. We may say simply that he takes his father as his ideal. This behavior has nothing to do with a passive or feminine attitude towards his father (and towards males in general); it is on the contrary typically masculine. It fits in very well with the Oedipus complex, for which it helps to prepare the way.[1]

For the identification thus defined to lead necessarily, mechanically, to a rivalry inconceivable as such, it suffices that the desires for *having* be made to depend on the desire for *being*, that all desire for possession be subordinated to the identification with the father. In the same Chapter 7 of *Group Psychology and the Analysis of the Ego*, Freud begins to envisage such a configuration: he tells us that the libidinal penchant for the mother undergoes a "reinforcement" at the moment when the identification with the father, initially independent, enters into contact with it.

How could this identification with the father, of which Freud emphatically affirms the absolute primacy, become concrete unless it translated into desires for having? How else could one conceive that "active" and "virile" character that Freud attributes to it?

But Freud does not uncover the mainspring of the myth because he cannot conceive of the rivalry without hostility on the part of the son. He is not able to dissociate rivalry from *consciousness of rivalry*, a very curious failing if we consider what Freud represents for us:

The little boy notices that his father stands in his way with his mother. His identification with his father takes on a hostile colouring and becomes identical with the wish to replace his father in regard to his mother as well.[2]

But Freud adds an observation that tends obscurely to undercut the assertion he has just made of a necessary weakening of the identification: "Identification, in fact, is ambivalent from the very first." If ambivalence is present from the very first, that means the rivalry is not incompatible with the identification. Far from being mutually exclusive, the two phenomena reinforce each other. It is not necessary to limit or diminish the identification to make room for the rivalry. Quite the contrary.

To be sure, the fact that the identification can arouse rivalry does not escape Freud. What does escape him, however, is that the identification can blind the son to the rivalry which it arouses. (This blindness is not the Freudian unconscious since nothing here is repressed.)

It is curious that after having assembled the elements that constitute it and having forcefully insisted on the order that determines it, Freud is not able to grasp this essential fact. Playing with those elements and changing that order means rendering the *skandalon* even less accessible, it means falling all the way back into the dissymmetry of the mythic vision. The son is cast once more as, first and foremost, the rival of the father; the identification is compromised by being subordinated to the rivalry itself. Jacques Lacan recognizes that there is a difficulty here: "The structural effect of identification with the rival does not go without saying, except at the level of fable."[3]

The way that psychoanalytic theory coincides here with "the level of fable" may be judged alarming. Real understanding is necessarily located at another level. The passages from Freud that we have just quoted, with their exemplary openmindedness and simplicity, are milestones on the path to such understanding.

Yet Freud himself falls back into the dissymmetry of the scapegoat. Not to make the desires for *having* hinge unequivocally on the desire for *being* ultimately means relegating this desire for *being* to the background, cutting it off from all reality and emasculating it little by little. Naturally, those interested in psychoanalyzing the psychoanalyst will find something to think about here.

Concrete observation is what is admirable in Freud. As soon as he turns his attention to the myth, we see the working of the mechanism which, however, he does not identify. If we take a close look at the definition of the superego, we will see that it too supposes the *skandalon*. The superego's relation to the ego

. . . is not exhausted by the precept: "You ought to be like this (like your father)."
It also comprises the prohibition: "You *may not be* like this (like your father)—that
is, you may not do all that he does; some things are his prerogative."[4]

This text reveals admirably what psychoanalysis is incapable of conceiving and accepting on a theoretical plane. In the Western world, there is no law. There is only the incomprehensible clash of contradictory imperatives. The distinction between the licit and the illicit is always made on empirical grounds. The superego is always a bastardized and precarious substitute that the son tries to rig up in order to escape from the *skandalon*. This passage from Freud converges with Kafka's great texts on the silence of the law, the cause of the son's misfortunes. The law is always absent insofar as difference, far from defining religion, is denied to men by religion itself. And it is ever more completely denied them as one moves from patriarchal religion to the Mosaic Law, from the Mosaic Law to prophetism, and finally from prophetism to Christianity—in other words, as the sacred, without escaping the city, is shaken and cast adrift by the very call of the scapegoat . . .

In the text on the identification with the father and the text on the superego, one and the same intuition is vainly seeking the light of day. Freud's observations affirm a truth, that of the myth, that his theoretical conclusions reject. Freud's thinking is therefore infinitely close to the myth; it is the myth itself right down to its obsessive insistence on patricide and incest. And since the *skandalon* is the key to the myth, it also guides us, through all of Freud's writings, to the outermost reach of Freudian thought, which comes very near the *skandalon* but does not succeed in grasping it.

All of this is lost with Freud's successors. What happens, for example, to the second identification with the father? It becomes the instrument of what is called "Oedipal normalization," meaning the child's definitive insertion into the cultural circuit. We are not told whether this identification raises any problem of rivalry. It is conceived more or less along the lines of a rite of passage. There is always an implicit assimilation of our society to those studied by anthropologists.

Just as before we had a rivalry without prior identification, we now have an identification without rivalry. The one never goes without the other in Freud, even if the articulation between them remains incomplete. Freud dimly respects the contradiction that shatters the rites of passage in the Western world by making this world, and it alone, the place where veneration and revolt have the same basis. It is always the best son—the best in the sense of the culture itself—and never the worst who is locked in struggle with the father. It is Jacob rather than Esau, it is the prodigal son, it is Oedipus.

The unease caused by an expression such as "Oedipal normalization" is not merely of an esthetic order. Neither the family nor Western society presents the son with a coherent norm.

If psychoanalysis conceives from the outset the relation to the father in terms of revolt, that is because it wants to destroy "prejudices," demystify family relationships, expel illusory difference. It wants to cure, but it also wants to be a living *scandal*, an insurmountable obstacle to the mediocre and conventional folk who surround it.

Freud does not see that the irreverence of revolt is still far too reverent towards its object. Namely, towards that Law of the father that we are always hearing so much about and that has even come to be associated nowadays with the Gospel expression *Name of the Father*—that is, with a religion which, on the contrary, systematically devalues alliance and kinship. Revolt is still much too submissive to the terrestrial father to see that his "Law" is not even fragmentary and chaotic but radically contradictory, null.

Every psychological genesis necessarily includes an element of myth. It is mythic to believe that the son sets himself up as a rival of the father, even if only in an unconscious, instead of being constituted as such by others. The genesis proposed here eliminates this element of myth, the most flagrant of all.

The psychoanalytic myth, the one that comes to full bloom in *Totem and Taboo*, is not quite the Oedipal myth; it is something more terrible, in a sense, but also more comical: it is the Oedipal myth reread—O irony— in the light of the biblical myth of the Fall. Psychoanalytic man is forever an Adam driven from paradise because he devoured or coveted the forbidden fruit. That is not the right way to relate the two myths. The terrestrial father must not be confused with the eternal Father. The Bible tells us that only the consequences of the Fall, not the Fall itself, are reproduced in all men. Let us try leaving the "law" out of it, then; let us not accuse the Bible of loading men down with burdens too heavy to bear: the accusation might turn back once more against the accuser.

Translated by Mark R. Anspach

CHAPTER 4

Doubles and the *Pharmakos*: Lévi-Strauss, Frye, Derrida, and Shakespeare

Structuralism can only collect differences. In order to vindicate the claim that it lays bare the true mechanisms of myth, it is necessary to show that differentiation is the whole of myth. If differentiation must be viewed as process, however, it cannot completely ignore the undifferentiated, at least as a starting point. Lévi-Strauss takes this necessity into account; the undifferentiated is present in his analyses but as precisely that and nothing more, as a mere starting point which is never questioned for its own sake.

In primitive religions taken as a whole, however, the undifferentiated looms too large to be entirely disregarded. We are told in *L'Homme nu* that the undifferentiated belongs to ritual and ritual to the undifferentiated. This is no more true, I believe, than the converse proposition, namely that differentiation is the whole of myth. In both myth and ritual we have first the undifferentiated, then differentiation. By exaggerating the role of the undifferentiated in rituals, Lévi-Strauss compensates for its minimization in the case of mythology. This minimization is needed to carve out a domain in which structuralism can be declared completely effective, even though it has strictly nothing to say about undifferentiation and the undifferentiated.

The present discussion has bearing on literary criticism. Literary structuralists take for granted that their object is sufficiently defined as differentiation, as the elaboration of a significant structure. What about those writers, Shakespeare, for instance, who are obsessed with chaos, with the destruction of institutions and hierarchies, the reversal and obliteration of even sexual identities, with countless phenomena which amount, in other words, to a dissolving of differences? Can a methodology which cancels out all that hope to reach anything truly Shakespearean? Lévi-Strauss, at least, is not blind to the problem even though he does not tackle it. He treats with open contempt and disgust all that big messy nonsense that lies too obviously beyond the grasp of his method. Literary structuralists have remained unaware of the difficulty; they take it for granted that great literary works are as alien to undifferentiation as Lévi-Strauss hopes myths are—already falsely in my view. Structuralism would be useful if it led critics to some real questioning of the undifferentiated. What is its status in the work of a writer like Shakespeare?

Is it really that big messy nonsense from which primitives and structuralists alike prefer to keep away, for fear it might contaminate them? In Shakespeare, as in the Greeks, the undifferentiated is closely associated with conflict. If this association is never given its due, it is partly, no doubt, because our minds rebel against it. To us, conflict is a matter of differences.

There is nothing irrational about the Shakespearean view. Desire is mimetic. It always focuses on some object already desired by the model and it necessarily brings disharmony and rivalry. *Troilus and Cressida* is obviously concerned with mimetic desire. There is nothing spontaneous in the passion of the two lovers. We might call them complete phonies if the standard by which they will be so branded, spontaneous passion, were not itself suspect of being the fruit of some mimetic suggestion. The Greek army is falling apart under the strains of mimetic rivalry. *Troilus and Cressida* is also a play in which culture is defined as a sytem of differences, of *degrees*, Shakespeare says, held together by Degree with a capital D. This common differential principle is a purely social transcendence. What we have here is a striking example of a structuralism *avant la lettre*, with one major discrepancy which is that Shakespeare is less concerned with systems than with their destruction, through mimetic rivalry.

Shakespeare talks of a shaking, a "wizarding" and finally a collapse of Degree which takes place through *hubris*, inordinate individual ambition that tries to appropriate Degree itself: this would be a neat trick, indeed, if it could be done but Degree vanishes as it becomes an object of rivalry, being nothing, really, but the mysterious absence of such destructive rivalry in times other than the crisis. *Hubris* and mimetic desire are one, in the sense that whoever appears to lay his hands on Degree becomes both the model and the rival. Mimetic rivalry, thus, is a quest for Difference that destroys whatever cultural reality there is to differences. Mimetic *hubris* is the equalizer *par excellence*, all the more powerful for going undetected. The end result of the struggle is the stupid reciprocity of reprisals between undifferentiated antagonists who go mad as they see Degree itself oscillate faster and faster from one to the other.

These antagonists are the protagonists of tragedy and comedy. We may define their relationship as one of *doubles* in the sense of a true reciprocity and concrete identity, a sense completely alien to the notion of doubles in Romantic literature, in Rank's essay on the double, or to Freudian narcissism.

When the Greeks, when Shakespeare, when Molière adapt a mythical theme, the differences which remain immutable and sacrosanct with the structuralists tend to dissolve into conflicts of doubles. This is the better interpretation, obviously so in the case of such fake specificities as mythical twins, often plainly produced through some divine intervention, a disguise, for instance, or a supernatural insemination (or both as in Amphytrion). The same goes for plagues and other scourges, for man-eating dragons and monsters of diverse kinds. Structuralism has nothing to say about the universality of these themes. We may assume that great tragedy and comedy revivify some crisis of degree from which myth has emerged in the first place. Shakespeare not only dissolves differences into crisis but, as he does it, he explains what he is doing. That is why, in *Troilus and Cressida*, to my mind at least, he is the greatest mythologist and interpreter of the Greeks ever.

Literary structuralism does just the opposite. It loses the violence of the doubles; it is quite literally mythical in the sense that it redifferentiates once more, just as mythology does, what the tragic writer takes such pains to undifferentiate.

Structuralism claims that its view of difference is truly scientific. But in the Lévi-Strauss of *Mythologiques*, no distinction is made between two types of differences which science, it would appear, cannot afford to confuse: 1) the difference between a real eagle and a real crow, 2) the difference between the two *moieties*, or the two *clans* of the eagle and of the crow. Lévi-Strauss will say the same thing of all these differences, that they are part and parcel of the "human mind."

If we choose science and objectivity, shouldn't we say that the difference between the real eagle and the real crow is part of nature before being a part of our minds? If we do, we immediately realize that the difference between the two *moieties* is something else again. As the scientist looks at the two *moieties*, he will surely find that they must be defined not by their differences but by their identities, or at least their similarities, in all possible areas, such as demography, institutions, even the space they occupy, even sometimes their physical shape. These identities are perpetuated by an explicit or *de facto* reciprocity in all types of exchange, matrimonial, economic, etc. This does not mean that the difference between the *moieties* is merely "subjective" or a matter of pure "classification"; it is experienced by the natives, even though in religious life as elsewhere reciprocity dominates. It is not without reason that the first explorers who discovered the *moieties* chose such a word for them, designating in them two *moitiés*, two identical halves of a single whole.

Historically, no doubt, all human cultures have tried to convince themselves and others that the differences they set up are as objective, stable and permanent as the differences between natural species. In this respect, totemism is exemplary. It exemplifies vividly what might be called, to use a Sartrian expression, the "project" of all human culture. The question is: should a scientific anthropology ratify and perpetuate that project? When it does so, of course, anthropology has not only totemism and mythology on its side but all of philosophy, implicitly or explicitly. It is Thomas Aquinas, I believe, who says somewhere that the differences between angels, if not yet human individuals,[1] are equivalent to the differences between species in the rest of nature. This of course is the type of statement a Kierkegaard would eagerly take up. And he did, only to be applauded by the French Heideggerian Jean Baufret who gives his imprimatur to the doctrine in his *Introduction aux philosophies de l'existence*: "things and animals are above all the representatives of a species whereas in man the reverse is true."[2] One wonders what meaning can be attached to such a statement. Biologically and culturally, individual men are much less autonomous than most individual animals of a same species. As for animals of different species, they usually treat or disregard each other in a way which men could not imitate, even for a single day, without endangering their survival. If something is specifically human, it is a mutual dependence with the consequence that human relations must include a good deal of reciprocity, reaching down to the most essential and intimate aspects of human existence.

Does this last observation contradict the universality of cultural differentiation? Rather than a mere contradiction, what we should perceive at this juncture may well be the essential paradox of human culture. In all human culture, reciprocity must be there, and it always is, but it is also inevitably covered up, at least in part, as well as distorted and often effectively suppressed.

Why? If the crisis of degree is taken not as an imaginary but as a real threat, an answer may suggest itself. Man cannot survive without reciprocity but, historically at least, he cannot survive either when reciprocity becomes too explicit. When mythical differences weaken, reciprocity breaks out in the open as the reciprocity of conflict rather than as the reciprocity of peace. Mimetic competition becomes so acute that social life itself is endangered and ritual rigidities come back to the fore, differences are reborn from their ashes.

Lévi-Strauss's statement about cultural differences being in the human mind cannot mean, of course, that cultures never die. It would be simply absurd. In order to become meaningful, if not unequivocal, this statement must signify that historically at least, men have never managed without cultural differences. Thus interpreted, this statement opens the possibility of *crises of Degree*, of a temporary dissolving of differences out of which these same differences or, if not the same, others will be somehow generated and stabilized once more. The question of cultural genesis, at least in relative terms, is not as farfetched as it appears; we are dealing not with history in the traditional sense but with a generative process which, in all likelihood, must be more standardized than the differences it produces. Myth and ritual tell us that differences are generated from that state of undifferentiation which we now identify with the reciprocal violence of the doubles. If we consider both this grounding in the uniform doubles and the fact that differences vary from culture to culture, we must wonder if there is not something random and haphazard in their production. Judging from the elaborate means sometimes devised in order to introduce an element of chance in the selection of the sacrificial victim, we must assume that ritualism may sometimes correctly observe this cultural throw of the dice and try to reproduce it while it mistakenly interprets it as an expression of some divine will.

The primordial event must be a murder, just as Freud magnificently surmised, not, however, the murder of a specific and identifiable individual as he erroneously added, but the murder of a random victim which must appear as the embodiment of the whole crisis, the sum total of all monstrous undifferentiation through a process of collective transfer made possible by the mimetic undifferentiation of the doubles.

It is thus, I believe, that totemic ancestors, gods and demons are generated. It is thus that Degree is restored, that the Difference is stabilized once more between a now sacralized violence and the community. All this, of course, is a complex hypothesis for the detailed exposition of which I refer my readers to *Violence and the Sacred*.[3] Once this hypothesis is clearly understood, the evidence from myth and ritual will be found, I believe, overwhelming.

I am well aware of the problems and objections this hypothesis must raise. Some have already been answered. Others are not suitable to the present occasion. I warn my readers, therefore, that a certain familiarity with *Violence and the Sacred* is necessary to a full understanding of the following—and preceding—remarks.

In order to prove its merit, the hypothesis should help demonstrate, among other things, that the thrust of our knowledge is in its direction. This is an enormous task, of course, which cannot be attempted here. We may think it impossible, on the grounds, perhaps, that anthropology and the other social sciences are retreating more and more from all broad questioning in the religious field, but we must be aware that progress, in such matters, may be realized in roundabout fashion and in unlikely fields, like literary and philosophical criticism.

Among other possibilities, I would like to single out, briefly, what looks to me like two outstanding instances of such progress. The first is *Anatomy of Criticism*. Northrop Frye includes among his "archetypes" the "figure of a typical or random victim" which

begins to crystallize in domestic tragedy as it deepens in ironic tone. We may call this typical victim the *pharmakos* or scapegoat. We meet a *pharmakos* figure in Hawthorne's Hester Prynne, in Melville's Billy Budd, in Hardy's Tess, in the Septimus of *Mrs. Dalloway*, in stories of persecuted Jews and Negroes, in stories of artists whose genius makes them Ishmaels of a bourgeois society. The *pharmakos* is neither innocent nor guilty. He is innocent in the sense that what happens to him is far greater than anything he has done provokes, like the mountaineer whose shout brings down an avalanche. He is guilty in the sense that he is a member of a guilty society, . . . or living in a world where such injustices are an inescapable part of existence.[4]

Just as Frazer gathered ritual analogies around the Jewish figure of the scapegoat, Northrop Frye gathers literary analogies around the Greek figure of the *pharmakos*. The reasons for going Greek in literature are as obvious as the reasons for going Jewish in religion but they are no more compelling in one case than in the other. The English word *scapegoat* designates a particular ritual form as well as the spontaneous violence that strengthens a threatened community at the expense of a random victim. Curiously enough, neither Frazer nor the Frazerians ever pondered the relationship between these two acceptations and their possible implications for cultural forms. The *pharmakos* of Northrop Frye inherits this double semantic polarity which remains unexplored. The need for radical analysis is hidden behind the catchall notion of "archetype."

At one extreme, the *pharmakos* looks like a literary theme, a traditional *topos*, readily identified by ordinary scholarly procedures. At the other extreme, the *pharmakos* is the non-ritual one, the random victim of spontaneous violence. A propos of the mystery story, for instance, the so-called "thriller," Frye writes that its "growing brutality" comes "as close as it is normally possible for art to come to the pure self-righteousness of the lynching mob."[5] Frye's most interesting insights, at least to me, cannot be subsumed under the ritual heading of the *pharmakos*. They are an implicit revelation of the lynching mob as a generative force behind all myth and ritual. In the demonic aspects of literature, "the social relation is that of the mob, which is essentially human society looking for a *pharmakos*, and the mob is often identified with some sinister animal image such as the hydra, Virgil's *Fama*, or its development in Spenser's Blatant Beast."[6]

The reason for which authors like Frye or Frazer privilege institutions like the *pharmakos*, or the Jewish *scapegoat* is, of course, that more of the original mechanism is visible in these rituals than in more recent forms; the writer's intuition gropes toward that mechanism itself; failing as it does to apprehend this mechanism, it falls back on the ritual forms that are closest to it.

Is there a connection between the "pure self-righteousness of the lynching mob" and the fact that the collective violence comes out as something other than itself, an animal image perhaps, or, why not, a plague-ridden city which can be cured only by the expulsion of a parricidal son? A lynching mob must believe in the malevolence of its victim. Which means that a lynching process described by the lynchers themselves must necessarily come out as something other than itself, as the Oedipus myth for instance. The reference to the *pharmakos* archetype, here, is only indirectly suggestive, and it is so for reasons which can become fully intelligible only through the generative effect of the single victim, if we assume that it is present behind everything.

The generative effect which remains for the most part hidden in

Anatomy of Criticism is more fully uncovered in the work of Jacques Derrida, notably in an essay which I read, of course, in the context of the above remarks, "Plato's Pharmacy."[7] Derrida shows, quite convincingly I believe, that, in the text of Plato, the difference between Socrates and the Sophists results from an arbitrary expulsion of the latter, invisible to both the author and the reader because it is effected through an unconsciously systematic use of certain semantic ambiguities. The pivotal word, lo and behold, is the word *pharmakos* itself and its cognates, notably *pharmakon* which means both good and bad drug, medicine and poison. The drug can work either way, just like violence itself which is poison but may become its own cure through the single-victim effect and the ritual reenactments of that effect.

Plato keeps shifting between the two opposite and yet related acceptations of *pharmakon* in the manner best calculated to confound the Sophists and justify Socrates, thus differentiating a relationship that is truly undifferentiated, a relationship of hostile reciprocity in that crisis of Degree that is Athens' golden age. In the case of physical violence, the cure is genuine insofar as the community is truly re-unified against the single victim, insofar, therefore, as the evil qualities of this random victim are unanimously and uncritically accepted. The same is true in the case of the Platonic text, except, of course, for the purely verbal means of the philosophical expulsion. Western philosophy, forever "Socratic" and "Platonic," has always depended for its existence on the expulsion of its sophistic double, an expulsion which remains unperceived as long as it is sanctioned by the unanimous consent of all philosophers. After more than two millennia, this unanimity has come to an end, first with Nietzsche, now with Derrida's "déconstruction." What is revealed is the dependence of philosophy on the same generative force, really, as sacrifice, a force that retains its binding power only for so long as the people bound are unanimously blind to its arbitrariness. The fact that we are dealing with a sacrificial displacement is spectacularly underlined, of course, by the pivotal role of *pharmakos*, a word which originally designates a human victim. Even though the displacement, substitution or metaphor, if you will, does not actually depend on any specific word, Plato's recourse to *pharmakos* is no mere coincidence. Even in the modern uses of *pharmakos*, or *scapegoat*, we have already observed a double semantic polarity so slippery as to provide an ever-ready instrument, a perfect cover and therefore, built into the language, a permanent incitement to the type of operation described by Derrida.

Frye seems fully cognizant of the sacrificial displacement that constitutes certain literary genres. In his eyes, this element of substitution makes literature more civilized than sacrifice. This is certainly correct and the terroristic conclusions some might be inclined to draw from analyses such as Derrida's are sacrificially regressive in their nihilistic self-righteousness. Frye is correct, therefore, but only up to a point; the vicarious element is not reserved to literature or baseball. It is already present even in the most gruesome forms of sacrifice. Being continuous in both directions, the chain of substitution may, at any time, reverse itself and all complacency is, to say the least, premature.

Are the present suggestions a blasphemy against literature? Would they, if followed, impoverish literary studies by limiting them to the identification of the right victim, as charged recently by a critic of my hypothesis?

Earlier, to reach our definition of the doubles, we had to resort to Shakespeare. Among modern critics, the dogma of difference remains too powerful for a recognition of the doubles. Shakespeare knows that the doubles can be reconciled only at the expense of a common victim and that is sacrifice. *Romeo and Juliet* is a case in point. The Montagues and the Capulets are the perfect doubles, totally undifferentiated in their stupid antagonism. A plague on both their houses! There is only one idea in the short prologue of the play, and it is repeated twice: the lovers, we are told,

> Do with their death bury their parents' strife.
> The fearful passage of their death-marked love,
> And the continuance of their parents' rage,
> Which, but their children's end, naught could remove,
> Is now the two hours' traffic of our stage.

Can one object that the absence of the word "sacrifice" makes my reading questionable? Let any sceptics move from the prologue to the conclusion where the same idea is repeated a third time and this time the word "sacrifice" is included. Talking to Capulet, Montague, or is it Capulet talking to Montague, defines the two lovers as "Poor sacrifices of our enmity."

There can be no such thing, of course, as a full and unambiguous revelation of the sacrificial mechanism. This revelation will immediately be turned into a reverse sacrifice. Let us suppose that Shakespeare is aware of this fact and annoyed by it. We may find that the enigmatic relationship between *Romeo and Juliet* on the one hand and, on the other, the play that immediately follows, *A Midsummer Night's Dream*, becomes intelligible.

In each play we have lovers and their predicament is the same. Two of the lovers in *A Midsummer Night's Dream* are separated by a father. In "Pyramus and Thisbe," the play within the play, the resemblance with *Romeo and Juliet* is closer still; it is their parents' strife, we are told, that erected the wall that keeps the lovers apart.

As we look closer, however, we must realize that, in all instances, the paternal obstacle is a sham. The lovers are left free to spend all their time together; they get into trouble, no doubt, but trouble of their own making: they are little erotic snobs who reduce each other to hysterics with their sado-masochistic shenanigans. They are a caricature and "Pyramus and Thisbe" is a caricature of this caricature, the mirror in which the protagonists are too stupid to recognize themselves.

Pyramus and Thisbe first lament loudly their cruel separation. Tired after awhile of their own wailing, they remember that lovers should have rendezvous. Theirs poses no more problem, it now appears, than a night in a motel for two of our horrendously oppressed teenagers. Pyramus asks: "Will you meet me straightway at Ninny's tomb?" Thisbe answers: "Tide life, Tide death! I come without delay!" (Act V, scene 1). The lion is not the cause of the disaster. Its roar is truly as gentle as that of the nightingale. The cause is a ludicrous misunderstanding, a stupid jumping to conclusion on the part of Pyramus who thinks Thisbe is dead. This ending is not even a parody of the one in *Romeo and Juliet.* It is exactly the same course of events, the same melodramatic nonsense, and Shakespeare is making fun of himself. We feel Romeo and Juliet are somehow murdered, their blood cries vengeance and yet they alone are responsible for their own death. The only one who shares in their romantic ineptitude is their asinine counsel, Friar Laurence. All are more or less guilty of generalized hysteria, compounded perhaps by a secret desire to monopolize the limelight.

What does it mean? The critics are still afraid to ask. They are afraid to let the two plays confront each other, as if both might be lost. Shakespeare knows that fiction is and must be a lie. The audience is looking for its *pharmakos*, as Northrop Frye tells us, and even the tiniest little sign in one direction or another will send everybody charging like raving buffaloes, so long as someone is there to be trampled to death. The doubles will be tilted one way or the other; better give them a strong and obvious tilt, in order not to be trampled oneself, or completely ignored, which is the same thing, really, for a playwright.

The truth is also there, not even hidden, in full view, enormously visible and yet invisible, as if Shakespeare had wagered to some friend he could make his audience swallow even the most outlandish nonsense.

From the very beginning, *Romeo and Juliet* would have to be read and obviously was read as the glorification of the young against the old, as the first great saga of the generation gap. Revolted by this first outpouring of Romantic self-righteousness, Shakespeare wrote *A Midsummer Night's Dream* as an antidote. The nature and circumstances of the comedy—and of all comedies—are such that he had to make his point covertly once more, and he turned this apparent liability into pure genius, devising his two-tier arrangement whereby the fantastic fairy tales and monstrous weddings on the upper level are secretly generated by the mad antics and wild scapegoating on the lower level.

In an age like ours, when the excesses of the youth cult are reaching tidal wave proportions, the secretly implacable comedy is the more refreshing play, but turning it into mere moralizing would be as un-Shakespearean as the opposite. If we look for Shakespeare himself, we will find him at the exact place where all the self-serving causes and ideological slants cancel each other out. He is absolutely not *relevant*.

In both plays, we must note, the author is visibly haunted by how little it takes to reverse the meaning of a text, to turn heroes into villains and villains into heroes, tragedy into comedy and comedy into tragedy. "A mote will turn the balance, which Pyramus, which Thisbe is the better" (Act V, scene 1). To change black into white, all you need is a half-turn of some Janus-like *pharmakos* or maybe a single comma moved an inch or two. Through mistaken punctuation, Quince's entire prologue, meant to be a compliment to Theseus and guests, turns into an insult. Such is the destiny of all language. In *Romeo and Juliet* the theme of the ambivalent drug remains trivial and Shakespeare should be blamed for giving it undue prominence unless we read it as an allegory of drama itself, a fitting one in view of the ending. Friar Laurence warns us about drugs: the most infinitesimal change in the dose and the substance that cured becomes the substance that kills. Like the dramatist, Friar Laurence is a sorcerer's apprentice, a philosophical pusher of sorts who hopes he has his dramatic cuisine well in hand. Everything should come out all right in the end. Just as the Friar said, however, the unholy brew has a power that cannot be controlled. Saying it so well in the first place, and being fooled anyway, only turns the Friar into a bigger fool.

Oh, mickle is the powerful grace that lies
In herbs, plants, stones, and their true qualities.
For naught so vile that on the earth doth live,
But to the earth some special good doth give;
Nor aught so good but, strained from that fair use,
Revolts from true birth, stumbling on abuse.
Virtue itself turns vice, being misapplied,
And vice sometime's by action dignified.
Within the infant rind of this small flower
Poison had residence, and medicine power.
For this, being smelt, with that part cheers each part,
Being tasted, slays all senses with the heart.
Two such opposed kings encamp them still
In man as well as herbs, grace and rude will;
And where the worser is predominant,
Full soon the canker death eats up the plant.
(*Romeo and Juliet*, Act II, scene 3)

In the explicitly sacrificial context of the play, none of this can be co-incidental. Friar Laurence sounds like Derrida's "Pharmacy" in a nutshell. Will a critic do to Shakespeare what Derrida has done to Plato? Shakespeare has already done it himself. We might see him perhaps as a Socrates who would be his own Aristophanes and more besides, as a Plato who would be his own Derrida. Where does that leave the rest of us?

CHAPTER 5

The Myth of Oedipus,
the Truth of Joseph

The city of Thebes is ravaged by a plague epidemic. A religious oracle announces that one single individual inside the city is reponsible for the disaster: he has offended the gods by killing his father and marrying his mother. A culprit is sought and a culprit is found. He is the new king. He had no knowledge of his own horrendous crimes and yet he really committed them. As a child, he had been cast out by his parents because of an oracle, once again, the same oracle already predicting the very thing that later happened, that he would kill his father and marry his mother. This he finally did when he returned to Thebes as an adult and a total stranger. Once more, as a result, Oedipus was cast out of his community.

A close examination will reveal similarities between this myth and the story of Joseph. Joseph had twelve brothers and Oedipus had none, but both heroes were rejected by their respective families, Oedipus by his parents and Joseph by his brothers. In both stories the hero was cast out: first, out of the community to which he belonged by birth; second, by the community to which he belonged by adoption.

Both Oedipus after his return to Thebes and Joseph when he was taken to Egypt can be described as highly successful immigrants. Through their skill in interpreting riddles, they both resolved difficult problems and, as a result, they both became great leaders. Oedipus was king of Thebes and Joseph something like the prime minister of Egypt.

Both heroes had to exercise their freshly acquired power against a natural disaster. In the case of Oedipus, it was the plague epidemic; in the case of Joseph, it was a great famine.

Oedipus, however, was guilty of parricide and incest. Joseph never committed such crimes but there is an incident in his career quite similar to the incest of Oedipus. The wife of his Egyptian master and benefactor falsely accused the young man of trying to seduce her. Her husband had treated Joseph as a son, and Joseph should have respected her as much as his own mother. The accusation is somewhat reminiscent of the mother incest. Because Joseph was a foreigner and the woman an Egyptian, the Egyptians believed her, and Joseph was imprisoned for awhile.

There are close similarities, therefore, and I think that we have to see the similarities rather than disguise them if we are to see the difference, the one difference that matters enormously.

Even as a little child Oedipus is already potentially guilty of the parricide and incest committed later. Therefore, his parents had a good reason to cast him out. The Thebans later on had a good reason to cast Oedipus out a second time. His presence among them was responsible for a plague epidemic.

In the case of Joseph, the matter is quite different. The brothers had no reason to cast Joseph out. They were simply jealous of him. The Egyptians had no reason to imprison Joseph. The wife of Joseph's benefactor was jealous of him, we are told.

As far as the plague is concerned, Oedipus is supposed to be guilty. Joseph might have been suspected by the foolish Egyptians of being responsible for the famine, but far from being guilty, the story of Joseph goes out of its way to tell us, he alone correctly predicted the catastrophe; and his excellent policy saved the country.

In both stories, two similar heroes are placed in similar circumstances and the consequences are similar up to a point. But in regard to the role of the hero, the interpretation of the myth and the interpretation of the Bible are poles apart.

Do the communities to which Oedipus and Joseph belong act justly when they expel these heroes from their midst? This is the question that I think dominates both texts, but it is only implicit in the Oedipus myth because the silent answer of the myth is always *yes*. Whatever Oedipus suffers, he suffers justly. In the Bible the question becomes fully explicit because the answer is a resounding *no*. Whatever Joseph suffers, he suffers unjustly; he is a victim of jealousy.

But what difference does it make, the reader might ask, if one story takes the side of the community against the victim, whereas the other takes the side of the victim against the violent community? These are only stories, after all. If the mythical story is fictional, is not the biblical story fictional as well? If the Oedipus story is a myth, the Joseph story may be a more humane, a more ethical myth. But nevertheless it must be a myth. This is the reasoning that most scholars would use in the face of what I say.

The difference between mythology and the Bible strikes us as ethical. The Bible is more concerned with victims than mythology is and with the possibility that individuals might be unjustly victimized. This ethical difference is obvious enough to be widely, although not universally, acknowledged. But even those who acknowledge it do not always feel that it is terribly important.

It is often regarded as inessential and superficial in our world because of the tremendous emphasis our modern society places on intellectual achievements and especially on scientific achievements. The essential opposition for our society is between science and mythology, and mythology here means religion. Most students of religion would maintain that the ethical difference in favor of the Bible is unrelated to the type of truth that the modern world is after, the social sciences, for instance. The Joseph story may be a more comforting myth but it must be just as fictional as the Oedipus myth.

I think this position is wrong. I believe that the difference in the Joseph story has implications of humaneness, of course, but they are not the only ones. They are absolutely one with enormous implications for knowledge in a scientific sense. I think that they are a revelation of the deceptive and violent nature of mythology.

In order to make my point clear, I will call attention once more to the themes of the Oedipus myth. Those who know the history of mob violence in the Middle Ages, or mob violence anywhere in the world, will realize that there is a great similarity between the themes of this myth and the distorted view that violent mobs have of their own victims.

During much of Western history, especially in times of great disasters such as plague epidemics or famines, many helpless individuals were the objects of a two-pronged accusation. They were accused of external moral turpitude in the style of the parricide and incest of Oedipus, and simultaneously they were accused of having caused the general disaster. The two accusations were connected to each other in the same irrational manner that they are in the Oedipus myth.

During the great medieval plague epidemics, for instance, the Jews were often the victims of these accusations, and so were the foreigners and strangers who happened to find themselves in some panic-stricken town. A century or two later, the same pattern of accusation reappears in the great epidemic of witch-hunting in the Western world. We find it again today in slightly different but still recognizable forms, in the totalitarian repression of dissidents.

During great disasters, irrational mobs turn violent against victims they regard as guilty even though they cannot be responsible for vast social catastrophes. Through its recourse to arbitrary violence, the helpless populace manages to forget its helplessness in the face of uncontrollable events.

When we understand this, we see that the victims are scapegoats. We are not really thinking of the ritual in Leviticus 16; we simply mean that the victims are innocent, that they are picked arbitrarily by their persecutors, who manage to convince themselves that they are guilty of Oedipus-like crimes.

Let us suppose that a mob has just performed a lynching of the type I alluded to. If you asked the participants to tell you what really happened, their account would resemble the Oedipus myth or countless other myths.

It makes sense, therefore, to suppose that the Oedipus myth must have originated in some collective violence of the type I have described. The fact that we have no historical proof is not very important. It does not matter where and when these things happened. What matters is that one can make sense out of all the themes and that one can bring everything together. Both Oedipus and Joseph are strangers in their communities. An additional clue, I think, in favor of the genesis I have just outlined is provided by the lameness of Oedipus. In a panicked community, an individual's chances of being selected as a victim are greatly increased if, in addition to being a highly visible and powerful stranger who became successful too fast, he is afflicted with some physical infirmity that the multitude regards as uncanny, such as Oedipus's lameness. The conjunction of themes that we find in mythology cannot be the product of a peaceful and purely poetic imagination.

Historians are fully aware of this when they deal with historical documents, but mythologists have not yet become aware of the possibility that mythology as a whole could be tied to the same type of phenomenon. If I were to examine other myths here, we would discover that they too very much resemble the perspective of deluded persecutors. My conclusion, therefore, is that mythology and the mythological religions are founded on this type of violence, which has an enormous cultural importance in primitive society.

A graphic way to illustrate the theory I have just outlined would be to take a myth and rewrite it in such a way as to rectify those points in the myth, and those points only, that are distorted by the blind hostility of a community against its scapegoats. It would not be an entirely new story. It would resemble a myth, therefore. Many things would remain the same. Only those aspects of the myth would be changed, I repeat, that prevent us from recognizing an innocent scapegoat in a mythical hero. There would still be a disaster such as a plague epidemic or a famine, but the hero would not be responsible for it. He would be accused of serious crimes such as incest or adultery, but he would not be guilty of them. This new story would not pretend that a scapegoating never happened; it would present it as unjust, as prompted by individual and collective envy against a too-successful stranger. This story already exists, of course. It is the Joseph story.

At every turn, the biblical story ridicules the nonsensical evidence against the scapegoat which we have in mythology and replaces it with arguments favorable to the victim. The repudiated mythology is repudiated as a lie. Each time Joseph becomes a victim, either of his brothers or of the Egyptians, the accusations against him are shown to be delusions arising from envy and hatred. So we have both the account given by the brothers to the father and the exposé of that account. After getting rid of their brother, they tell their father that he was killed by a wild beast. In many myths the scapegoat process is described in terms of destruction by a group of animals that hunt together or by a single animal. The brothers' story is, I believe, such a myth.

It is not only the Joseph story in the Bible that repudiates the deceptions and violence of myth. I could go to other biblical stories and show every time that the absolutely essential difference I have been discussing is present. I would never say that this is *the* truth of the Bible, its whole truth, but its *anthropological* truth. The Bible stories say what I have tried to say, but much better. They are a more graphic, a more intelligible instrument for destroying the credibility of mythology than any theoretical construction. They expose the belief on which mythology relies as a coherent and cruel system of representation. The mythical hero is guilty and punished rightly even if he is a god and even if he later restores order, whereas the biblical figure is punished wrongly; he is innocent.

The Bible itself is perfectly aware of its opposition to all mythological religions. It brands them as idolatrous, and I think that the revelation of scapegoat delusion in mythology is an essential part of the fight against idolatry. Here we could go, for instance, to the story of Cain and Abel, and compare it to the myth of Romulus and Remus. In the story of Cain and Abel, the murder of one brother by the other is presented as a crime that is also the founding of a community. But in the Roman story this foundation story cannot be viewed as a crime. It is a legitimate action by Romulus. The point of view of the Bible about such events differs enormously from that of myth.

I do not believe, therefore, that the theory of mythology I have outlined here is new. I do not think that it is mine at all. I think that it is nothing more than a weak, scholarly translation and transposition of the anthropological content of the Bible. I also believe that the ability we have in the modern world not to be fooled by scapegoat persecutions of the type I have discussed, those in the Middle Ages, or the ones today in the totalitarian world—our ability not to be deceived by such collective persecution comes from the Bible. The fact that many people are fooled but that ultimately in our world the truth of persecution always comes out is the one thing that makes us entirely different from all previous societies. It is not the fruit of unaided human reason as the *philosophes* of the eighteenth century and the humanists would like us to believe, but it is the influence of the Bible on us, an influence that is not perceived most of the time.

Comparative religion has failed to acknowledge the superiority of the biblical perspective because it has remained lost in a dream of "science and objectivity" which, if interpreted in a certain way, is the modern myth par excellence, the myth of a middle ground between the persecutors and the victims that cancels out the differences between the infinite diversity of the persecutors' delusions and the uniqueness of the victims' truth. Not only is the Bible not myth; it is the source of whatever "demythologization" has occurred in our world and will occur in the future. At the same time the Bible is aware of the enormous ethical demand that this makes on humanity.

To conclude, I will turn to the last episode, the last moment in the Joseph story, which is so beautiful and reveals so clearly that the question of the victim paying for the others in an unjust fashion is really the subject of the story. In the last episode, we see Joseph, as prime minister, engineer a kind of scapegoat testing of his brothers. He wanted to test the possibility of a change of heart in them. They had first come to Egypt in order to beg for grain because in Palestine they had none, and Joseph, now the prime minister, in charge of everything, had warned them that they would not be supplied with that grain a second time unless they brought with them their youngest brother, Benjamin, whom they had left at home. Besides Joseph, Benjamin was the only other son of Jacob by his most cherished wife, Rachel, and they did not want anything to happen to him, especially anything of the sort that had already happened to Joseph.

But the famine becomes so serious that the brothers come back, and this time they return with Benjamin. On Joseph's orders a precious cup that belonged to him is placed in Benjamin's bag. When the eleven brothers are searched on their way back to Palestine, the youngest appears guilty of theft and Joseph announces that he will be detained. At this point, Judah, one of the ten remaining brothers, one of the ten who had expelled Joseph in the first place, offers to take Benjamin's place as a prisoner of Joseph, for fear, he says, that his father might die of grief. This dedication of Judah stands in symmetrical opposition to the original deed of collective violence which it cancels out and reveals. As he hears Judah, Joseph is moved to tears and identifies himself.

This conclusion is profoundly moving because it unites the ethical and the powerful intellectual dimensions of the Bible. It tells us that the Bible looks forward to a world where all men will treat each other not as rival brothers but as real brothers, a world in which the cultural violence that has divided and separated human communities in the past will be entirely revealed and abolished.

Notes

INTRODUCTION

1. "Chu-bu and Sheemish" (1912), reprinted in Lord Dunsany, *Beyond the Fields We Know*, ed. L. Carter (London: Pan/Ballantine, 1972), pp. 245–50.

2. "*Oedipus* Analyzed," in this volume.

3. Ibid.

4. "The Plague in Literature and Myth," in René Girard, *"To double business bound": Essays on Literature, Mimesis, and Anthropology* (Baltimore: Johns Hopkins University Press, 1978), p. 136.

5. Thucydides, *The Peloponnesian War*, Book 2, excerpted in L. Berkowitz and T. F. Brunner, eds., *Oedipus Tyrannus* (New York: Norton, 1970), p. 39. Helene P. Foley notes for her part that Thucydides analyzed the Athenian plague "in terms that suit Girard's," linking it "to the breakdown of the social and religious order"; see Helene P. Foley, *Ritual Irony: Poetry and Sacrifice in Euripides* (Ithaca: Cornell University Press, 1985), p. 59.

6. Frederick Ahl, *Sophocles' Oedipus: Evidence and Self-Conviction* (Ithaca: Cornell University Press, 1991), p. 35.

7. René Girard, *Violence and the Sacred*, trans. P. Gregory (Baltimore: Johns Hopkins University Press, 1977), p. 76.

8. Ahl, p. 46.

9. Ibid., p. 68.

10. Suzanne Saïd, "La tragédie de la vengeance," in G. Courtois, ed., *La vengeance* (Paris: Cujas, 1984), 4: 64.

11. Ibid., 4: 63.

12. John Jones, *On Aristotle and Greek Tragedy* (New York: Oxford University Press, 1962), excerpted in Berkowitz and Brunner, p. 146.

13. Géza Roheim, "Teiresias and Other Seers," *Psychoanalytic Review* 33 (1946): 314–34; cited in Richard S. Caldwell, "The Blindness of Oedipus," *International Review of Psycho-Analysis* 1 (1974): 209.

14. In a series of medieval variants on the Oedipus story centered on the legendary Pope Gregory, the incestuous hero is himself the product of an incestuous union. See Lowell Edmunds, *Oedipus: The Ancient Legend and Its Later Analogues* (Baltimore: Johns Hopkins University Press, 1985), p. 20; see also Thomas Mann's novel on the same theme, *The Holy Sinner* (*Der Erwählte*).

15. Maria Daraki, *Dionysos* (Paris: Arthaud, 1985), p. 135.

16. "*Oedipus* Analyzed."

17. "Symmetry and Dissymmetry in the Myth of Oedipus," in this volume.

18. Jean-Pierre Vernant, "Ambiguity and Reversal: On the Enigmatic Structure of *Oedipus Rex*," trans. P. du Bois, *New Literary History* 9 (1978): 493 (the translation of Tiresias's words has been modified to restore the original reference to Oedipus's equality with himself; cf. Jean-Pierre Vernant, "Ambiguïté et renversement: Sur la structure énigmatique d'*Œdipe-Roi*" (1970), in Jean-Pierre Vernant and Pierre Vidal-Naquet, *Mythe et tragédie en Grèce ancienne* (Paris: Maspero, 1981), p. 128.

19. J. T. Sheppard, *The Oedipus Tyrannus of Sophocles* (Cambridge: Cambridge University Press, 1920), excerpted in Berkowitz and Brunner, p. 192.

20. On this point, see Jacques-Jude Lépine, "Agatha Christie: Maîtresse du soupçon," *Stanford French Review* 16, no. 1 (1992): 95–109.

21. Northrop Frye, *Anatomy of Criticism* (Princeton: Princeton University Press, 1971), p. 47.

22. "The Myth of Oedipus, the Truth of Joseph," in this volume.

23. Ibid.

24. Ibid.

25. "Doubles and the *Pharmakos*," in this volume.

26. "Andrej," translated by R. Pardyjak from N. Kostomarov, *Pamjatniki Starinnoj Russkoj Literatury* ("Monuments of Old Russian Literature," first published in St. Petersburg in 1860), in Edmunds, pp. 188–92.

27. See Edmunds, pp. 202–5. Alain Moreau has located intriguing circumstantial evidence that the original Oedipus story may once have included an episode in which he unwittingly ate his own offspring. Although the existence of such an episode cannot be proven, Moreau concludes that Oedipus's crimes must be understood within a Greek mythic context in which patricide and incest bore a "close, essential and universal" relationship to cannibalism; see Alain Moreau, "A propos d'Œdipe: La liaison entre trois crimes—parricide, inceste et cannibalisme," in S. Saïd et al., *Etudes de littérature ancienne* (Paris: Presses Universitaires de l'Ecole Normale Supérieure, 1979), p. 120.

28. He studied at the venerable Ecole Nationale des Chartes.

29. For an extended comparative analysis of myths and medieval persecution texts, see the first four chapters of René Girard, *The Scapegoat*, trans. Y. Freccero (Baltimore: Johns Hopkins University Press, 1986).

30. "The Myth of Oedipus, the Truth of Joseph."

31. *The Scapegoat*, p. 29; cf. René Girard, *Le bouc émissaire* (Paris: Grasset, 1982), pp. 45–46 (in this and subsequent notes, the reference to the French text is provided whenever an English translation has been modified to better reflect the original meaning).

32. Ahl, p. x.

33. *Violence and the Sacred*, p. 73.

34. Ahl, p. x. For a detailed critique of Ahl's reasoning, see R. Drew Griffith, "Oedipus Pharmakos? Alleged Scapegoating in Sophocles' *Oedipus the King*,"

Phoenix 47, no. 2 (1993): 95–114. But note that Griffith wrongly ascribes to Ahl the thesis that "Oedipus is totally innocent of the crime" and "never laid a finger on Laius" (Griffith, p. 95). While Ahl casts doubt on the belief "that Oedipus' guilt is proved" (p. 265), he does not claim to prove his innocence, suggesting instead that Sophocles has made Oedipus's guilt or innocence an open question.

35. Sandor Goodhart, "*Lêistas Ephaske*: Oedipus and Laius' Many Murderers," *diacritics* 8, no. 1 (March 1978): 58; this essay has since been reprinted in Sandor Goodhart, *Sacrificing Commentary: Reading the End of Literature* (Baltimore: Johns Hopkins University Press, 1996).

36. Ahl, p. 62.

37. Goodhart, pp. 59–60.

38. See lines 1026, 1038–40.

39. Ahl, p. 206.

40. Ibid.

41. R. D. Dawe, *Sophocles: Oedipus Rex* (Cambridge, 1982), p. 192; quoted by Ahl, p. 161.

42. Ahl, pp. 171, 174.

43. Ibid., p. 207.

44. William Chase Greene, "The Murderers of Laius," *Transactions of the American Philological Association* 60 (1929): 81. Greene nonetheless assumes that Oedipus committed both crimes.

45. *The Scapegoat*, pp. 64–65; cf. *Le bouc émissaire*, pp. 94–95.

46. René Girard, *Job: The Victim of His People*, trans. Y. Freccero (Stanford: Stanford University Press, 1987), pp. 35–36.

47. E. F. Watling, *The Theban Plays* (Harmondsworth, Middlesex: Penguin, 1947), p. 59.

48. Michel Foucault, "La vérité et les formes juridiques," *Chimères* 10 (Winter 1990–91): 21 (the text of a lecture originally delivered in Brazil in 1973).

49. Quoted by Goodhart, p. 70, from René Girard, "Dionysus and the Violent Genesis of the Sacred," *boundary* 2 (1977): 487–505; this essay has since been reprinted in J. G. Williams, ed., *The Girard Reader* (New York: Crossroad, 1996).

50. Goodhart, pp. 66, 67.

51. In "Doubles and the *Pharmakos*," Girard credits Shakespeare with devising a "two-tier arrangement," an argument fully developed in René Girard, *A Theater of Envy: William Shakespeare* (New York: Oxford University Press, 1991). In an interview originally published in the same issue of *diacritics* as Goodhart's essay, Girard expressed his own uncertainty regarding a possible parallel between Shakespeare and Sophocles: "I do not find the position of Sophocles as clear as I do that of Shakespeare, perhaps because of the greater cultural distance. I may be mistaken. Sandor Goodhart thinks that Sophocles is as fully in charge as Shakespeare. He may be right" ("An Interview with René Girard," in *"To double business bound,"* p. 223).

52. Ahl, p. 217.

53. *Job*, p. 40; cf. René Girard, *La route antique des hommes pervers* (Paris: Grasset, 1985), pp. 62–63.

54. After he offered up his shorn hair and fingernails, the rain came, ending the drought that had followed his overthrow of the previous ruler. See Marcel Granet, *Danses et légendes de la Chine ancienne* (Paris: Presses Universitaires de France, 1959), 2: 451–52; quoted in Françoise Lauwaert, "Le saint, le boiteux et l'héritier: A propos de la fonction impériale en Chine," *L'Homme* 148 (Oct.–Dec. 1998): 86.

55. Simon Simonse, *Kings of Disaster: Dualism, Centralism and the Scapegoat King in Southeastern Sudan* (Leiden: Brill, 1992): "When the country is hit by disaster or enemies, the King is there to receive the blame. In theory he can be killed for each failure to maintain the community's immunity. In practice the sentence is suspended as long as there is a possibility to restore the relationship between King and people. . . . Negatively his power is defined as the capacity to allow enemies and disasters to enter the community, positively he is the community's patron against these dangers" (p. 428).

56. "Ambiguity and Reversal," pp. 489–90; cf. "Ambiguïté et renversement," pp. 122–23.

57. As a *tyrannos*, a ruler exercising unrestrained power obtained outside of normal legal channels, Oedipus was already well suited to embody disorder. In *Il tiranno e l'eroe: Per un'archeologia del potere nella Grecia antica* (Milan: Bruno Mondadori, 1996), Carmine Catenacci demonstrates a systematic association between tyranny and disordered sexuality (pp. 142–70) and explores the mythic and ritual dimensions of the tyrant's typically violent and untimely end, which he compares to that of a *pharmakos* (pp. 241–55).

58. Jones, *On Aristotle and Greek Tragedy*, in Berkowitz and Brunner, p. 142.

59. See "Doubles and the *Pharmakos*."

60. "The Plague in Literature," p. 146.

61. Ahl, p. 264.

62. A financial panic spreads by contagion, each investor imitating the behavior of the others; see André Orléan, "Money and Mimetic Speculation," trans. M. R. Anspach, in P. Dumouchel, ed., *Violence and Truth* (Stanford: Stanford University Press, 1988), pp. 101–12.

63. David Camroux, "Il nazionalismo corrotto della Malesia," *Le Monde Diplomatique / Il manifesto* (Feb. 1999), p. 13.

64. *Job*, p. 35.

65. François Tricaud, *L'accusation: Recherche sur les figures de l'agression éthique* (Paris: Dalloz, 1977), p. 27.

66. Marie Delcourt, *Œdipe ou la légende du conquérant* (Paris: Belles Lettres, 1981 [1944]), pp. 12–13.

67. Ibid., pp. 13, 59–60.

68. Ibid., pp. 1, 23, 66.

69. "Symmetry and Dissymmetry."

70. "The Scapegoat" (ll. 1–8), in Sylvia Townsend Warner, *Selected Poems* (Manchester: Carcanet Press, 1985), p. 46.

71. "Symmetry and Dissymmetry."

72. Ibid.

73. "From the Novelistic Experience to the Oedipal Myth," in this volume.

74. Frye, p. 41.

75. *Violence and the Sacred*, pp. 73–74.

76. "An Interview with René Girard," p. 223.

77. Sigmund Freud, *The Interpretation of Dreams*, trans. J. Strachey, excerpted in Berkowitz and Brunner, pp. 70, 71.

78. Ibid., p. 71.

79. Friedrich Nietzsche, *The Birth of Tragedy*, trans. F. Golffing, excerpted in Berkowitz and Brunner, p. 136.

80. René Girard, *Deceit, Desire, and the Novel: Self and Other in Literary Structure*, trans. Y. Freccero (Baltimore: Johns Hopkins University Press, 1965), pp. 28–29, 38.

81. Ibid., pp. 73, 74; cf. René Girard, *Mensonge romantique et vérité romanesque* (Paris: Grasset, 1961), p. 80.

82. Quoted from Marcel Proust, *Swann's Way*, trans. C. K. Scott Moncrieff (New York: Random House, 1934), in *Deceit, Desire, and the Novel*, p. 55.

83. *Deceit*, pp. 10, 34; cf. *Mensonge*, p. 19.

84. *Deceit*, pp. 1–3, 8–9.

85. Ibid., pp. 9–12.

86. Ibid., pp. 92, 222–23; cf. *Mensonge*, p. 225.

87. *Deceit*, pp. 99, 279.

88. Ibid., p. 271.

89. *Deceit*, pp. 299–300; cf. *Mensonge*, pp. 298–99.

90. *Deceit*, p. 298; cf. *Mensonge*, p. 297.

91. Freud, *The Interpretation of Dreams*, in Berkowitz and Brunner, p. 70.

92. "Strategies of Madness—Nietzsche, Wagner, and Dostoevski," in *"To double business bound,"* p. 67.

93. *Violence and the Sacred*, pp. 188, 190.

94. "Strategies of Madness," p. 67.

95. *Deceit*, p. 83. Girard's approach holds significance for the anthropological debate over the universality of Oedipal triangles in world folklore and mythology. In *Oedipus Ubiquitous: The Family Complex in World Folk Literature* (Stanford: Stanford University Press, 1996), Allen Johnson and Douglass Price-Williams conclude that the results of their wide-ranging, cross-cultural survey largely confirm the relevance of the Freudian model. However, the authors allow for great variation in the identity of the protagonists who instantiate the primordial triangle: "Father can be substituted for by any senior male," such as a king or priest or even a lion or dragon; "mother is frequently substituted for by a queen, animal, or devil woman," not to mention an aunt, stepmother, mother-in-law or grandmother; less commonly, "any handsome youth" may substitute for the son (p. 43). The mechanism posited by Girard makes it possible to account for such variety within a universal framework without resorting to the assumption that every senior male or female other than the father or mother is necessarily a substitute for the father or mother.

96. *Deceit*, p. 44.

97. Ibid., pp. 105–6.

98. Ibid., p. 35.

99. Marcel Proust, *Swann's Way*, trans. C. K. Moncrieff and T. Kilmartin, rev. D. J. Enright (London: Vintage, 1996), p. 41. As Viviane Forrester notes, Marcel's mother then "spends the night by his side, reading to him *François le Champi*, a novel which ends with the marriage between an adoptive mother and her son" ("Marcel Proust: le texte de la mère," *Tel Quel* 78 [winter 1978]: 73).

100. *Deceit*, p. 35.

101. *Swann's Way*, 1996, p. 34.

102. "Symmetry and Dissymmetry."

103. "*Oedipus* Analyzed."

104. *Deceit*, p. 8.

105. "*Oedipus* Analyzed."

106. *Deceit*, p. 10.

107. Ibid., p. 92.

108. René Girard, *Things Hidden since the Foundation of the World*, trans. S. Bann and M. Metteer (Stanford: Stanford University Press, 1988), p. 385.

109. *Deceit*, p. 93.

110. Ibid.

111. Fyodor Dostoevsky, *Notes from Underground*, trans. M. R. Katz, 2d ed. (New York: Norton, 2001), p. 34.

112. Ibid., p. 36.

113. Ibid., pp. 37, 39.

114. *Deceit*, pp. 93, 179; cf. *Mensonge*, p. 184.

115. "Symmetry and Dissymmetry."

116. "*Oedipus* Analyzed."

117. Karl Abraham, "The Rescue and Murder of the Father in Neurotic Phantasy-Formations" (1922) in *Clinical Papers and Essays on Psycho-Analysis*, quoted in John Murray Cuddihy, *The Ordeal of Civility: Freud, Marx, Lévi-Strauss, and the Jewish Struggle with Modernity* (Boston: Beacon Press, 1974, 2d ed., 1987), pp. 55–56.

118. Sigmund Freud, in *A Psycho-Analytic Dialogue: The Letters of Sigmund Freud and Karl Abraham*, quoted in Cuddihy, p. 56.

119. Karl Abraham, "'The Trifurcation of the Road' in the Oedipus Myth" (1922), in *Clinical Papers and Essays on Psycho-Analysis*, quoted in Peter L. Rudnytsky, *Freud and Oedipus* (New York: Columbia University Press, 1987), pp. 261–62.

120. Quoted in Rudnytsky, pp. 40–41.

121. Ernest Jones, *The Life and Work of Sigmund Freud*, vol. 1, quoted in Cuddihy, p. 102.

122. Quoted from *The Interpretation of Dreams* in Rudnytsky, p. 40.

123. Cuddihy, pp. 51–53. The passage from Sophocles' *Oedipus* is a composite constructed by Cuddihy from *Oedipus Rex*, trans. F. Storr, in *Sophocles* (Cambridge: Harvard University Press, 1951), 1: 75, and *Oedipus the King*, trans. D. Grene, in *Sophocles* (Chicago: University of Chicago Press, 1954), 1: 45–46.

124. Cuddihy, pp. 53, 62.

125. Peter L. Berger, "Excursus: Alternation and Biography," in *An Invitation to*

Sociology (Garden City, N.Y.: Doubleday Anchor, 1963), p. 60; quoted in Cuddihy, p. 58.

126. Cuddihy, pp. 54, 62.

127. Ibid., pp. 54–55.

128. Quoted in Rudnytsky, pp. 49–50.

129. Rudnytsky, pp. 15–16 (Jones's words are quoted from *The Life and Work*, 1: 11).

130. Quoted in Rudnytsky, p. 42.

131. Quoted in Rudntysky, p. 33.

132. Rudnytsky, pp. 34–35.

133. Ibid., p. 33.

134. As a young man, Freud almost came to blows over a point of philosophy with the father of his future patient Dora. According to Ernest Jones, Freud "behaved very rudely to his philosophical opponent and obstinately refused to apologize; there was even for the moment some talk of a duel" (*The Life and Work*, 1: 43; quoted in Cuddihy, pp. 45–46).

135. Jones, *The Life and Work*, 3: 100, and Merton, "The Ambivalence of Scientists," in N. W. Storer, ed., *The Sociology of Science* (Chicago: University of Chicago Press, 1973), p. 386; quoted in Cuddihy, p. 94.

136. Quoted in Rudnytsky, p. 25.

137. Lucien Scubla, "Pour une archéologie du texte freudien," *Cahiers du C.R.E.A.* 2 (May 1983): 150. On the rivalry of brothers in Freud's circle—including what Freud himself referred to as "quarrels of priority" between Abraham and Jung—see François Roustang, *Dire Mastery: Discipleship from Freud to Lacan*, trans. N. Lukacher (Baltimore: Johns Hopkins University Press, 1982).

138. Marthe Robert, *D'Œdipe à Moïse* (Paris: Hachette, 1978), p. 119; quoted in Scubla, p. 148.

139. Scubla, p. 149.

140. Cuddihy, pp. 49, 57 n.

141. Ibid., pp. 18–19.

142. Fear of the same accusation prompted James Strachey to spend a fruitless hour pleading with Ernest Jones—the last Gentile among Freud's original followers after Jung's defection—not to translate *das Es* as "the id": "I said that I thought that everyone would say 'the Yidd,'" he explains, but "Jones said there was no such word in English. . . . Simply because that l.b. [little bastard] hasn't ever heard it"; quoted in Cuddihy, p. ix, from P. Meisel and W. Kendrick, eds., *Bloomsbury/Freud: The Letters of James and Alix Strachey 1924–1925* (New York: Basic Books, 1985), p. 83.

143. *Deceit*, p. 54.

144. Fyodor Dostoyevsky, *Notes from the Underground*, trans. C. Garnett (New York: Dial Press, 1945), quoted in *Deceit*, p. 54.

145. Cuddihy, pp. 65–66; Freud's words are quoted from a 1912 paper in *Collected Papers, Papers on Metapsychology, Papers on Applied Psycho-Analysis*, trans. J. Rivière (New York: Basic Books, 1959).

146. According to Lowell Edmunds, the tale of an Oedipal Judas "was extremely popular in the Middle Ages. It is preserved in more than forty-two Latin

manuscripts" (p. 18). Edmunds furnishes three medieval versions (pp. 61–67), as well as a number of variants from modern European folklore (pp. 89–93, 138–41, 143–48, 155–60, 197). See also Hyam Maccoby, *Judas Iscariot and the Myth of Jewish Evil* (New York: Free Press, 1992), pp. 102–7. Like "the Jews in medieval and later Nazi propaganda," Maccoby comments, the Oedipal Judas "is imagined as rampant in his sexual desires and unimpeded by moral restraints" (p. 106).

147. For an extended analysis of the Joseph story as a "deconstruction of sacrificial thinking," see Sandor Goodhart, "'I am Joseph': René Girard and the Prophetic Law," in P. Dumouchel, ed., pp. 53–74.

148. For a critical discussion of Girard's interpretation of the New Testament, see Lucien Scubla, "The Christianity of René Girard and the Nature of Religion," trans. M. R. Anspach, in P. Dumouchel, ed., pp. 160–78. On the respective attitudes of Judaism and Christianity toward violence and sacrifice, see Henri Atlan, "Founding Violence and Divine Referent," trans. M. R. Anspach, in P. Dumouchel, ed., pp. 192–208.

149. *Deceit*, pp. 10–11.

150. Dunsany, p. 249.

CHAPTER 1

1. Marcel Proust, *Contre Sainte-Beuve* [Paris: Gallimard, 1954], p. 344.

2. Ibid., pp. 301–2.

3. Paris: José Corti, 1961.

4. René Girard, "Camus's Stranger Retried," *P.M.L.A.* 79 (Dec. 1964), pp. 519–33 [reprinted in René Girard, *"To Double Business Bound"* (Baltimore: Johns Hopkins University Press, 1978), pp. 9–35].

5. ["Calme bloc ici-bas, chu d'un désastre obscur"—Stéphane Mallarmé, "Le Tombeau d'Edgar Poe."]

CHAPTER 2

1. Translator's note: The word for "competitors" in the French text, *concurrents*, is nearly the same as the Latin *concurrentes*. The French verb *con-courir*, which literally means "to run together," is an ambivalent term, signifying either "to compete" or "to cooperate."

2. Friedrich Hölderlin, *Remarques sur Œdipe/Remarques sur Antigone* (Paris: Plon, 1965).

3. ["Mais rendre la lumière/Suppose d'ombre une morne moitié"—Paul Valéry, "Le cimitière marin."]

4. These observations were inspired by Eugenio Donato.

5. F. Hölderlin, *Remarques sur Œdipe*.

CHAPTER 3

1. [*The Standard Edition of the Complete Psychological Works of Sigmund Freud*, ed. and trans. James Strachey, 24 vols. (London, 1953–66), vol. 18, *Group Psychology and the Analysis of the Ego*, p. 105.]

2. Ibid.

3. J. Lacan, "L'agressivité en psychanalyse" [*Ecrits* (Paris: Seuil, 1966), p. 117].

4. [*Standard Edition*, vol. 19, *The Ego and the Id*, p. 32.]

CHAPTER 4

1. I thank Professor C. Morón-Arroyo for setting me straight on this point.

2. Paris: Denoël, 1971, p. 83.

3. [René Girard, *Violence and the Sacred* (Baltimore: Johns Hopkins University Press, 1977).]

4. Northrop Frye, *Anatomy of Criticism* (Princeton: Princeton University Press, 1971), p. 41.

5. Ibid., p. 47.

6. Ibid., p. 149.

7. [In Jacques Derrida, *Dissemination*, trans. B. Johnson (London: Athlone, 1981).]

Index

Prison, 12, 19
Projection, 33–34, 39, 46
Prophetism, Jewish, 56–57, 88–89, 93
Proust, Marcel, xxxiiiff, xxxviii–xl, xli,
    1–4, 8–12, 19–20, 22, 24
Prynne, Hester, 100
Psychoanalysis, xxxii, 4, 15–16, 39, 49, 55,
    57, 81, 83. *See also* Freud; Latency pe-
    riod; Oedipus complex
Psychopathology of Everyday Life, The, xlvi
Pyramus and Thisbe, 104–105

Rank, Otto, 97
Rationalism, 24ff, 37, 88
Realism, 5, 7, 12, 22, 26, 78
Red and the Black, The, 5–8, 10ff, 23f. *See
    also* Julien
Regicide, xiii, xvii. *See also* King, killing
    of; Laius, murder of
Remembrance of Things Past, xxxiii–xxxiv,
    xxxviii–xl, xli, 1–4 passim, 8–12 pas-
    sim, 18, 19–20, 120n99
Rênals, the (*The Red and the Black*), 19;
    Madame de, 6–7
Resurrection, 10, 12, 21
Réveillons, the (*Jean Santeuil*), 3
Revolt, 29, 87–88, 93f
Riddle-solving, 38, 47, 66, 77, 107
Rieux, Docteur, 17
Rites of passage, 93
Ritual, 47, 52, 95, 99–102 passim
Rivalry, mimetic, 96. *See also* Enemy
    brothers
Robert, Marthe, l
Roheim, Geza, xii
Romanticism, xxxiiiff, xl, 97, 105
Romeo and Juliet, 103–106
Romulus and Remus, 35, 112
Rougement, Denis de, xli, lii
Roustang, François, 121n137
Rudnytsky, Peter L., xlvi–xlvii,
    xlviii–xlix
Russian folktale, xviif

Sacred, the: and difference, 70, 74,
    75–76, 77, 84, 89, 93; and oracle, 24,
    49, 52, 54, 75
Sacrifice, 45–46, 47, 52–53, 56, 63, 86, 89,
    99, 102f, 122n148
Saïd, Suzanne, x–xi
Sand, George, see *François le Champi*
Sartre, Jean-Paul, 37, 98
Satan, 68f
Scandal (*Skandalon*), 68–70, 73–75,
    79–86 passim, 92–94
Scapegoat, xxii–xxxii, liif, 45–46, 49–93
    passim, 100–102, 110–112; consent of,
    86, 88–89; Freud and, lii, 92; identifi-
    cation with, 49, 55–57; king as,
    xxiv–xxv, 118n55; ritual of, 45,
    100–101, 110
Scubla, Lucien, l, 122n148
Septimus (*Mrs. Dalloway*), 100
Servant of Yahveh, 56, 89
Shakespeare, 95–97, 103–106, 117n51
Shelley, Percy Bysshe, xvi
Sheppard, J. T., xv
Sheriff and outlaws, 61
Simonse, Simon, xxv, 118n55
Singleton, Charles S., 23
Sisyphus, 27
Snobbery, 3f, 9, 13, 104
Socrates, 102
Solomon's judgment, 50
Sophocles, ix–xiii passim, xx–xxvi pas-
    sim, 15f, 26f, 33, 35, 40, 49–56 passim,
    60–65 passim, 70, 75, 77f, 85, 87f,
    117n51; *Antigone,* 53; *Electra,* xi. See
    also *Oedipus at Colonus*
Sophists, 102
Sorel, Julien, *see* Julien
Spenser, Edmund, 101
Sphinx, 13, 27, 29–30, 35–36, 38, 47, 67,
    69, 76, 83
Stendhal, xxxv, 5–8, 10–12, 14, 19, 20–21,
    22ff
Strachey, James, 121n142